Construction Grammar and its Application to English

to English

Edinburgh Textbooks on the English Language – Advanced

General Editor
Heinz Giegerich, Professor of English Linguistics, University of Edinburgh

Editorial Board
Laurie Bauer (University of Wellington)
Olga Fischer (University of Amsterdam)
Rochelle Lieber (University of New Hampshire)
Norman Macleod (University of Edinburgh)
Donka Minkova (UCLA)
Edgar W. Schneider (University of Regensburg)
Katie Wales (University of Leeds)
Anthony Warner (University of York)

TITLES IN THE SERIES INCLUDE:

Corpus Linguistics and the Description of English
Hans Lindquist

A Historical Phonology of English
Donka Minkova

A Historical Morphology of English
Dieter Kastovsky

Grammaticalization and the History of English
Manfred Krug and Hubert Cuyckens

A Historical Syntax of English
Bettelou Los

English Historical Sociolinguistics
Robert McColl Millar

A Historical Semantics of English
Christian Kay and Kathryn Allan

Construction Grammar and its Application to English
Martin Hilpert

Visit the Edinburgh Textbooks in the English Language website at
www.euppublishing.com/series/ETOTELAdvanced

Construction Grammar and its Application to English

Martin Hilpert

EDINBURGH
University Press

Edinburgh University Press Ltd
The Tun – Holyrood Road
12 (2f) Jackson's Entry
Edinburgh EH8 8PJ
www.euppublishing.com

Typeset in 10.5/12 Janson by
Servis Filmsetting Ltd, Stockport, Cheshire,
and printed and bound in Great Britain by
CPI Group (UK) Ltd, Croydon CR0 4YY

A CIP record for this book is available from the British Library

ISBN 978 0 7486 7584 5 (hardback)
ISBN 978 0 7486 7585 2 (paperback)
ISBN 978 0 7486 7586 9 (webready PDF)
ISBN 978 0 7486 7588 3 (epub)

Contents

List of tables and figures

Acknowledgements

I would like to write a few words of thanks to my colleagues, friends, and students who have been involved in the project of writing this book. First of all, I need to thank Heinz Giegerich, general editor of the ETOTEL series, for giving me the opportunity to write a textbook on Construction Grammar. Through the writing process, I discovered that I only half-knew a couple of things that I thought I did know, so at least one reader of this book has learned something from it. I also want to thank Graeme Trousdale, who read the entire manuscript and provided critical comments, and two not-so-anonymous referees, who commented on the book proposal. A big round of thanks goes to Florian Dolberg and his students at the University of Mainz for testing out the manuscript and pointing me towards issues that needed clarification. By the same token, my own students at the universities of Freiburg, Zurich, and Neuchâtel have offered their critical feedback. Thank you all! Finally, I would also like to express my gratitude towards the researchers whose ideas form the backbone of this book.

I would like to dedicate this book to the memory of P.P., who was always ready to listen, and who was prepared to change his mind if the argument was good enough.

To readers: Why you shouldn't pick up, let alone read, this book

So, you have found this book, an introduction to a linguistic theory called *Construction Grammar*, on a shelf in a library or bookshop, or you are reading these lines on your computer screen. Chances are that you somehow came across the term *Construction Grammar*, perhaps in connection with a sentence such as *John sneezed the napkin off the table*, and you were curious to find out more. Before you read any further, let me tell you why that would be a bad idea.

Most importantly perhaps, Construction Grammar is not one of those topics in linguistics where decades of work have produced a solid stock of ideas that most researchers in that area can more or less agree on. Take phonology, for instance, or sociolinguistics. Yes, there are important differences between current approaches to these topics, issues that give rise to fierce debates and the occasional ad-hominem attack. However, few of those arguments concern the ideas that are laid out in an introductory textbook. Adherents of optimality-theoretic phonology and followers of exemplar theory would both expect a textbook of their subject to introduce ideas such as the phoneme, complementary distribution, syllable structure, assimilation, dissimilation, and the like. They could sit down together and draw up a list of topics to represent the common bedrock of their respective research areas. Things are a little different when it comes to Construction Grammar. Researchers in Construction Grammar broadly agree that their work is 'different from work in generative grammar' and that 'constructions are important'. A necessary caveat to this statement is that Construction Grammar shares a fair number of ideas with the generative enterprise and that the notion of 'constructions' is rather hotly contested. That being the case, I have to warn you, dear reader, that this book will present a view of Construction Grammar that is not necessarily shared by the majority of researchers working in this field, which is still very young, highly diverse, and undergoing rapid development. I am writing these lines in early 2013, and the more time elapses between now and the moment in which you are reading them, the more likely you are to find a view that is not only disputed, but also hopelessly outdated.

Another point I would like to offer in order to discourage you from any further engagement with this book is that there are excellent texts out there that you can profitably use to get an overview of the kind of work that is being done in Construction Grammar. Let me mention the work of Adele E. Goldberg (1995, 2006), which has been extremely influential, and which offers an authoritative and highly accessible starting point for the interested novice. Also, *The Oxford Handbook of Construction Grammar* has recently been published (Hoffmann and Trousdale 2013). This hefty tome of some 650 pages, written by experts in the respective topics, is in a much better position to do justice to the complexities of the field than a slim introductory book such as this one. Another resource that I would like to mention is the excellent textbook *Syntactic Theory*, in which Ivan Sag, Thomas Wasow, and Emily Bender give a detailed account of how constructions can be usefully formalised (Sag et al. 2003). Formalisation is completely disregarded in this book, but it is essential in many areas of research, not least in computational linguistics. Oh, one more thing. If you are passing through Northern California in the not-too-distant future, you could stop by at Copy Central, 2560 Bancroft Way, in Berkeley, and ask for a copy of the text-book manuscript written by Charles J. Fillmore and Paul Kay, who are the main architects of Construction Grammar and whose ideas literally inform every page of this book.

Lastly, you will note that the title of this book is *Construction Grammar and its Application to English*. What this book aims to do is to lay out an inventory of English constructions and to explain how these can be analysed, using the framework of Construction Grammar. The focus on English constructions comes at the price of neglecting all other languages that are currently the subject of constructional research and, importantly, comparisons between them. Construction Grammar has been devised as a framework for the analysis of the general human capacity for language. It is a basic assumption that knowledge of language will be organised according to the same principles across different languages, but to what extent this assumption is correct is still very much a matter of investigation. This book will completely ignore this interesting issue, focusing instead on English constructions, many of which are actually quite well described in existing treatments of English grammar, idioms, and vocabulary.

You're still reading? Well, don't say I didn't warn you.

1 Introducing Construction Grammar

1.1 What do you know when you know a language?

What do speakers of English have to know in order to produce utterances that other speakers will understand? For many linguists, across different theoretical persuasions, working out what speakers know when they know a language is *the* most important task in their field of study. So, what do speakers know? If you had to come up with a number of bullet points with the most important aspects of linguistic knowledge, your list would be likely to show some overlap with the following ones.

(1) What speakers have to know:
- must know words
- must know how to combine words into phrases and sentences
- must know how to put the right endings on words
- must be able to understand newly coined words
- must know that sometimes what is meant is different from what is said
- must know that language varies across different contexts
- must know idiomatic expressions

Clearly, more items could be added to this list. In order to get a working model of linguistic knowledge, it would further be necessary to work out how each item on the list interacts with all the other ones. For instance, how does knowledge of idioms relate to knowledge of the words that occur in them? How does knowledge of syntactic patterns relate to knowledge of morphological inflections of the words in a sentence? Given that modelling speakers' knowledge of language is a highly complicated task, it will be likely to come to you as a surprise that linguistic knowledge, according to Construction Grammar, can be captured by a list that is considerably shorter than the one shown above.

(2) What speakers have to know, according to Construction
     Grammar:
     • must know constructions

Yes, you have read correctly. All that speakers need to have, according
to the constructional view, is knowledge of **constructions**. This claim
is expressed by Adele E. Goldberg, one of the central developers of
Construction Grammar as a theory of linguistic knowledge, in the following way (2003: 219):

> The totality of our knowledge of language is captured by a network of
> constructions: a 'construct-i-con'.

At this point you will probably wonder what a construction is. This
chapter will offer a comprehensive definition, but as a first approxima-
tion, Goldberg and other researchers in Construction Grammar view
constructions as units of linguistic knowledge that pair a linguistic
form with a meaning. This means that you are in fact familiar with a
very common kind of construction, namely words. Words, by virtue
of being symbolic form–meaning pairings, are constructions. The
construct-i-con, as the name suggests, thus contains everything that
would be contained in a lexicon, but in addition to that a large number
of symbolic units that are larger in size than single words. The remaining parts of this chapter will characterise these units in some more
detail, but let us for the moment return to the fundamental claim of
Construction Grammar, namely that knowledge of language consists of
a large network of constructions, *and nothing else in addition.* Everything
that speakers know about words, about syntactic patterns, about pre-
fixes and suffixes, about idioms, and about the intricacies of what is
said and what is meant, everything of this is to be recast as knowledge
of constructions. At first, this may seem an outrageous proposition.
What motivates a claim that departs so drastically from the seemingly
obvious conclusion that speakers need many different kinds of linguistic
knowledge? The short answer is that all of that knowledge is thought
to be represented directly at the level of constructions. The constructions that speakers know are directly associated with phonological,
morphological, and syntactic properties, along with conventionalised
meanings, possible variants, and the social contexts in which you are
likely to use and hear them. In the simplest of terms, your knowledge of a construction is the sum total of your experience with that
construction.

   This view of linguistic knowledge may be hard to stomach at first,
because it militates against an idea that is widely shared, both among

laypeople and among professional linguists. That idea goes by the name of the **dictionary-and-grammar model** (Taylor 2012: 8), which is a model of linguistic knowledge in which knowledge of vocabulary is neatly separated from knowledge of grammatical rules. (You will recognise the first two bullet points from our laundry list of linguistic knowledge.) And indeed, you might say, is it not obvious that children learn words and, in a second step, rules to combine those words into phrases and sentences? The central challenge for the dictionary-and-grammar view of linguistic knowledge is one that has plagued generations of second language learners, namely idiomatic expressions. (You recognise the last, seemingly less important bullet point from the list.) In the dictionary-and-grammar model, idioms form a kind of 'appendix' to the dictionary, a list that contains expressions such as *beat it, hit the road,* or *make like a banana and split*. These expressions need separate entries in the mental lexicon because speakers have to learn that each of the three means 'to leave', and that each of them is appropriate for slightly different contexts of use. Knowledge of the individual words and their meanings will not lead a speaker to that particular conclusion. The constructional view of linguistic knowledge originates with the observation that relegating idioms to an appendix is not satisfactory. The following sections outline why this is the case.

1.1.1 Idiomatic expressions permeate ordinary language

Contrary to what you might think, idiomatic expressions are no particularly peripheral phenomenon in naturally occurring data. Consider the following snippet from the British National Corpus (BNC), which is a large text collection that documents the usage of British English in the second half of the twentieth century.

(3) In winter you can look out of the window and tell it's 2 °C outside. How? Because the crocuses are coming into bloom. Crocuses are plants that nature has provided with a biological thermometer. It's very accurate, reacting to temperature differences of as little as 0.5 °C. As the weather gets warmer the flowers open. But when the temperature drops, they close again.

On the face of it, the text excerpt seems to be entirely unremarkable. You would be hard pressed even to find an expression in the text that would qualify as an idiom. However, a closer look reveals a number of expressions that would be difficult to explain with a dictionary-and-grammar model of linguistic knowledge. Take the very first words, *In winter.* This is a conventional way of saying *during the time of winter, in general*, as opposed to *in the winter of 2012*. Knowing this is part of your linguistic knowledge, and a second language learner of English might not necessarily know it, opting for *in the winter* instead. Moving on, the sentence *you can look out of the window and tell it's 2 °C outside* is not as straightforward as you might initially think. Note that the verb *tell* in this sentence does not have its usual meaning of 'narrate', as in *tell a story*, but rather, the sentence conveys that the listener can *infer* that the temperature is 2 °C. Again, you understood that without any problems, but how so? The answer is that you know an idiomatic usage pattern with *tell*, which is important enough to receive its own entry in the *Oxford English Dictionary* as '*preceded by* can: *To be able to state; to know; to discern, perceive, make out, understand*' (*OED*: tell, v.). An example that would almost count as a real idiom is the expression *coming into bloom*, said of the crocuses. Plants in general can be *coming into leaf, coming into flower*, or *coming into fruit*, but crucially not into *leaves, flowers*, or *fruits*, even though that might be a more accurate description of what happens. Proficient speakers of English are aware that the singular is required; learners have to work that out, but cannot bank on the help of a dictionary or grammar book in that endeavour. Two sentences later, the text mentions *temperature differences of as little as 0.5 °C*. Here, we have an expression that many second language learners of English are actually taught, namely the use of *as . . . as* with an intervening adjective. This expression typically serves to make a comparison, as in *John is as tall as Bob*, but note that here, the expression connects a scale with a value on that scale, so that the phrase *differences of as little as 0.5 °C* is an example of a schema that is also at work in *interest rates of as high as 100 per cent*, or *microcredit loans of as small as £40*. What is conveyed by these examples is that some measure is comparatively high, or comparatively low, but the standard against which the respective measurements are compared remains implicit, to be understood by the reader. You know that, but neither because you know what the individual words mean, nor because you know how to combine words into phrases. Again, the dictionary-and-grammar model is at a loss.

What emerges from the discussion of the short text excerpt is that ordinary language is fully permeated by a large number of idiomatic expressions whose forms and meanings are not entirely predictable on the basis of either the word meanings recorded in a dictionary or the rules of syntax provided by a grammar. The appendix to the dictionary, listing expressions such as *in winter, coming into bloom*, or *differences of as little as 0.5 °C*, would have to be of a substantial size in order to reflect speakers' knowledge of language fully.

1.1.2 Idiomatic expressions are more than fixed strings

Besides the sheer size of the appendix that would have to be added to the lexicon, the dictionary-and-grammar model faces difficulties that are less easily resolved. Representing speakers' knowledge of idiomatic expressions would be a relatively straightforward task if those idioms were just fixed strings of words such as *bite the dust*, *let off steam*, or *jump the gun*. However, many idiomatic expressions cannot be analysed as memorised strings, as two examples from the following BNC excerpt illustrate.

(4) 'Clients tell me that they are not worried about their property as long as their pets are all right,' says William Lewis, managing director of Home & Pet Care. 'We often get asked to look after elderly pets whose owners are worried that going into kennels may be too big a shock.' Most sitters are over 60, sensible and probably have pets of their own.

Sentences such as *going into kennels may be too big a shock* have been discussed under the heading of the BIG MESS construction (Van Eynde 2007).[1] Clearly, understanding a phrase such as *too big a shock* does not come about because speakers have memorised that very phrase. Rather, what speakers know is a more abstract pattern that also allows them to identify sentences such as *That's quite useful a lesson* or *How big an area are we talking about?* as conventional expressions. You can think of this abstract pattern as a cognitive schema, that is, a mental representation that captures the construction's general traits. In the case of the BIG MESS construction, this schema deviates in some ways from general syntactic patterns of English. For instance, in an ordinary English noun phrase, an attributive adjective follows the determiner and precedes the head noun, as in *a big shock*, rather than *big a shock*. Importantly, the BIG MESS construction has a certain grammatical systematicity, which is to say that it is sensitive to distinctions that, under the dictionary-and-grammar model, would be handled by the grammar, rather than by the dictionary. To illustrate, the nominal in the big mess construction must be indefinite. Replacing the indefinite article in *too big a shock* or *quite useful a lesson* with the definite determiner *the* or a demonstrative such as *this* renders the examples highly unconventional. Likewise, the nominal must be in the singular, so that it is not possible to replace *a shock* with

---

[1] Throughout this book, you will find the names of constructions printed in SMALL CAPITALS, as in the DITRANSITIVE construction, the BE GOING TO construction, or the S-GENITIVE construction.

two shocks, some shocks, or *a few shocks.* Lastly, the schema that represents speakers' knowledge of the BIG MESS construction must include some information on the pre-adjectival modifiers that are acceptable in the construction. It is easy to find authentic examples with the degree modifiers *quite, rather, too, somewhat,* and *pretty;* examples with interrogative *how* are quite common; but examples with *very* are surprisingly rare, and even unacceptable to some speakers (Van Eynde 2007). Speakers' knowledge of the BIG MESS construction is thus more than a fixed string of words, or perhaps a list of fixed strings, but rather a generalisation over such strings that specifies what works and what does not.

The second example from the excerpt that is worth some consideration is the sentence *Most sitters are over 60, sensible and probably have pets of their own.* The crucial phrase here is *have pets of their own,* which illustrates another idiomatic expression with internal grammatical systematicity. The elements *of* and *own* are invariant, but between the two, any possessive determiner (*my, your, his, her,* etc.) may enter the expression. The construction, which we may call the N OF ONE'S OWN construction, includes a nominal that must be indefinite. The sentence *John now has a car of his own* is a conventional expression, but replacing the indefinite determiner with the definite determiner *the* leads to an ungrammatical, perhaps even uninterpretable result. By contrast, a constraint on the number of the nominal, as observed in the BIG MESS construction above, does not apply. *John now has three cars of his own* is just as good an example as the one in which he owns only one car.

Summing up this particular argument, there is evidence to suggest that many idioms cannot be stored as fixed strings, which makes it necessary to think of idiomatic expressions as schemas with slots that can be filled with certain elements but not others. The slots of some idioms are sensitive to grammatical distinctions, such as the distinction between singular and plural, or the distinction between definite and indefinite. These observations put the dictionary-and-grammar model of linguistic knowledge in a rather awkward position: Should the appendix to the dictionary perhaps include a bit of grammatical information, so that these expressions could be accounted for? Doing this is possible, but you see how that decision would start blurring the line between dictionary and grammar. If grammar enters the appendix, a large grey area emerges between dictionary and grammar in which the patterns that are memorised show characteristics of lexical entries, but also of grammatical rules. It is this grey area that researchers in Construction Grammar call the construct-i-con.

1.1.3 Idiomatic expressions are productive

A good reason for keeping vocabulary and grammar apart as separate forms of linguistic knowledge is that words can be thought of as 'building blocks' that are highly numerous, but essentially fixed and atomic, whereas syntactic rules and morphological word formation processes are productive, that is, they allow speakers to create structures that are new and original. Vocabulary is thus just a finite collection of building material; grammar is what gives language the power to produce an infinite variety of new utterances.

The dictionary-and-grammar model of linguistic knowledge would be much more convincing if the idioms of a language were essentially like words: fixed and learnable as strings. The previous section has argued that this is an impoverished view. Many idiomatic expressions do not fully specify the lexical elements that can occur in them, and a good number of them even allow different grammatical elements into the variable slots that can be filled. For example, the phrase *the more, the merrier* instantiates a schema that has given rise to many expressions that are structurally identical but contain other adjectives in the comparative, such as *the bigger, the better* or *the redder, the deadlier*. It appears that *the more, the merrier*, also known as the COMPARATIVE CORRELATIVE construction (Culicover and Jackendoff 1999) or THE *X*-ER THE *Y*-ER (Fillmore et al. 1988), is productive, allowing speakers to produce creative utterances. The productivity, however, does not stop with different types of adjective that are inserted into that construction, but it extends to variation of grammatical forms. In an example such as *The darker the roast, the stronger the taste*, each adjective is followed by a nominal. In *The stronger a voice we have, the more effective we are*, each adjective forms part of a clausal structure. In *The more carefully you do your work, the easier it will get*, the first part is in fact adverbial, rather than adjectival. Hence, speakers' knowledge of this construction is not limited to the fact that there are open slots for different kinds of adjective, but rather, speakers have an active command of the kinds of grammatical unit that are acceptable in the construction. The fact that speakers know how to use idiomatic expressions productively makes it necessary to abandon the strict separation of lexical and grammatical knowledge.

1.1.4 The growth of the appendix

The considerations that were presented in the previous sections make one thing very clear. The commonsensical view of linguistic knowledge as divisible into knowledge of vocabulary and knowledge of grammar suffers from a painful growth of the appendix, requiring an emergency procedure. Should the appendix perhaps be surgically removed, so that the patient can recover? In a paper that has since become one of the central references of the Construction Grammar literature, Charles J. Fillmore and colleagues suggest a solution that takes a surprisingly different route. In the conclusion to their study of the LET ALONE construction (*I don't eat fish, let alone raw oysters*), they propose the following (1988: 534):

> It appears to us that the machinery needed for describing the so-called minor or peripheral constructions of the sort which has occupied us here will have to be powerful enough to be generalized to more familiar structures, in particular those represented by individual phrase structure rules.

In other words, if it is the case that idiomatic expressions are abundant in language, if they cannot be characterised as fixed strings, and if speakers can be observed to use them productively, then these expressions deserve to be given a proper analysis. Since idiomatic expressions accommodate different words and show structural variation, the tools for such an analysis will have to be sensitive to both lexical and grammatical distinctions. Hence, and this is the punchline of Fillmore et al.'s argument, these tools can just as well be used for the 'more familiar structures', that is, everything that used to be part of the grammar component of the dictionary-and-grammar model. Instead of dictionary and grammar, all that is needed for the description of linguistic knowledge is the 'construct-i-con'. Essentially, this means that after the operation, the surgeons watch in astonishment as the severed appendix gets up, thanks everybody in the room, and walks out of the hospital, all on his own.

Up to now, the discussion in this chapter has dealt with linguistic knowledge in fairly general terms. What is still missing from the picture is a more detailed account of what constructions actually are. The following sections will focus on precisely that topic.

1.2 What is a construction?

The term **construction** is used not only in Construction Grammar, but in almost any area of research that is concerned with language. Hence, you will probably already have an idea of what a construction is, but your idea might not fully correspond to the way in which the term will be used in this book. In pedagogical language textbooks, a construction is typically a complex linguistic form that serves a grammatical function. Examples would be the PASSIVE construction (*The village was destroyed*), the IMPERATIVE construction (*Go to your room and stay there!*), or the PAST PERFECT construction (*I had already heard the news*). The examples of idiomatic expressions that were discussed in the sections above would seem to suggest that the term means something similar in Construction Grammar. Perhaps, you might reason, the term is used a little more broadly, including not only grammatical constructions such as the past perfect, but also idioms and words. That is a good enough guess, but one important issue is missing from this view of constructions. Recall that Construction Grammar is a theory of linguistic knowledge. Hence, constructions are first and foremost something cognitive, that is, a piece of speakers' linguistic knowledge. More specifically, we can say that a construction is a generalisation that speakers make across a number of encounters with linguistic forms. Let's take another look at a few examples of the COMPARATIVE CORRELATIVE construction:

(5) the more, the merrier
     the bigger, the better
     the redder, the deadlier
     the younger, the messier
     The darker the roast, the stronger the taste.
     The larger the company, the worse is the service.
     The stronger a voice we have, the more effective we are.
     The more that Mrs Bell reflected upon the subject, the more at a
     loss she was.
     The less he knows, the better.
     The more carefully you do your work, the easier it will get.

As was pointed out in the discussion above, the construction displays substantial variation in the lexical items that can appear, but also in the grammatical units that instantiate it. Nonetheless, you will probably agree that all of the examples above are 'the same' in that they belong to a common constructional pattern. If you do agree, that is evidence that your experience with language led you to abstract away from individual differences between sentences like these ones and to form a generalisation. It is this generalisation that Construction Grammarians talk about when they discuss the COMPARATIVE CORRELATIVE construction.

1.2.1 Defining constructions: a first try

The preceding discussion has mentioned several characteristics of constructions, but it has not yet presented a satisfying definition of the term that would allow us to identify a construction as such when we look at linguistic data. A widely cited definition of constructions has been offered by Adele E. Goldberg (1995: 4):

C is a CONSTRUCTION iff$_{def}$ C is a form–meaning pair $<F_i, S_i>$ such that some aspect of F_i or some aspect of S_i is not strictly predictable from C's component parts or from other previously established constructions.

This definition captures three important notions. First, a construction pairs a linguistic form with a meaning. (In the definition, *F* stands for *Form*, *S* is for *Semantics*). Second, by virtue of being a form–meaning pair, a construction is a unit of knowledge, rather than a form that could be described without reference to speakers' knowledge of language. Third, the definition introduces a criterion that we have not explicitly mentioned up to now, namely the criterion of non-predictability. A construction is defined as a form–meaning pair in which either an aspect of form or an aspect of meaning is non-predictable. What does that mean? With regard to meaning, this criterion captures the common characteristic of idioms that the interpretation of the whole idiom is more than just a combination of the meanings of its component words. Consider the following idioms that carry non-compositional and hence non-predictable meanings:

(6) We're back to square one.
    Will and Jenny finally tied the knot.
    His theory is totally off the mark.
    Let's call it a day.

Non-compositional meaning is perhaps the most widely used diagnostic to identify constructions, but note that the definition does not only talk about non-predictable meanings. Constructions can also be identified on the basis of non-predictable aspects of their *form*. A form of a construction is non-predictable if it is not an instance of a more general formal pattern, say, a particular sentence type or a morphological schema. The following examples illustrate the idea of constructions with non-predictable forms.

(7) all of a sudden
    by and large
    the more, the merrier
    Try as I might, I just couldn't grasp the principle.
    How big an area are we talking about?
    I have waited many a day for this to happen.

These examples defy typical phrase structure rules that would model the structure of phrases such as *the large sandwich with egg salad*. In fact, for several of the examples it is not even possible to determine the parts of speech for every component word. Into what word class would we categorise *sudden* in *all of a sudden*? Is the *by* in *by and large* a preposition, and if so, why is it not followed by a nominal (*by the lake*), or at least coordinated with another preposition (*made by and for dog-owners*)? In some of the examples, the component parts are clearly identifiable, but their order seems to revolt against ordinary syntactic patterns. For instance, there is no general phrase structure rule that would allow speakers to conclude that *many a day* is a conventional expression of English. Usually, *many* occurs with plural nouns, or as a pronominal form by itself. In those contexts, *many* can be replaced by *few*, but this does not work in *many a day*. Fillmore et al. (1988: 506–10) describe these kinds of examples when they speak of 'familiar pieces, unfamiliarly arranged', and 'unfamiliar pieces, unfamiliarly arranged'. In pedagogical works on idioms, these two categories are often relegated to the relative background, with the focus being on expressions such as *set the record straight*, *tie up loose ends*, or *show someone the ropes*. These idioms, as you will notice, have non-compositional meanings, but are formally 'familiar pieces, familiarly arranged', that is, there is nothing idiomatic about their form, only about their meaning.

   With all of these observations in place, we are in a position to look at linguistic data and to decide whether or not a given expression qualifies to be called a construction. Since formal or semantic non-predictability is a required criterion in the definition proposed by Goldberg (1995), this gives us a reason to exclude all kinds of expressions that are both semantically compositional and formed according to general phrase structure rules or word formation processes, as illustrated in the following examples:

(8) John enjoys playing the piano.
   Strawberries are more expensive than apples.
   I wonder why he keeps wearing that hat.
   Harvey's taunting of the bear was merciless.

   Saying that these are not constructions does of course raise the question what else they might be. And, you might add, was Construction Grammar not founded on the premise that knowledge of language was knowledge of constructions, and nothing else in addition? How can this claim be reconciled with the assessment that a certain linguistic expression is no construction? So, when we say that *John enjoys playing the piano* is not a construction, what is meant is that this particular example is not a construction in its own right, because first, the meaning of the whole is fully derivable from the meaning of the parts, and second, the structure of the whole is fully explicable from constructions that are known to exist in English. The sentence thus instantiates several more general constructions. At the most general level, this concerns the SUBJECT–PREDICATE construction, which is instantiated by all sentences that combine a subject noun phrase with a predicate verb phrase. Somewhat more specifically, the sentence exemplifies the TRANSITIVE construction, which pairs a verb such as *enjoy* with a structure that serves as a direct object. In *John enjoys playing the piano* that object is not a noun, but rather a participial clause, which means that the sentence also instantiates the PARTICIPIAL *-ing* CLAUSE construction. Within that participial clause, we find another instance of the TRANSITIVE construction, as *the piano* is the direct object of *playing*. Finally, the phrase *the piano* instantiates the DEFINITE NOUN PHRASE construction. In summary, saying that a particular sentence is no construction boils down to the statement that every part of that sentence can be analysed in terms of a more general construction. There is even a term for expressions that are not in themselves constructions: phrases and sentences that instantiate more general constructions are called **constructs**. Dwelling on this term for a minute, you will notice that *by and large* is a construction because it does not instantiate any pattern that would be more general than itself. The same holds for *all of a sudden*. However, the phrase *many a day* in the sentence *I have waited many a day for this to happen* is a construct: it instantiates a more general pattern, namely the MANY A NOUN construction, which also gives rise to the expressions *many a time* or *many an Englishman*. The distinction between constructions and constructs is thus one between generalisations and concrete instances, between abstract types and the tokens that instantiate them. You could memorise the rule of thumb that constructions are relatively more abstract, whereas constructs are relatively more concrete, which will serve you well as a general principle. However, note that patterns such as *by and large* or *all of a sudden* are constructions that are not any more abstract than their instantiations. For these patterns, the constructs, that is, the actual tokens that appear in language use, have the exact same form as the constructions on which they are based.

1.2.2 Defining constructions: beyond non-predictability

The criterion of non-predictability in meaning or form is a very powerful diagnostic. If the meaning of an expression cannot be inferred from the meanings of its parts, then there is simply no alternative to the conclusion that speakers *must* have learned this expression as a form–meaning pair in its own right, that is, as a construction. Nonetheless, researchers in Construction Grammar these days have largely abandoned the idea that non-predictability should be a necessary criterion for some expression to qualify as a construction. The reason for this assessment is that there are many expressions that are semantically and structurally transparent, but which nonetheless seem to qualify as constructions. Consider the following set of expressions.

(9) I love you.
    I don't know.
    Take a seat!
    Can I ask you something?
    How has your day been?

As you will agree, all of these expressions would have to be viewed as constructs because they instantiate highly general syntactic patterns. The sentence *I love you* illustrates the most basic form of the TRANSITIVE construction, *I don't know* is an instance of the NEGATION WITH *Do* construction, and so on and so forth. Still, despite the fact that these examples are structurally transparent, and despite the fact that their meanings can be compositionally derived, there is a reason for viewing these expressions as constructions. That reason is the fact that all of those expressions are highly frequent, highly conventionalised ways of saying things. The question *How has your day been?* literally asks for the information how someone's day turned out, but note that it is very different from *Of what quality has your day been?*, which would seem to be a rough paraphrase, but which is inadequate for opening a conversation of small talk. Some expressions may thus superficially look like constructs, but through repeated use, they have become the default option for a specific communicative situation. Taylor (2012: 100) offers the conspicuous example of *How old are you?*, which simply cannot be replaced with *How long ago were you born?* to ask for the interlocutor's age. As a proficient speaker of English, you know this, and hence this kind of information needs to be represented in the construct-i-con. Knowledge of language does not only include the ability to understand everything that is said, but it crucially also involves the ability to speak idiomatically. In order to accommodate this important aspect of linguistic knowledge, Adele E. Goldberg has proposed a modified version of her earlier definition of constructions (2006: 5):

> Any linguistic pattern is recognized as a construction as long as some aspect of its form or function is not strictly predictable from its component parts or from other constructions recognized to exist. In addition, patterns are stored as constructions even if they are fully predictable as long as they occur with sufficient frequency.

You recognise the prior definition in the first sentence: non-predictable constructions are still recognised as such. However, the second sentence opens up the definition to cover forms that are frequent enough to be remembered as such. These include sentence-level expressions such as *How old are you?* and *I don't know*, but crucially also many inflected word forms such as *cats*, *walked*, or *easier*. In the dictionary-and-grammar model of linguistic knowledge, these forms would not be stored as such, and also under Goldberg's earlier definition, these would have been viewed as constructs of the PLURAL construction, the PAST TENSE construction, and the MORPHOLOGICAL COMPARATIVE construction. In short, if you know the word *cat*, and if you know how the plural is formed, there is technically no need for you to remember the form *cats*. However, the view that regular, but sufficiently frequent expressions are stored in the construct-i-con is not only theoretically viable, but also receives empirical support from psycholinguistic studies (Stemberger and MacWhinney 1988; Arnon and Snider 2010). We will come back to psycholinguistic evidence for Construction Grammar later in this book.

1.3 Identifying constructions

Armed with our definition of what a construction is, we are now in a position to analyse linguistic data in the pursuit of finding and identifying constructions. Think of it what you like – many researchers in Construction Grammar are genuine language lovers who enjoy nothing more than finding a construction with peculiar non-predictable characteristics, preferably one that no one has investigated before. Occasionally, Construction Grammarians even acknowledge their love of 'butterfly collecting' (Hilferty 2003: 49), though usually they hasten to add that finding generalisations is the ultimate purpose of their endeavours. Finding constructions is an activity that requires some practice, although there are people who seem to have a natural talent for sniffing out grammatical oddities. This section discusses a number of strategies that are useful for the detection and identification of constructions.

1.3.1 Does the expression deviate from canonical patterns?

A first strategy relates to Goldberg's criterion of non-predictability, especially the formal side of that criterion. If a linguistic expression exhibits formal characteristics that deviate from more canonical grammatical patterns, then you have an argument for calling that expression a construction. Formal deviation from canonical patterns can be identified in different ways. Take for instance the expression *by and large*. A first observation would be that a phrase consisting of a preposition, a conjunction, and an adjective, in that order, is unique in the grammar of English. You do find sequences of those parts of speech in phrases such as *acquainted with and supportive of the school aims*, but note that *with and supportive* does not form a constituent in that expression. A second piece of evidence would be that *by and large* becomes completely unintelligible if the adjective *large* is replaced with the synonymous adjective *big*. Taken together, these pieces of evidence lead to the conclusion that there is no broader generalisation that would allow speakers to produce or comprehend the expression *by and large*. See for yourself if you can apply the same logic to the examples that are offered in (10).

(10) There was cat all over the road.
      The tractor was driven by a 16 year old boy.
      John is best friends with Eddie Murphy.

The first example, which describes the unfortunate result of a car accident involving a feline, is probably the easiest to analyse. The lexical item *cat* is, in most contexts of use, a count noun. In the example above, it behaves structurally as a mass noun. Constructions in which count nouns are used as mass nouns are aptly called GRINDING constructions (Fillmore et al. 2012). Two structural characteristics of the example are worth some consideration. First, *cat* occurs here without a determiner. Second, when used as a mass noun, *cat* disallows pluralisation. The sentence *There were cats all over the road* would enforce a count noun interpretation and thus refer to numerous intact felines occupying the road. Turning to the second example, the final noun phrase *a 16 year old boy* instantiates what could be called the MEASUREMENT AS MODIFIER construction. The idiosyncrasy that can be observed here is that the noun *year* is in the singular, despite the fact that *years* might be expected, given that the boy is 16 years old. This peculiarity is systematic, as is evidenced by expressions such as *a twelve-inch-thick wall* or *a six-foot-tall athlete*. The third example expresses a reciprocal relation between *John* and *Eddie Murphy*: the two are best friends. What is remarkable about the structure of the example is that we have a singular subject, *John*, but a plural subject complement, *best friends*. In canonical predicative constructions, subject and subject complement have to agree in number, as in *John is a doctor* or *They might be giants*. Note also that the RECIPROCAL PREDICATIVE construction, unlike canonical predicative constructions, requires a prepositional phrase such as *with Eddie Murphy*. Summing up, even though formal non-predictability is not a required criterion for constructions, finding formal idiosyncrasies is an excellent source of evidence for calling something a construction.

1.3.2 Does the expression carry non-compositional meaning?

The second strategy that will help you to find and identify constructions relates to Goldberg's criterion of non-predictable meaning. Can hearers work out the meaning of an expression by combining the meanings of its individual parts, or does the whole expression signify something in addition that cannot be worked out? If the meaning of an expression is 'more than the sum of its parts', there is evidence to speak of a construction. Non-compositional meanings are self-evident in idioms such as *get your act together*, *make waves*, or *call the shots*. A second language learner of English would be likely to know all component words of these idioms, but this would not allow her to work out their overall meanings. In the preceding sections, we have discussed expressions that may be less salient than these figures of speech, but which nonetheless convey non-compositional meanings. Recall that *in winter* conveys the idea of 'in winter, generally', or that *How has your day been?* is used as a conventional way to strike up a conversation. A second language learner would have little trouble understanding these expressions, but she would have no way of knowing beforehand that these are typical, idiomatic ways of expressing the respective meanings. Identifying non-compositional meanings essentially requires you to 'play dumb', pretending not to understand anything that cannot be worked out on the basis of the component parts of an expression. Use the following examples to get some practice.

(11)   During the game John broke a finger.
       The result was not much of a surprise.
       The Royal Shakespeare Company is a tough act to follow.

The first example conveys that John had an accident that left him with one of his fingers broken. Crucially, he did not break someone else's finger, even though there is nothing in the words of the example that would preclude that interpretation. In the second example, the phrase *not much of a surprise* does not refer to 'a small part of a surprise', whatever that might be, but rather, it is to be understood as 'no surprise at all'. Taylor (2012: 60) calls this the (NOT) MUCH OF A NOUN construction and points out some of its structural and semantic characteristics. The last example may be a little trickier than the two previous ones. What we are dealing with here is a special case of what has been called the TOUGH-RAISING construction (Langacker 1995). Adjectives such as *tough*, *difficult*, or *hard* occur in sentences such as *Proust is tough to read*, which ascribe toughness to 'reading Proust', rather than to 'Proust' himself. In the example above, the Royal Shakespeare Company is not 'a tough act', as a second language learner might conclude. Rather, following an act such as the Royal Shakespeare Company is considered a tough challenge.

At this point, we need to introduce a concept that is of central importance for the idea of non-compositional meaning in constructions. This concept is called **coercion**, and it describes the phenomenon that the meaning of a lexical item may vary systematically with the constructional contexts in which it is found. Laura Michaelis has formulated a **principle of coercion** that captures this phenomenon (2004: 25):

> If a lexical item is semantically incompatible with its morphosyntactic context, the meaning of the lexical item conforms to the meaning of the structure in which it is embedded.

What this means is that constructions may override word meanings, creating non-compositional constructional meanings in the process. The 'morphosyntactic context', that is, the construction in which a lexical item is found, thus has the power to change or suppress certain semantic characteristics of that lexical item. When word meanings can be observed to change within a constructional context, we speak of **coercion effects**. The principle of coercion can be seen at work in the examples below.

(12) Three beers please!
     John sauced the pizza.
     Frank played the piano to pieces.

The first example illustrates the converse of expressions such as *There was cat all over the road*. The noun *beer* is usually a mass noun, and hence semantically incompatible with the plural inflection and the numeral *three*. The morphosyntactic context thus imposes an interpretation that differs from the default meaning of *beer*: instead of a mass, the example refers to three units of beer, as served in a bottle or a glass. Constructions that convert mass nouns to count nouns will be discussed in this book as INDIVIDUATION constructions. In the second example we find the noun *sauce* used as a verb. The entire expression conveys the meaning that John applied sauce to the pizza. This meaning cannot be derived from the individual words, and a second language learner might arrive at different interpretations, assuming for instance that John dipped a piece of pizza into sauce, or that John, using a heavy-duty blender, turned a pizza into a thick, unappetising sauce. Meanwhile, proficient speakers of English arrive at the intended interpretation because their linguistic knowledge includes a subpattern of the TRANSITIVE construction with denominal verbs that shows itself in expressions such as *pepper the steak*, *butter the toast*, or *egg and breadcrumb the fish*. The construction coerces the lexical meanings of *pepper*, *butter*, *egg*, and *breadcrumb* into the meaning 'apply to a surface', which is a substantial semantic enrichment. Finally, the third example illustrates the English RESULTATIVE construction. What is conveyed by the example is that Frank played the piano in such a violent manner that it ultimately fell to pieces. The lexical meaning of *play* does make reference to an instrument that is played, but it does not specify a possible change of state in that instrument. It is the morpho-syntactic context of the resultative construction that coerces *play* into the meaning 'bring about a change of state by means of playing'.

Spectacular coercion effects, as for instance in *John sneezed the napkin off the table* or in *She smiled herself an upgrade*, have served as a very com-pelling argument for the idea that constructions are symbolic units that carry meaning. After all, the only alternative explanation for the meanings of the above examples would be that verbs such as *sneeze* or *smile* have highly specific secondary senses, namely 'cause to move along a path by means of sneezing' or 'cause a transfer of a good between an agent and a recipient by means of smiling'. Goldberg (1995: 9) points out that Construction Grammar obviates the need to posit such implausible verb senses. In the dictionary-and-grammar model of linguistic knowl-edge, there would be no other choice.

1.3.3 Does the expression have idiosyncratic constraints?

So far, we have discussed two strategies that allow the detection and identification of constructions: we could be looking for non-predictable formal aspects or for non-compositional meanings. This section will discuss a third strategy, which relates to both form and meaning of a construction. Suppose that we come across an expression that, on a cursory glance, would seem to be entirely unremarkable, such as *The dog over there is asleep*. In terms of its structure, every part of that sentence can be analysed as instantiating more general patterns of the grammar of English: *the dog over there* is a DEFINITE NOUN PHRASE construction that incorporates a prepositional phrase, not unlike *the book on the table*. The entire expression instantiates a PREDICATIVE construction, which gives rise to expressions such as *The book on the table is new*. Still, there is something about the example that necessitates a constructional analysis. To let the cat out of the bag, the adjective *asleep* belongs to a class of English adjectives that exhibit an idiosyncratic constraint: they cannot be used attributively. Whereas you could speak of *an interesting book*, the grammar of English does not allow you to refer to **the asleep dog*. Evidently, restrictions of this kind have to be learned, and there is evidence to suggest that language learners pay close attention to the contexts in which elements such as *asleep* do and do not appear (Boyd and Goldberg 2011). At any rate, the positioning constraint on adjectives such as *asleep* is something that constitutes knowledge of language, and hence it needs to be included in the construct-i-con. The following examples show constraints that affect other English constructions.

(13) I brought John a glass of water.
      *I brought the table a glass of water.

      Mary is a smarter lawyer than John.
      *Mary is the smarter lawyer than John.

      She elbowed her way through the room.
      *She elbowed her way.

      I have long known your father.
      *I have long read this book.

The first pair of examples illustrates a constraint on the English DITRANSITIVE construction, namely that the referent of the recipient argument be animate when actual transfers are at issue. In metaphorical examples such as *Give the table a good scrub!* that constraint is relaxed. Note that this is a semantic constraint, rather than a formal one. The second pair of examples shows a constraint on a DEGREE MARKER construction. As is shown by the examples, there is a constraint with regard to definiteness: only the example with the indefinite article is acceptable. In the third pair of examples, we see an example of the English WAY construction (Goldberg 1995). In present-day usage, this construction requires the presence of an argument that specifies a path, here instantiated by *through the room*. As was shown in a historical study by Israel (1996), this was not always the case: the WAY construction used to occur without path arguments, but as such arguments became increasingly frequent, a constraint developed that is categorical for present-day speakers of English and that renders the second member of the pair ungrammatical. Finally, the fourth pair of examples shows a use of *long* as an adverb with the meaning 'for a long time'. Whereas it could be presumed that all sentences of the structure *I have V-ed NP for a long time* could be paraphrased as *I have long V-ed NP*, the unacceptability of the second example suggests otherwise. There are constraints on the HAVE LONG V-*ed* construction, and they form part of what speakers of English know about their language.

Discovering idiosyncratic constraints on the use of constructions is not as straightforward a task as the identification of non-predictable formal aspects or non-compositional meanings. Mainly, this is because finding an example such as *The dog over there is asleep* or *I have long known your father* in a corpus will not tell you anything about constraints that might affect parts of those expressions. In the words of Noam Chomsky, 'A corpus never tells you what is impossible. In fact, it does not even tell you what is possible' (Aarts 2000: 6). Contrary to what Chomsky suggests, corpora in fact do both if quantitative tools of analysis are applied (Stefanowitsch 2008, 2011; Goldberg 2011). Still, Chomsky would have a point if the quote were altered to 'A single, isolated example never tells you what is impossible. In fact, it does not even tell you what is possible.' So, if that is the case, how can we determine what is possible and impossible? For a long time, linguists have approached the issue by constructing examples and judging the grammaticality of those examples, using their intuitions. Using intuitions as the only source of evidence is methodologically highly problematic (Schütze 1996), and for readers of this book who are non-native speakers of English it might not even be feasible. Still, it would be wrong to demonise linguistic intuitions. Intuitions are in fact necessary for the analysis of idiosyncratic constraints, but they are only half of the story. What I recommend for the analysis of constructions and their constraints is to use intuition to construct examples and to check those examples against a large database, such as Mark Davies' suite of corpora, which is freely accessible on the world wide web (e.g. Davies 2010). If your experience in doing corpus analyses is limited, Lindquist (2009) is an excellent resource to use. For a start, try to work out some restrictions on the constructions that are illustrated in (14). First, search for expressions that conform exactly to these sentences, altering at most the concrete lexical items. Determine the parts of speech for all components of the respective expressions. Then, move on to change some of their formal aspects and see if the results point to restrictions.

(14) Most at risk are the very young and the elderly.
      I check my email once every ten minutes.
      I'm willing to go thermonuclear war on this.

Even if your own intuitions at first do not generate the 'right' predictions about what is found in a corpus and what is not, chances are that you will get a clearer idea of how the respective constructions are used and what restrictions might be at play.

1.3.4 Does the expression have collocational preferences?

There is one strategy for finding constructions that we still need to discuss. Even if an expression seems formally regular, semantically transparent, and without noticeable constraints on its behaviour, it might still be a construction in its own right, rather than an instantiation of a more general pattern. Take the following example.

(15) I will call you tomorrow morning.

The sentence is an example of the English WILL FUTURE construction. Let us for a moment ponder the question on what grounds, if any, we could make the case that a sentence-level construction with the auxiliary verb *will* and a following non-finite verb phrase should be called a construction. Evidently, pedagogical grammars call it a construction, but is it a construction according to the definitions and criteria that we have set up in the preceding sections? The argument from non-predictable structural criteria appears to fail: there is a more general pattern according to which auxiliary verbs can be paired with non-finite verbal complements. The argument from non-compositional meanings will not get us any further. The overall meaning of the example in (15) can clearly be worked out from the meanings of the individual words, for *will* we rely on the *OED* and adopt the definition 'auxiliary of the future tense with implication of intention or volition' (*OED: will*, v., 11). Can we identify constraints? It appears that *will* combines rather freely with verbs in the infinitive. Consequently, there would be nothing left for us to do but to concede that we are looking at a construct instantiating what we might call the AUXILIARY PLUS INFINITIVE construction.

However, there is evidence to suggest otherwise. Even though *will* is technically combinable with just about any verb of the English language, data from corpora show that *will* occurs more frequently with some verbs than with others. Well, you might say, is that not to be expected, given that some verbs, like *be*, are very frequent, and others, like *procrastinate*, are used less often? That is of course the case. But if you control for the respective frequencies of *be*, *procrastinate*, *arrive*, *eat*, *copy*, *argue*, and all the other verbs that are used with *will*, it turns out that some verbs occur more frequently than expected whereas others occur less frequently than expected. Gries and Stefanowitsch (2004a) have analysed the collocational preferences of *will* and *be going to*, finding that these two expressions of future time have markedly different preferences with regard to the verb types that occur with them. The basic result, which is replicated in Hilpert (2008), is that *be going to* exhibits a tendency to occur with verbs that are agentive, punctual, and high in transitivity. Conversely, *will* attracts verbs that are non-agentive, durative, and low in transitivity. Gries et al. (2005) present experimental evidence that speakers are acutely sensitive to the relation between constructions and their typical collocates. The construct-i-con, it turns out, stores information about language use in a highly detailed fashion that includes rich information about how linguistic units combine with others. Hence, it is absolutely warranted to speak of WILL PLUS INFINITIVE as a construction. The question whether a construction has collocational preferences can be addressed with relative frequency counts on the basis of corpus data. Stefanowitsch and Gries (2003) have developed an elegant method that goes by the name of **collostructional analysis**, and that has been applied to a variety of English constructions (cf. Gries and Stefanowitsch 2004a; Gries and Wulff 2005; Hilpert 2006; Stefanowitsch 2006; inter alia).

1.4 Summing up

In this chapter, we have raised the question what speakers have to know when they know a language such as English. Common sense suggests that linguistic knowledge consists of several different kinds of knowledge. In linguistics, this idea has given rise to what is called the dictionary-and-grammar model of linguistic knowledge (Taylor 2012), which makes a clear distinction between knowledge of vocabulary on the one hand and knowledge of grammar on the other. Construction Grammar is a theory that takes a radically different perspective: knowledge of language is to be modelled as knowledge of constructions, and nothing else in addition. The main reasons for adopting such an approach are the following. First, it is observed that idiomatic expressions fully permeate ordinary language. Listing all idiomatic expressions in an appendix to the mental lexicon would greatly inflate its size. But a second point is more problematic. Many idioms cannot be reduced to fixed strings that could be memorised and represented as such. Rather, idiomatic expressions have slots that can accommodate different lexical items, and different grammatical structures. Furthermore, many idiomatic expressions are clearly productive, so that speakers can generate new and original utterances with them. The overall conclusion of these observations is that the line between the mental lexicon, containing knowledge of words, and the mental grammar, containing knowledge of rules, becomes increasingly blurry; so much so that Construction Grammarians propose to abandon it altogether. Instead, knowledge of language is seen as a large inventory of constructions, a construct-i-con.

Constructions, on this view, are defined as linguistic generalisations that speakers internalise. Specifically, this book adopts a definition of constructions under which they are form–meaning pairs which have either non-predictable formal characteristics, non-compositional meanings, or a high enough frequency to be remembered as such (Goldberg 2006: 5).

This chapter also discussed four strategies that allow you to identify constructions. The first strategy is to look out for structural traits of an expression that deviate from more canonical patterns. Second, constructions can be identified on the basis of non-compositional meanings. Third, idiosyncratic constraints that involve meaning or form serve as a powerful and flexible diagnostic. Fourth, even if the first three strategies fail to identify an expression as a construction, an analysis of collocational preferences may reveal that the expression in question does in fact have the status of a construction.

1.5 Outline of the following chapters

It was the aim of this chapter to give you a rough overview of the enterprise that is Construction Grammar. In the remaining chapters of this book, that overview will be successively fleshed out in order to address the many open questions that will be on your mind right now. So, what lies ahead? The rest of this book is structured into two main parts. Chapters 2–5 will further familiarise you with the central concepts of Construction Grammar. They will do so by describing a repertoire of constructions that illustrates how these concepts are applied. Specifically, we will be concerned with argument structure constructions (Chapter 2), abstract phrasal and clausal constructions (Chapter 3), morphological constructions (Chapter 4), and information packaging constructions (Chapter 5). What you can expect is thus a grand tour of English grammar. That tour will include several stops at locations that may seem more or less familiar, but I promise that these will appear in a new light. The second part of the book, comprising Chapters 6–8, will focus on interfaces between Construction Grammar and specific areas of linguistic study. What makes Construction Grammar attractive as a linguistic theory is not least that it connects usefully to many areas of research that may interest you. We will discuss constructional work in psycholinguistics (Chapter 6), research on language acquisition (Chapter 7), and language variation and change (Chapter 8). A concluding chapter will try to connect the most important ideas of this book, sending you off with a number of suggestions for research projects.

Study questions

• What is the dictionary-and-grammar model of linguistic knowledge?
• What is the construct-i-con?
• How are constructions defined?

- What are the reasons for rejecting non-predictability as a definitional criterion of constructions?
- What is the difference between a construction and a construct?
- What strategies can you use to identify a construction?
- What is meant by the term 'coercion'?

Further reading

The work of Adele E. Goldberg (1995, 2006) has been extremely influential. An excellent starting point for further reading is her synopsis article of Construction Grammar (Goldberg 2003). All of the issues raised in the present chapter are discussed in greater depth in *The Oxford Handbook of Construction Grammar* (Hoffmann and Trousdale 2013). I also highly recommend the chapters on Construction Grammar that are found in two introductory works on cognitive linguistics (Croft and Cruse 2004; Evans and Green 2006). The first two chapters in Fried and Östman (2004) provide further information on the intellectual background of Construction Grammar and on formalisation, the latter of which is also treated in Sag et al. (2003). Among the foundational works of Construction Grammar, Fillmore et al. (1988) and Kay and Fillmore (1999) stand out. Working through these papers is not easy, but very rewarding.

2 Argument structure constructions

2.1 Analysing 'simple sentences'

The last chapter made the point that language use is full of idiomatic expressions that exhibit idiosyncrasies with regard to form and meaning. Constructions of this kind have been addressed in many classic studies in Construction Grammar, for instance in Fillmore et al. (1988), who focus on sentences such as *I don't eat fish, let alone raw oysters.* Idiomatic expressions constitute the central theoretical motivation for Construction Grammar as a theory of language: if speakers have to memorise a large number of idiosyncratic, semi-fixed constructional schemas, then the dictionary-and-grammar model of linguistic knowledge cannot be maintained. Given the importance of idioms, it may come as a surprise to you that one of the most influential studies in Construction Grammar addresses 'simple sentences' that at first glance appear to behave much more regularly than constructions such as *let alone.* In her book *Constructions: A Construction Grammar Approach to Argument Structure,* Adele Goldberg (1995) discusses expressions such as the following.

(1) Pat gave Bill a book.
     John threw the ball over the fence.
     Bob hammered the metal flat.

On the face of it, these sentences seem to fail the most important criteria for constructionhood that were developed in the last chapter, as there does not appear to be anything unusual about either the form or the meaning of these examples. A learner of English who knew all of the words in these sentences would have no trouble understanding what they mean. Still, there is good evidence for viewing these examples as instances of a special kind of construction, namely **argument structure constructions**. This chapter will discuss what these constructions are and it will explain why these constructions continue to attract substantial attention in current research.

The remaining sections of this chapter are organised in the following way. The next section will introduce the term **argument structure** and flesh out its role in a constructionist theory of linguistic knowledge. The subsequent section will discuss a number of valency-increasing constructions, that is, constructions that can add arguments to the event structure of a verb. The RESULTATIVE construction is one such construction, but there are quite a few more of them in English. The section after that will focus on the inverse process and discuss valency-decreasing constructions. In such constructions, a role that is present in the event structure of a verb is 'suppressed', that is, it is not overtly expressed. Perhaps the most conspicuous example of a valency-decreasing construction is the PASSIVE. In a sentence such as *Mistakes were made*, which passivises the verb *make*, the person making the mistakes is not identified. The PASSIVE construction thus reduces the valency of *make* by suppressing its agent argument. As this chapter will discuss, there are other constructions that behave in similar ways. The final section of this chapter will discuss relations between argument structure constructions, introducing the concept of **syntactic alternations**.

2.2 Argument structure

The phenomenon that is described by the term **argument structure** is often also referred to as **valency**. The term 'valency' is borrowed from chemistry, where it describes how many different atoms a chemical element can bind to itself to form a complex molecule. Chemical elements differ in this regard, such that hydrogen for instance can only bond with a single other atom, whereas carbon can bond with several others, thus forming larger molecules. The words of a language can be likened to this behaviour of chemical elements: the verb *yawn* usually forms a bond with just one element, namely its subject (*The cat yawned*). The verb *send* typically bonds with three elements, namely its subject and two objects (*Sylvia sent me a message*). Valency is first and foremost a characteristic of verbs, but the concept can also be applied to adjectives and nouns. For instance, the adjective *certain* can form a bond with a *that*-clause (*I'm certain that he left*) or an infinitival clause (*John is certain to win the election*). Nouns such as *fact* or *suspicion* can bond to *that*-clauses as well (*the fact that he left, the suspicion that sausages contain dog meat*). Hence, the terms 'argument structure' and 'valency', as used in linguistics, refer to a relationship that holds between a **predicate** denoting an activity, state, or event and the respective participants, which are called **argu-**

Table 2.1 Thematic roles

Role	Definition	Example
AGENT	the initiator of an action	**Pat** ate a waffle.
PATIENT	the participant undergoing an action or a change of state	Pat ate **a waffle**.
THEME	the participant which is moving	Pat threw **the rope** over.
EXPERIENCER	the participant who is aware of a stimulus	**Pat** heard a sound.
STIMULUS	the participant that is experienced	Pat heard **a sound**.
BENEFICIARY	the participant who benefits from an action	Pat sang for **me**.
RECIPIENT	the participant receiving an item	Pat gave **me** a waffle.
INSTRUMENT	the participant serving as a means to an action	Pat opened it with **a knife**.
LOCATION	the place of an event	Pat was born in **Florida**.
GOAL	the end point of a movement	Pat threw it into **the fire**.
SOURCE	the starting point of a movement	Pat came home from **work**.

ments. In the sentence *John threw the ball over the fence*, the verb form *threw* is the predicate, and *John, the ball*, and also the prepositional phrase *over the fence* would be its arguments. Arguments are thus not only expressed by nominal structures; other phrase types and clauses may also express them.

What makes argument structure a difficult term to deal with is that it can be understood in two ways: semantically and syntactically. A verb such as *eat* evokes a scene with two participants, someone who is eating and something that gets eaten. This would be the semantic argument structure of *eat*, which is sometimes also called its **event structure**. In order to talk about event structure, linguists have developed a vocabulary that abstracts away from individual verbs and describes different semantic roles, which are sometimes also called thematic roles. Table 2.1 lists eleven semantic roles that are frequently referred to (Saeed 2003: 153).

Naturally, this list is open-ended, the roles are not necessarily mutually exclusive, and it would be possible to make finer distinctions or to construct more abstract roles. For instance, recipients and beneficiaries share certain characteristics with patients, and goals and sources both encode locations. The event structure of a verb specifies the kinds of roles that may appear with that verb. As is illustrated by the first two examples in the table, the verb *eat* typically occurs with an agent and with a patient, but other configurations are possible. Importantly, *eat* also has a syntactic argument structure. Speakers know that the verb *eat* usually occurs with a subject and a direct object, but they also know that *eat* is sometimes used intransitively, as in *Thanks, I have already eaten*. In the dictionary-and-grammar model of linguistic knowledge, the dictionary entry for a lexical element such as *eat* would include information on its event structure, including the roles of someone who is eating and something that is eaten, and information on syntactic argument structure patterns. Typically, there will be several patterns. For instance, the entry for *sweep* would list the following ones, amongst others:

(2) We still have to sweep.
     We still have to sweep the tiles.
     We still have to sweep the tiles squeaky clean.
     We still have to sweep the mud off the tiles.

It seems very natural to assume that speakers' knowledge of a verb such as *sweep* includes knowledge of the structures in which that verb typically appears. However, Goldberg (1995) argues that argument structure cannot be wholly explained in terms of lexical entries alone. An important piece of evidence in this regard is that speakers occasionally use verbs 'creatively', that is, with argument structures that are not conventionally associated with the respective verbs. The following examples illustrate that phenomenon.

(3) John played the piano to pieces.
     He pulled himself free, one leg at a time.
     No matter how carefully you lick a spoon clean, some goo will cling to it.

The verb *play* can be used intransitively (*The kids were playing*), transitively (*Sylvia played a Schubert sonata*), and in the PREPOSITIONAL DATIVE construction (*John played the ball to the centre forward*), to illustrate just three of its conventional argument structure patterns. It is typically the case that the meaning of a verb is not quite the same across different patterns. In the examples just mentioned, intransitive *play* evokes the idea of 'interacting with toys', transitive *play* conveys the meaning of 'using a musical instrument', and *play* in the PREPOSITIONAL DATIVE construction simply means 'pass'. Despite these differences, the respective activities of the kids, Sylvia, and John all count as instances of playing. With the use of *play* that is given in (3), things are not quite as straightforward. The example conveys that John's playing had an effect on the piano, such that it fell to pieces. This meaning cannot be explained as a conventional sense of the verb *play*. Rather, it is the syntactic form of the sentence that leads hearers to understand this non-compositional meaning. Goldberg (1995) calls this form the English RESULTATIVE construction. Compare the phrase *played the piano to pieces* to *pulled himself free* and *lick a spoon clean*. In each case, the verb combines with a direct object and a predicate that expresses a resultant state. The RESULTATIVE construction is an argument structure construction, because it 'adds' an element to the conventional argument structure of verbs such as *play, pull*, or *lick*. In the case of the above example with *play*, this extra element is the prepositional phrase *to pieces*. Goldberg argues that syntactic constructions, such as the RESULTATIVE construction, are not just structural templates that are used to arrange words into phrases and sentences, but carry meaning. That is, speakers of English know that there is a syntactic pattern that conveys the meaning 'X causes Y to become Z', independently of the actual verb that is found in this pattern. This pairing of form and meaning is stored in the construct-i-con, and it allows speakers to create and understand sentences in which verbs are used resultatively, regardless of whether their conventional argument structure specifies a result, or even a direct object. The verbs *play*, *pull*, and *lick* frequently occur with direct objects, but even intransitive verbs such as *run, sneeze*, or *worry* can be inserted into the RESULTATIVE construction, as the following examples show.

(4) John ran his feet sore.
Frank sneezed his cat soaking wet.
Bob's mother worried herself sick.

In these examples, the RESULTATIVE construction contributes not only a result argument, but also a patient argument. The phrases *his feet, his cat*, and *herself* denote patients, which undergo a change of state as a result of an action. One can take the argument even further and construct example sentences with invented words, which are associated neither with a conventional argument structure nor with a particular semantic event structure. The following examples draw on some nonce words that Lewis Carroll used in his famous poem *Jabberwocky*.

(5) The children were gimbling the cat frumious.
Chortle the toves into small pieces. Season liberally with salt and pepper.
David has whiffled my borogoves completely vorpal again!

Naturally, the interpretations of these sentences depend on contextual cues, such that hearers try to link the words *gimbling* and *frumious* to activities and states that ensue when children and cats interact in prototypical ways. Note, however, that the third example is largely devoid of such contextual cues, and still, you are likely to have come up with an idea of what David might have done. Regardless of the specifics, your interpretation of the sentence will be consonant with the idea that David whiffled the borogoves, and that this act of whiffling made them vorpal again. Given that you have no idea what the words by themselves mean, this is a remarkable achievement!

To summarise these observations, the 'simple sentences' of English matter deeply to Construction Grammar because they instantiate argument structure constructions. These constructions have to be part of speakers' knowledge of language for two reasons. First, they can change the conventional valency patterns of verbs, thus generating expressions that are formally idiosyncratic. A verb such as *sneeze* does not usually take a patient argument, but it does take one in the RESULTATIVE construction. Second, argument structure constructions convey meanings that cannot be explained compositionally. The resultative meaning of the example sentences in (4) and (5) does not simply follow from combining the individual word meanings. Rather, it is the syntactic construction as such that imposes this meaning on the words. Goldberg (1995) points out that the combination of verbs and constructions is not entirely unconstrained. A verb can only be inserted into a given construction if the event structure of that verb and the argument structure of the construction match semantically. To illustrate, it is possible to insert *sneeze* into the resultative construction because both *sneeze* and the resultative construction require an agent argument in the subject position. Hence, the respective roles can be 'fused'. This idea is rendered more precise in what is called the **semantic coherence principle** (Goldberg 1995: 50):

> Only roles which are semantically compatible can be fused. Two roles r_1 and r_2 are semantically compatible if either r_1 can be construed as an instance of r_2, or r_2 can be construed as an instance of r_1.

The semantic coherence principle explains why verbs such as *hear* or *sink* cannot readily be inserted into the resultative construction. Sentences such as **John heard his ears deaf with loud heavy metal* or **John sank himself drowned* are odd because neither of the verbs specifies in its conventional event structure the agent role that the resultative construction requires for its subject. The verb *hear* specifies an experiencer in its event structure, and the verb *sink* specifies a theme.

Argument structure constructions are important to the Construction Grammar enterprise for yet another reason. The 'simple sentences' of a language tend to have very basic meanings that reflect recurrent types of everyday experience. In other words, languages have a simple

sentence pattern to express the result of an action because acting on
one's environment in order to bring about a result is a basic, recurrent, and important pattern of human behaviour: on any given day,
you will probably start your morning by dragging yourself out of bed,
drawing the curtains open, and getting the coffee maker up and running.
Several other resultative actions may follow before you have even had
a shower. Similarly, languages have ditransitive constructions because
situations of giving, sending, offering, and showing are just so central
to the interaction between human beings. The general idea that grammatical structures reflect the realities of daily life has been captured in
the slogan that 'Grammars code best what speakers do most' (Du Bois
1985: 363). Goldberg (1995: 39) translates this idea into what is called
the **scene-encoding hypothesis**:

> Constructions which correspond to basic sentence types encode as their
> central senses event types that are basic to human experience.

The scene-encoding hypothesis predicts that across many languages,
there should be basic syntactic patterns that express ideas such as
bringing about a result, transferring an object, moving along a path,
undergoing a change of state, or experiencing a stimulus. Of the
English argument structure constructions that Goldberg discusses,
the RESULTATIVE construction, the DITRANSITIVE construction, and the
CAUSED MOTION construction do correspond closely to basic scenes of
human experience.

2.3 Valency-increasing constructions

Across languages, constructions that increase the valency of verbs tend
to have similar kinds of meanings, most notably RESULTATIVE constructions, CAUSATIVE constructions, and APPLICATIVE constructions
(cf. Payne 1997 for a cross-linguistic overview). In English, valency-
increasing constructions are exemplified by the RESULTATIVE construction that was discussed above, the DITRANSITIVE construction (*Sylvia
wrote me an email*), the CAUSED MOTION construction (*John sneezed the
napkin off the table*), and the WAY construction (*Frank cheated his way into
Harvard*). The following sections will discuss each of these in turn.

2.3.1 The DITRANSITIVE construction

The DITRANSITIVE construction is exemplified by the following
sentences.

(6)   I gave John the keys.
      Sylvia wrote me an email.
      Sally baked her sister a cake.
      Could you draw me a picture of the suspect?

The construction links a verb with three arguments, that is, a subject and two objects. These arguments map onto three distinct semantic roles. The subject argument is understood to be the agent of a transfer. This action involves the second object, which receives the role of the transferred object. This object is transferred from the agent to a recipient, who is expressed by the first object. Whereas *give, send, offer,* and many other English verbs conventionally include two objects in their argument structure, the same cannot be said of other verbs that occur with the DITRANSITIVE construction. The verbs *bake* and *draw*, although perfectly acceptable in the construction, only rarely occur with two objects in corpus data. In order to explain the acceptability of such examples, it is thus necessary to posit a construction that forms part of speakers' grammatical knowledge. By the same token, the verbs *bake* and *draw* can in no way account for the overall meaning of the respective examples, which convey the idea of a transfer. If *Sally baked her sister a cake*, that means that Sally produced a cake so that her sister could willingly receive it. Unless we assume an ad-hoc sense of *bake* along the lines of 'apply heat to an item of food with the purpose of creating a product that can then be transferred to a willing recipient', the overall meaning of the example cannot be derived from the respective word meanings. Alternatively, we can posit the DITRANSITIVE construction as a symbolic unit that carries meaning and that is responsible for the observed increase in the valency of *bake*. In this case, *bake* contributes its usual lexical meaning while the construction augments its argument structure to include a recipient argument.

   Several semantic idiosyncrasies of the construction are worth pointing out. First, it appears that the agent needs to carry out the transfer consciously and willingly. For instance, it would be highly misleading to state that *Sylvia wrote me an email* when in fact Sylvia unintentionally hit 'reply to all', sending out a private message that I was never supposed to read. Second, it is equally necessary that the recipient be willing to receive the transferred objects. The sentence *We threw the squirrels some peanuts* evokes the idea of squirrels willingly accepting their peanuts. The example could not be used to describe the activity of throwing peanuts at dead squirrels. In the following examples, the respective recipients fail the criterion of being 'willing to accept'. The examples are therefore judged as odd by proficient speakers of English.

(7) ?Bill threw the coma victim a blanket.   (I threw John a blanket.)
    ?John gave the house new windows.   (I gave John a new key.)
    ?I left the baby some beer in the fridge.   (I left John some beer in
                                                the fridge.)

One might of course object that there are many uses of the DITRANSITIVE construction in which the recipient does not want to receive the transferred object, and which are nonetheless perfectly acceptable.

(8) The professor gave the student an F.
    The plumber mailed me another invoice.
    The criminals sent him a ransom note, asking for a million pounds.

It is probably fair to say few people enjoy receiving bad grades, unexpected bills, or ransom notes. In the light of these examples, it seems more adequate to say that the recipient has to be able to receive the transferred object, and perhaps conventionally expected to do so, which motivates the label of a 'socially qualified recipient'. But even so, there are further examples that seem to contradict what we have said so far about the DITRANSITIVE construction.

(9) The noise gave me a headache.
    The music lent the party a festive air.
    The flood brought us the opportunity to remodel our old bathroom.

A first thing to notice about these examples is that the 'transferred object' is immaterial. Headaches and opportunities are not the kind of thing that could be physically exchanged. Likewise, the examples contain subject noun phrases that refer to noise, music, and a flood, none of which can be said to be a volitional agent. Goldberg (1995: 144) argues that these examples metaphorically extend the basic meaning of the DITRANSITIVE construction. Whereas the basic meaning of the construction conveys the idea of a physical transfer, the examples in (9) express the relation between a cause and an effect. Causal relations are thus metaphorically understood as events of giving and receiving. A noise that causes a headache can be described as 'giving me a headache'. A flood that causes the destruction of a bathroom could, under a rather optimistic outlook on life, be construed as 'bringing an opportunity for remodelling'. The semantic spectrum of the DITRANSITIVE construction further includes transfers that will only occur in the future, acts that facilitate reception of an object, and acts that block a potential transfer.

(10) John ordered Margaret a gin and tonic.
     The doctor allowed me a full meal.
     The banks refused him a loan.

So far, we have identified a number of semantic idiosyncrasies that
pertain to the DITRANSITIVE construction. Other idiosyncrasies of the
construction concern the collocational behaviour of the construction. Specifically, there are certain verbs that do not occur in the
DITRANSITIVE construction despite having a lexical meaning that would
fit the constructional meaning.

(11) *Sally shouted John the news.
     *John explained me the theory.
     *Margaret donated the Red Cross £100.

Why do these verbs 'not work' in the DITRANSITIVE construction? While
it could be suspected that we are seeing verb-specific idiosyncrasies here,
some generalisations have been found. For instance, *shout* behaves just
like a range of other verbs that describe manners of speech, including
scream, murmur, whisper, or *yodel* (Goldberg 1995: 128). The verbs *explain*
and *donate* have in common that they represent Latinate, specialised
vocabulary. Gropen et al. (1989) show that a number of morphophono-
logical traits that characterise Latinate vocabulary, notably involving
stress patterns and affixation, can to some extent predict which verbs
do occur in the DITRANSITIVE construction and which ones do not.
However, many open questions remain, and there is even considerable
inter-speaker variation with regard to the acceptability of verbs such as
obtain or *purchase.* Goldberg (1995: 129) marks *Chris purchased him some food*
as ungrammatical, but *Hannah purchased him a microscope* is one of several
attested examples from corpus data. In Construction Grammar, idiosyncratic lexical preferences of constructions and even differences between
speakers with regard to such preferences can be modelled as part of individual speakers' linguistic knowledge. Constructions will exhibit some
regularities with regard to the kinds of verbs that they accommodate, but
some amount of collocational idiosyncrasy is fully expected.

Summing up, the DITRANSITIVE construction conveys, as its basic
sense, the meaning of a transfer between an intentional agent and a
willing recipient. The construction conventionally occurs with verbs
such as *give, send,* and *offer;* its occurrence with verbs such as *bake, feed,*
or *leave* demonstrates that the construction can actively increase the
valency of verbs that do not usually occur with two objects. Besides its
basic sense, the construction metaphorically expresses relationships of
cause and effect; additional meanings include future transfers, 'enabled'

transfers, and blocked transfers. The construction exhibits collocational restrictions so that it does not readily combine with several specific classes of verbs.

2.3.2 The CAUSED MOTION construction

The following examples illustrate the CAUSED MOTION construction.

(12) The audience laughed Bob off the stage.
John chopped carrots into the salad.
The professor invited us into his office.

Like the DITRANSITIVE construction, the CAUSED MOTION construction can alter and augment the argument structure of the verbs with which it combines. In the examples given above, the construction adds arguments to the verbs *laugh*, *chop*, and *invite*. Whereas the event structure of *laugh* merely specifies someone who is laughing, the example with *laugh* adds an argument of someone who is being moved, what is called a theme, and the goal of that movement. The event structure of *chop* includes a patient argument, that is, something that is being chopped. In the example above, this argument has a double role: the carrots are being chopped, for sure, but in addition to being a patient argument, they are further understood to be moving towards a goal, in this case into the salad. It is therefore appropriate to characterise the role of the carrots as both patient and theme in the context of the CAUSED MOTION construction. The construction can thus increase the valency of verbs, either by adding a path/goal argument, or by adding a theme and a path/goal argument.

Semantically, the construction indicates that an agent carries out an activity that causes a theme to move along a path or towards a goal. More succinctly, the construction conveys the meaning that 'X causes Y to move along or towards Z'. Laughter is hence presented as the ultimate cause of Bob's movement off the stage, even if it is presumably the case that Bob was walking. The CAUSED MOTION construction thus harmonises best with verbs such as *throw*, *kick*, or *pull*, which are conventionally associated with an event structure containing a theme argument and a path/goal argument:

(13) John threw the ball over the fence.
Franz kicked the ball into the goal.
She pulled a handkerchief out of her pocket.

Besides its central sense, the construction conveys the meanings of assisted motion (*John helped Mary out of the car*), prevented motion (*John locked the dog into the bathroom*), enabled motion (*Mary allowed the dog out of the bathroom*), and prompted motion (*The professor invited us into his office*).

Speakers' knowledge of the CAUSED MOTION construction includes knowledge of the following constraints. First, the agent argument cannot be an instrument. Whereas instruments are commonly found as subjects of active clauses such as *The key opened the door* or *This knife chops and slices beautifully*, the CAUSED MOTION construction requires that the agent act autonomously.

(14)   *The key allowed John into the house.
      *The gun threatened the hostages into the back office.
      *The knife chopped the carrots into the salad.

Another constraint on the CAUSED MOTION construction is that the path of the theme is usually intended. Hence, it is not possible to chop carrots onto the floor or pour milk next to one's glass. However, if the action that is specified by the verb is unintentional to begin with, as for instance with the verb *sneeze*, unintended paths do not pose any problem.

(15)   *John chopped the carrots onto the floor.
      *Bob poured milk next to his glass.
      He sneezed his tooth right across town. (Goldberg 2006: 6)

The CAUSED MOTION construction is further constrained with regard to the path of the motion. Specifically, the causal event must fully determine the path of the theme. Paths with very specific goals, or goals that require independent movements along a path, therefore lead to the unacceptability of the following examples.

(16)   *The audience laughed Bob home.
      *Mary allowed the dog to the next village.
      *Bob threw the stone to the bottom of the lake.

To summarise, the CAUSED MOTION construction conveys the meaning that 'X causes Y to move along or towards Z'. The construction can add the arguments of a theme and a path or goal to the event structure of a verb, and it is associated with a range of senses that relate to the basic scenario of caused motion. The construction is chiefly constrained with regard to the subject, which cannot be an instrument, and the path, which must be fully determined by the causal action.

2.3.3 The WAY construction

The English WAY construction differs from the constructions that have been discussed up to now in this chapter because it specifies the lexical element *way* and a possessive determiner such as *his, her,* or *their,* in its form. The following examples serve to illustrate the construction.

(17) Frank dug his way out of prison.
John elbowed his way across the room.
She slowly climbed her way up through the branches.

Just like the previously discussed constructions, the WAY construction can add arguments to the event structure of lexical verbs. The construction evokes a scenario in which an agent moves along a path that is difficult to navigate. The verbs that occur in the WAY construction can be verbs of directed movement, such as *climb,* but also verbs such as *dig* or *elbow,* which do not inherently convey the idea of movement along a trajectory. The WAY construction thus imposes this meaning on its component words, adding up to two arguments in the process: the *way* argument and a path/goal argument not unlike the argument that was discussed in connection with the CAUSED MOTION construction. With a verb such as *dig,* which conventionally takes a direct object (*digging a hole, digging your own grave*), it could be argued that 'his way out of prison' is simply a noun phrase instantiating a direct object, so that nothing out of the ordinary would be going on with that example. However, the example states more than that Frank has dug a tunnel out of prison. What the example conveys is that Frank succeeded in actually traversing the tunnel, thus escaping from prison. Goldberg (1995: 200) points out that the WAY construction entails motion, so that examples such as the following are nonsensical.

(18) *Frank dug his way out of prison, but he hasn't gone yet.
*Staying behind the counter, the bank robbers shot their way through the crowd.

Verbs such as *climb* do specify a path argument in their event structure, but the construction adds the *way* argument, which cannot be replaced by other lexical elements that refer to paths or trajectories more broadly. The following examples are therefore unacceptable, despite their superficial similarity to the example with *climb* given above.

(19) *She quickly climbed her escape route down the stairs.
*She steadily climbed her track up to the summit.

In the basic sense of the WAY construction, the verb conveys the means by which a path is being forged: through digging, climbing, elbowing, or even shooting. In many instances of the WAY construction, the path along which the agent moves is thus not pre-existing, but has to be created, prototypically with some effort. This aspect of the constructional meaning explains that basic motion verbs such as *move* or *step* are not acceptable in the WAY construction.

(20) *She moved her way into the room.
      *She stepped her way down the stairs.

The WAY construction is very commonly used metaphorically, such that completing a demanding task is talked about in terms of the creation of a path and movement along that path. The following examples illustrate metaphorical usages of the construction.

(21) Sally was crunching her way through a bag of potato chips.
      Bob worked his way to the top of his profession.
      The three girls sang their way into the hearts of the audience.

The WAY construction is further used with a meaning that does not make reference to the means by which a path is created, but that rather describes the manner in which a movement is performed. In the examples below, the action denoted by the verb occurs simultaneously to a movement, but that action neither causes nor enables that movement. Discussions of the WAY construction hence distinguish the more common means interpretation from the manner interpretation of the construction.

(22) Sam joked his way into the meeting.
      John was whistling his way down the street.
      Triathlete Paula Finlay cried her way across the finish line.

Goldberg (1995: 212) identifies several semantic constraints on the WAY construction that have to do with the difficulty of creating a path or moving along that path. First, the activity denoted by the verb has to be unbounded or repetitive. Hence it is possible *to climb one's way up a cliff* but not *to jump one's way off a cliff*. A second constraint pertaining to the movement demands that it be self-propelled. Speakers therefore reject *The snow melts its way into the river*, in which the movement is not self-propelled, but they accept *The probe melts its way through the glacier*, in which the probe moves of its own accord. Third, Goldberg (1995: 214) suggests that the WAY construction encodes motion that is directed, not aimless. This is certainly the prototypical case, but many examples, including *James Bond womanising his way across the globe* or *young people drifting their way through life*, suggest that this constraint can be violated fairly easily.

To conclude this section, the WAY construction can be characterised as an argument structure construction that can increase the valency of a verb to include a lexically specified *way* argument and another argument that expresses a path or a goal. There are two basic interpretations of the WAY construction, namely the more common means interpretation, in which the verb encodes the means by which a path is created and/or traversed, and the manner interpretation, in which the verb specifies the manner of an action that occurs simultaneously to a movement. In the means interpretation of the construction, the agent's action is commonly quite difficult, which imposes a number of constraints on the kinds of movements that can be expressed by the WAY construction.

2.4 Valency-decreasing constructions

In the Construction Grammar literature, the discussion of argument structure constructions has been dominated by the topic of valency-increasing constructions. It is not hard to see why this should be the case: constructions that can add multiple arguments to the event structure of otherwise intransitive verbs provide compelling evidence for the idea that knowledge of language must include knowledge of constructions and for the idea that constructions can override lexical meanings. Specifically, speakers must know that it is acceptable to utter a sentence such as *Sally baked her sister a cake* and that the lexical meaning of the verb *bake* is enriched by the constructional context to convey the idea of a transfer. In the introductory chapter, the constructional override of lexical meaning was discussed as the principle of coercion (Michaelis 2004). Yet valency-increasing constructions only represent one half of the set of valency-changing constructions in English. It will be argued in this section that valency-decreasing constructions are no less important to the Construction Grammar enterprise than their more famous relatives.

Cross-linguistically common constructions that decrease the valency of a verb are PASSIVE constructions (*Mistakes were made*), REFLEXIVE constructions (*John shaved*), RECIPROCAL constructions (*Let's meet again soon*), and IMPERATIVE constructions (*Go!*). This section will further discuss NULL INSTANTIATION constructions, which can be illustrated with examples such as *Tigers only kill at night* or *I know*. In these examples, central participants of the actions that are described are left unexpressed, but are nonetheless understood.

2.4.1 The PASSIVE

The English PASSIVE construction with *be* is most often discussed as the marked counterpart of ACTIVE sentences with transitive verbs. The following examples thus form corresponding pairs.

(23) The reviewer rejected the paper.
      The paper was rejected (by the reviewer).
      John paid the bill.
      The bill was paid (by John).

Because of the close relation between pairs such as these, and because
the ACTIVE clearly represents a construction that is applicable in a much
wider set of contexts, characteristics of the PASSIVE are typically phrased
in terms of how PASSIVE sentences deviate from the less marked ACTIVE
sentences. Huddleston and Pullum (2002: 1428) point out three correspondences. First, the subject of the ACTIVE (*the reviewer, John*) appears
in the corresponding PASSIVE sentences as an oblique object marked
with the preposition *by*. As the parentheses in the examples indicate, it
is possible, and indeed the default option in actual language use, to omit
this argument in the PASSIVE. It is this type of omission that justifies
categorising the PASSIVE as a valency-decreasing construction. Second,
the object of the ACTIVE (*the paper, the bill*) appears as the subject of the
corresponding PASSIVE sentences. The PASSIVE thus functions to reverse
the relative prominence of the two arguments in the event structure of
a transitive verb. Whereas normally the agent of a transitive verb has to
be expressed and the patient argument can be omitted under certain circumstances (*Thanks, I have already eaten*), the PASSIVE construction makes
the patient argument obligatory and the agent argument optional.
Third, the verb of the PASSIVE construction is more complex in form
than the corresponding verb in the ACTIVE. It appears in the form of a
past participle that is preceded by a form of the auxiliary *be*.

   Given these clear-cut correspondences, it is a tempting idea to think
of the PASSIVE as a grammatical rule that takes a transitive ACTIVE
sentence as its input and yields a passivised counterpart. However,
Huddleston and Pullum offer a range of examples that differ from the
above description in several respects, but that arguably still instantiate
the PASSIVE construction.

(24) John was given a large data set for the analysis.
      *A large dataset was given John for the analysis.
      Sally's papers are referred to a lot.
      *The children are looked to a lot.

In the first example, the verb *give* is a ditransitive verb, not a transitive
one. As the second example shows, only the recipient, not the theme,
can appear as the subject of a PASSIVE sentence. This is not per se a
problem for a putative passivisation rule: the rule would just have to
include the additional information that theme arguments are not avail-

able for passivisation. The example with *Sally's papers* illustrates what is called a prepositional passive. In the example, the prepositional object of the verb *refer* appears as the subject of a passivised sentence. By contrast, this does not work with *look*. The difference between *refer* and *look* is difficult to explain with recourse to a general grammatical rule, but it can be made sense of if the PASSIVE is viewed as a construction that has distinct collocational preferences. As a rule of thumb, it appears that prepositional passives work well with highly entrenched or idiomatic combinations of verbs and prepositional objects. Hence, *approve of a plan, pay for everything,* or *deal with issues* are good candidates for prepositional passives, whereas *search under a bed, walk across a hallway,* or *choose between two theories* yield questionable examples.

(25) The plan was approved of by my mother.
Everything was paid for in advance.
These issues will be dealt with in another paper.
?The bed was thoroughly searched under.
?This hallway was walked across by George Washington.
?These two theories have to be chosen between.

Examples of the PASSIVE also show varying degrees of acceptability in cases where clausal structures appear as the subject of the passivised sentence. The following examples show instances of -*ing* clauses, infinitive clauses, and *wh*-clauses. For each of these categories, it is possible to find examples that sound fully idiomatic and, conversely, other examples that seem rather unacceptable.

(26) Texting a marriage proposal is not recommended.
*Texting a marriage proposal was remembered (by John).
Not to go would be considered rude.
*Not to go was decided (by John).
Whether it was feasible had not yet been determined.
*Whether it was feasible was wondered (by John).

A general passivisation rule would be of limited use to account for such asymmetries. The only viable solution in a dictionary-and-grammar model of linguistic knowledge would be to inscribe these restrictions into the lexical entries of the respective verbs in an ad-hoc fashion. This, however, raises further questions, specifically with regard to novel verbs. Take for instance the recent verb *blog.* The verb is regularly passivised, and even if your experience with such examples is limited, you will probably agree that *Our wedding was blogged about!* is an idiomatic sentence of English whereas *That we married was blogged by John* is not. If you do, this suggests that your knowledge of language includes knowledge of how *blog* behaves as a verb, how this behaviour compares to that of other verbs, and in what kind of PASSIVE constructions those verbs appear. This kind of knowledge can be accommodated by the construct-i-con in a straightforward way.

Finally, Huddleston and Pullum (2002: 1435) note that there are verbs which seem to be restricted to the PASSIVE, among them *be reputed to, be said to,* and *be rumoured.*

(27)   Pat is reputed to be very rich.
Kim is said to be a manic depressive.
It is rumoured that there will be an election before the end of the year.

The fact that some examples of the PASSIVE cannot be transformed into a corresponding ACTIVE clause makes it difficult to maintain the idea of a grammatical rule that systematically links both constructions. To be sure, speakers will be aware that the two constructions correspond in important ways, that they often paraphrase one another, and that they express similar states of affairs. All of this does not run counter to the idea that the PASSIVE is a construction in its own right, a generalisation that speakers have to learn as an independent unit of grammatical knowledge.

2.4.2 The IMPERATIVE construction

The English IMPERATIVE construction is shown in the following examples.

(28)   Call me after lunch.
For next time, please read chapters three and four.
Take one of these in the morning, and another one before bedtime.

The IMPERATIVE is a valency-decreasing construction because it suppresses a central argument of the respective verbs, namely the agent. It is easy to construct paraphrases of the above examples in which such an agent is overtly expressed. The sentence *I would ask you to call me after lunch* makes explicit that it is the addressee who is expected to perform the action denoted by the verb. The meaning of the IMPERATIVE construction is thus non-compositional. It cannot be derived from the lexical meanings of the words alone that the agent of *Call me after lunch* should be the addressee. Besides this basic observation, there are several other pieces of evidence that the IMPERATIVE is a construction. Most importantly perhaps, there are constraints on the combination of the

IMPERATIVE with other constructions. Proficient speakers of English find the following examples questionable.

(29) *Must/should/got to leave!
      *Be called later!

The first example suggests that combining the IMPERATIVE with a modal auxiliary yields an intelligible but ungrammatical utterance. There is nothing semantically odd about such a request; it is the structure that speakers find unacceptable. Second, Takahashi (2012: 124) observes that some combinations of the IMPERATIVE with the PASSIVE yield unacceptable examples. Examples that do work would include *Be checked over by a doctor* or *Stand up and be counted for what you are about to receive.* The IMPERATIVE further occurs relatively rarely with the perfect (*Have your homework done by 5!*) and the progressive (*Be waiting in the lobby at 9!*). Huddleston and Pullum (2002: 932) explain this by pointing out that requests typically prompt dynamic actions rather than states. The grammatical behaviour of the IMPERATIVE in this regard is thus a consequence of real-world circumstances.

An unpredictable semantic trait of the construction concerns its interpretation in coordinations of imperative clauses and declarative clauses. In the following examples, the initial IMPERATIVE clauses are understood as having conditional meaning.

(30) Take an aspirin and you'll feel better.
      Ask him about his dissertation and he will be rambling on for hours.
      Do that again and you will regret it for the rest of your life.

What is noteworthy about these examples is that quite often, their overall meaning directly contradicts the IMPERATIVE clause. Whereas the first example suggests that the hearer take an aspirin, the two other examples are meant to discourage the hearer from complying with the initial request.

The English IMPERATIVE further exhibits strong collocational preferences. Takahashi (2012: 24) observes that the verbs *let, tell, look,* and *come* are among the most frequently used verbs in the construction. Some of these even have preferred argument realisation patterns, for instance *tell,* which usually combines with *me,* as in the example below.

(31) Let's not argue any more.
      Tell me about it.
      Look, we all make mistakes sometimes.
      Come on!

Takahashi's frequency results indicate that the function of the IMPERATIVE is not so much that of a vehicle for giving orders as that of the rather polite organisation of discourse, as in expressions such as *let's see, look, listen, trust me*, or *guess what*. This observation echoes a similar finding by Stefanowitsch and Gries (2003).

2.4.3 NULL INSTANTIATION

The term NULL INSTANTIATION refers to the phenomenon that not all arguments that a verb has in its event structure are overtly expressed. In many cases, the possibility of NULL INSTANTIATION has to be seen as a property that is inscribed in the lexical entry of a verb. For instance, the verb *eat* allows omission of the patient argument (*The children ate noisily*) whereas the verb *devour* does not (**The children devoured noisily*). An interesting aspect of NULL INSTANTIATION is that verbs differ with regard to the definiteness of the argument that can be omitted. Ruppenhofer (2005) distinguishes INDEFINITE NULL INSTANTIATION (INI), which can be observed with the verb *read*, from DEFINITE NULL INSTANTIATION (DNI), which shows itself in uses of the verb *understand*. The crucial difference is whether the speaker knows the exact identity of the omitted argument. Compare the following examples:

(32) Kim was reading. I just don't remember what.
      Kim understood. *I just don't remember what.

While it is perfectly acceptable for me to say that *Kim was reading* and to have only a vague idea of what it was that she was reading, saying that *Kim understood* conveys that I know more or less exactly what she understood. The behaviour of INI verbs and DNI verbs makes for an interesting topic, but this section will focus instead on a third type of NULL INSTANTIATION, namely cases in which a construction licenses the omission of an argument. Ruppenhofer and Michaelis (2010) report on several such constructions, which they find to be genre-specific, that is, tied to very specific communicative situations. Consider, for instance, the LABELESE construction.

(33) Contains sulphites.
      Creates visibly fuller, thicker hair.
      Eliminates pet odours.

The LABELESE construction suppresses the subject argument of a verb. This does not create any communicative problems because the construction can only appear printed on the very referent that is left unexpressed by the construction. The LABELESE construction not only occurs

with verbs but also works with a whole range of PREDICATIVE constructions, as is evidenced by statements such as *easy to use, for children 4
years and up, made in China,* and *dietary supplement.* In these examples, the
reader understands that an expression such as *made in China* describes a
characteristic of the product on which the expression is found.

Another NULL INSTANTIATION construction is confined to the language of cooking recipes.

(34) Season liberally with salt and pepper.
      Chill before serving.
      Cut into one-inch-thick slices.

Ruppenhofer and Michaelis (2010: 181) call this the INSTRUCTIONAL
IMPERATIVE construction. Like the LABELESE construction, it represents
a generalisation that speakers must have learned. Whereas it might be
argued that quite generally, an argument can be omitted in contexts
where its identity is glaringly obvious, this theory fails to explain why
Cut into one-inch-thick slices is fine as a written instruction but decidedly odd as a spoken request. The next time you are preparing a meal
together with a friend, sprinkle your conversation with something like
Fry until lightly brown, and see what happens.

2.5 Relations between argument structure constructions

Many argument structure constructions in English can be paraphrased
in terms of another, formally and semantically related argument structure construction. The previous section has discussed the example of
ACTIVE and PASSIVE sentences, which are mutually linked through a
number of correspondences. A further example of an argument structure construction with a close paraphrase is the DITRANSITIVE construction, which has a 'twin' construction in the PREPOSITIONAL DATIVE
construction. Consider the following examples.

(35) John gave Mary the book.
      John gave the book to Mary.

Another close relation exists between the CAUSED MOTION construction and what one might call the *With*-APPLICATIVE construction.

(36) John brushed barbecue sauce onto the ribs.
      John brushed the ribs with barbecue sauce.

Linguists of different theoretical persuasions have long been interested in the relations between these constructions. Pairs of constructions such as the ones given above have come to be known as **syntactic**

alternations; the pairs in (35) and (36) are known respectively as the DATIVE ALTERNATION and the LOCATIVE ALTERNATION. As with ACTIVE and PASSIVE sentences, the correspondences between the two members of those pairs invite the idea of a grammatical rule that systematically links one to the other. In a dictionary-and-grammar model of linguistic knowledge, such a rule would allow speakers to use one member of the pair as the input from which the second member of the pair can be derived as an output. The rule would apply across the board, for all manners of verbs, unless the lexical entry of a verb specifically disallows its application. For both the DATIVE ALTERNATION and the LOCATIVE ALTERNATION, there are what are called non-alternating verbs, as shown in the following examples.

(37) John took his son to the doctor.
*John took the doctor his son.
John filled the glass with water.
*John filled water into the glass.

The verb *take* does not readily enter the DITRANSITIVE construction, and the fact that *fill* cannot be used in the CAUSED MOTION construction is even being taught to learners of English as a second language. As you may guess, researchers in Construction Grammar view the idea of a grammatical rule linking the members of a pair of constructions as problematic. The alternative view is expressed by Goldberg under the heading of the **surface generalisation hypothesis** (2006: 25):

> [T]here are typically broader syntactic and semantic generalizations associated with a surface argument structure form than exist between the same surface form and a distinct form that it is hypothesized to be syntactically or semantically derived from.

The phrase 'a surface argument structure form' here paraphrases the term 'construction' in a theory-neutral fashion. What the hypothesis claims is that each member of a pair of paraphrasable constructions is best analysed on its own terms, all correspondences notwithstanding. The hypothesis further predicts that each member of such a pair will exhibit systematic differences with regard to the other member and systematic generalisations that pertain to its own form and meaning. Both of these points can be illustrated with the behaviour of the DITRANSITIVE construction. Interestingly, examples of the DITRANSITIVE construction correspond not only to examples of the PREPOSITIONAL DATIVE construction, but also to examples of the *For*-BENEFACTIVE construction.

(38) John gave the book to Mary.   John gave Mary the book.
John poured a scotch for Mary.   John poured Mary a scotch.

On the dictionary-and-grammar view of linguistic knowledge, these pairs would need to be linked by two separate rules, which implies that the two DITRANSITIVE sentences on the right would in fact not instantiate the same construction, despite having the same surface argument structure form. This conclusion, however, is questionable. Goldberg (2006: 27) presents the examples shown in (39) to make the case that DITRANSITIVE sentences corresponding to PREPOSITIONAL DATIVE examples and DITRANSITIVE sentences corresponding to *For*-BENEFACTIVE examples show exactly the same behaviour. When one is fine, so is the other; when one is questionable or ungrammatical, so is the other.

(39) *Ditransitives*   *Paraphrases*
Mina bought Mel a book.   Mina bought a book for Mel.
Mina sent Mel a book.   Mina sent a book to Mel.
??Mina bought Mel it.   Mina bought it for Mel.
??Mina sent Mel it.   Mina sent it to Mel.
??Who did Mina buy a book?   Who did Mina buy a book for?
??Who did Mina send a book?   Who did Mina send a book to?
*Mina bought Mel yesterday a book.   Mina bought a book yesterday for Mel.

*Mina sent Mel yesterday a book.   Mina sent a book yesterday to Mel.

Goldberg concludes that the similarities between examples that show the surface form of the DITRANSITIVE construction are greater than similarities between the member constructions of a syntactic alternation. In her own words, '[t]he robust generalizations are surface generalizations' (2006: 33).

2.6 Summing up

This chapter introduced the idea of argument structure, which is a synonym for the term 'valency'. Argument structure describes the number and character of elements that can bond to a given linguistic item, and is a term that pertains both to the meaning of the bonding elements and to the form of those elements. The former aspect was called the event structure; the latter was called syntactic argument structure. The chapter introduced thematic roles such as agent, patient, and experiencer. It was argued that argument structure constructions are items of linguistic knowledge that allow speakers to use verbs in syntactic contexts in which they are not conventionally used. 'Famous' examples such as *John sneezed the foam off his capuccino* illustrate this phenomenon.

Argument structure constructions are syntactic constructions that can be filled by all manners of lexical material and that convey some meaning of their own that goes beyond the meaning of their component words. There are hence two main pieces of evidence for argument structure constructions: first, they allow non-conventional combinations of verbs and syntactic contexts; second, they convey non-compositional meanings. The combination of verbs and argument structure constructions is not unconstrained: Goldberg's semantic coherence principle states that a verb can only be combined with a construction if the participants that are evoked by the verb and the construction match semantically. There are hence limits on the possible combinations of verbs and constructions. The importance of argument structure constructions to Construction Grammar at large was discussed in connection with the scene encoding hypothesis, that is, the idea that the basic syntactic patterns of a language encode recurrent event types that are basic to human experience.

The chapter then drew a distinction between valency-increasing constructions and valency-decreasing constructions. Valency-increasing constructions such as the RESULTATIVE construction, the DITRANSITIVE construction, the CAUSED MOTION construction, and the WAY construction can augment the argument structure of lexical verbs. The constructions thus add participants to the event structure of the verb. By contrast, valency-decreasing constructions such as the PASSIVE, the IMPERATIVE, the LABELESE construction, and the INSTRUCTIONAL IMPERATIVE construction suppress the expression of participants that are there in the event structure of the respective verb. Quite often, the suppressed arguments are easily recoverable from the context. Examples of the LABELESE construction such as *Contains sulphites*, read on a bottle of red wine, leave little doubt as to what could be meant. However, it was argued that contextual recoverability is not the only constraint on the use of these constructions.

The chapter closed with a discussion of relations between paraphrasable constructions, called syntactic alternations. In contrast to the idea of grammatical rules that systematically link argument structure patterns with similar meanings, what is called the surface generalisation hypothesis expresses the view that argument structure constructions are best analysed in their own right because similarities will be greater between examples with the same surface form than between members of a syntactic alternation.

In summary, despite the fact that 'simple sentences' such as *Pat gave Bill a book* or *Bob hammered the metal flat* give the initial impression of being completely regular and semantically compositional, they illustrate constructions that yield strong evidence for a constructional view of linguistic knowledge. Any theory of grammar needs to have an explanation for the fact that *John cut the rope in half with a knife* is a fine sentence of English whereas *John heard his ears deaf with loud heavy metal* is not. Positing argument structure constructions, in connection with principles that constrain possible combinations of verbs and constructions, provides an intuitive and testable account.

Study questions

- What is argument structure?
- Can you give an example of an expression where the event structure of a verb and its syntactic argument structure do not match?
- What are thematic roles?
- What does the surface generalisation hypothesis predict? What data would cast doubt on the hypothesis?
- What are the two main pieces of evidence for recognising argument structure constructions?
- What is the principle of semantic coherence?
- What is meant by the term NULL INSTANTIATION?
- Can you come up with an example of an English valency-changing construction that was not discussed in this chapter?

Further reading

The central reference for this chapter is Goldberg (1995). Chapters 2 and 9 in Goldberg (2006) represent continuations of that work. Boas (2003, 2005) and Goldberg and Jackendoff (2004) discuss English RESULTATIVE constructions. Foundational work on the topic of verbs and their argument structure is found in Pinker (1989), Levin (1993), and Levin and Rappaport Hovav (2005). A very useful resource is the *Valency Dictionary of English* (Herbst et al. 2004); see also Herbst and Götz-Votteler (2007). General overviews of valency-changing constructions are found in Payne (1997) and Haspelmath and Müller-Bardey (2004). These include many examples from languages other than English, which helps to put the English data into perspective.

3 Inside the construct-i-con

3.1 Meaningless constructions?

The previous two chapters presented the view that knowledge of language should be modelled as a construct-i-con, that is, as a large network of form–meaning pairs that accommodates words, idioms, semi-specified patterns such as THE *X*-ER THE *Y*-ER, and also argument structure constructions such as the DITRANSITIVE construction or the RESULTATIVE construction. For all of these constructions, it is fairly straightforward to make the case that aspects of their form or meaning cannot be predicted from more general patterns that exist in the grammar of English. In short, it is intuitively clear that words such as *dog* or *green* are forms that have lexical meanings; it is equally clear that the phrase *pushing up daisies* has an idiomatic meaning; and the non-compositional meaning of an example such as *John sneezed his cat soaking wet* is evidence for including the English RESULTATIVE construction as part of speakers' knowledge of language. However, you might wonder, is this enough evidence to make the case that *all* of linguistic knowledge consists of form–meaning pairs? Do all syntactic forms carry meaning? On the view that knowledge of language is a large repository of symbolic units, the answer would have to be a 'yes' – a symbol is only a symbol by virtue of having a form *and* a meaning. At the same time, there are syntactic forms for which it is quite difficult to establish a meaning in anything but the most general of terms. Consider the following examples.

(1) John sings.
    Bob heard a noise.
    One sock lay on the sofa, the other one under it.

The first example illustrates what must be one of the most fundamental principles of English grammar: verbs agree with their subjects, showing inflections that correspond to the categories of number and person. A third person singular subject, in the simple present tense, combines with verb forms that end in the suffix /-s/. Speakers obviously know this, but does that knowledge represent a construction? The second example, *Bob heard a noise*, combines a verb with a subject and an object, thus forming a transitive clause. The previous chapter discussed argument structure constructions as units of linguistic structure that have meaning. By analogy with the DITRANSITIVE construction and the RESULTATIVE construction, does the example represent something that could be called the TRANSITIVE construction? If so, what would be its meaning? One answer to the latter question, motivated by examples such as *Bob hit the nail* or *Bob ate the sandwich*, would be to characterise the prototypical transitive clause as one in which an agent intentionally affects an individuated, inanimate patient argument (cf. Hopper and Thompson 1980; Thompson and Hopper 2001). But if the TRANSITIVE construction were to include examples such as *Bob remembered his appointment*, *Bob walked a mile*, or *Bob weighed 15 stone*, such a semantic characterisation would be difficult to maintain. Moving on to the third example, *One sock lay on the sofa, the other one under it* illustrates a syntactic pattern in which two clauses are coordinated and the second clause omits an element that is common to both, in this case the verb form *lay*. Evidently, speakers know that this particular pattern is an acceptable way to express a given idea, whereas **One sock lay on the sofa, the other one under* would not be acceptable, despite only a seemingly minor difference. Is this kind of knowledge still knowledge of constructions?

The fundamental question whether all constructions are meaningful has been answered in conflicting ways in the Construction Grammar literature. Goldberg (2006: 166-82) takes the position that even highly abstract patterns are meaningful. She discusses the example of SUBJECT–AUXILIARY INVERSION, which is a syntactic pattern that occurs in questions, conditionals, and exclamatives, amongst several other construction types. A few examples are shown below.

(2) Would you mind if I smoke in here?
Had I known this, I would have stayed at home.
May he rest in peace!
Rarely have I heard such nonsense.

Whereas earlier research had pointed to this large range of contexts as evidence that SUBJECT–AUXILIARY INVERSION is a purely formal phenomenon with no semantic substance (Green 1985), Goldberg argues that all construction types that share this particular syntax also share semantic traits, notably the characteristic of non-assertiveness. Especially, questions, conditionals, and wishes describe states of affairs that are not factual. Arguing against this idea, Fillmore et al. (2012: 326) explicitly proclaim 'the legitimacy of semantically null constructions'. Constructions without meanings would be linguistic generalisations not unlike traditional phrase structure rules, such as the generalisation that noun phrases can be formed through the combination of a determiner, an attributive adjective, and a noun. All that such a generalisation specifies is that a certain configuration of syntactic structures yields a grammatically acceptable phrase of English. Note that we are talking about precisely the kind of thing that would be handled by the grammatical component in the dictionary-and-grammar model of linguistic knowledge. So, is there something to the distinction of grammar and lexicon after all? Would the construct-i-con be able to accommodate purely formal generalisations? In order to answer these questions, we need to have a closer look at 'meaningless' constructions.

Fillmore et al. (2012) identify three construction types that they view as meaningless. The first kind is exemplified by examples such as *John sings*, which combines a subject with an agreeing verb in what is called the SUBJECT–PREDICATE construction. This construction reflects a formal generalisation, but it does not contribute any meaning of its own that would go beyond the combined meanings of the component lexical items. Fillmore et al. even reject the idea that the SUBJECT–PREDICATE construction might evoke a highly general meaning, such as 'the establishment of a topic about which something is said': in examples such as *There's a problem* or *It's a shame* the subject constituents (*there, it*) are not referential and hence cannot be topics. The case for viewing the SUBJECT–PREDICATE construction as meaningful is thus highly tenuous. Another purely formal construction would be the MODIFIER–HEAD construction, which is instantiated by the combination of an adjective with a noun (*red ball*), or an adverb and an adjective (*completely full*). What the construction formally specifies is that the first element modifies the second and that the second element determines the type of phrase that the whole construct represents. Whereas one might be tempted to argue that the construction conveys the meaning of 'an X that has the quality of being Y', it turns out that this paraphrase only works for a subset of all examples that instantiate that construction. Consider the following examples.

(3) John smoked a fat cigar.
     I never see any of my old friends any more.
     The judge found the alleged murderer innocent.
     Bob's restaurant was closed down for hygienic reasons.

Whereas *a fat cigar* is 'a cigar that is fat', *old friends* are not 'friends that are old', and an *alleged murderer* is no more 'a murderer who is alleged' than *hygienic reasons* are 'reasons that are hygienic'. So even though the syntactic mechanism of combining a modifier with a head is the same across these examples, the respective interpretations differ.

The second type of construction that Fillmore et al. discuss is not so much meaningless in itself as highly heterogeneous in the meanings that are associated with different examples of the respective constructions. In this category, Fillmore et al. include SUBJECT–AUXILIARY INVERSION, criticising Goldberg's account of a common core meaning as too vague (Fillmore et al. 2012: 327). While there may be common semantic traits of questions, conditionals, and exclamatives, Fillmore et al. doubt that ordinary speakers of English entertain semantic generalisations at such high levels of abstractions. However, they maintain that speakers know the formal pattern of SUBJECT–AUXILIARY INVERSION. Another highly abstract formal generalisation that maps onto a variety of separate meanings is exemplified by FILLER-GAP constructions (Sag 2010). These constructions have in common that an argument of a verb, typically a direct object, appears in a place that differs from its canonical position in a simple declarative clause. For instance, in the sentence *Bob ate the sandwich*, the object directly follows the verb. Compare that to the following sentences that include the verb *eat*.

(4) What kind of sandwich did you eat?
How many sandwiches he ate!
Keep track of all the sandwiches you eat!
Normally the kids don't touch sandwiches, but this one they'll eat.
The more sandwiches you eat, the hungrier you get.

The examples above illustrate different constructions, namely *WH*-QUESTIONS, EXCLAMATIVES, RELATIVE CLAUSES, the TOPICALISATION construction, and the THE *X*-ER THE *Y*-ER construction. In each of these examples, the thing that is eaten is expressed, but it appears in a place before the verb, not after it. As a technical way of referring to this state of affairs, we can say that the thing eaten, the 'filler', appears in a non-argument position. The argument position, which directly follows the verb *eat*, is not taken up by any linguistic material in these examples, so that we speak of it as a 'gap'. In the published literature on FILLER-GAP constructions you will often find example sentences in which filler and gap are co-indexed and shown as such, as illustrated in the example below.

(5) [What kind of sandwich]$_i$ did you eat __$_i$?
    filler   gap

As with Subject–Auxiliary Inversion, it does appear that Filler-Gap constructions reflect a broad syntactic generalisation specifying that an argument of a verb may appear in a non-argument position. A linguistic theory would be considered 'elegant' if it could state that generalisation and explain, in one fell swoop, the syntactic behaviour of the whole range of construction types that are shown in (4). By the same token, it is clear that these construction types do not share a common semantic core. Fillmore et al. (2012) thus posit Filler-Gap as an abstract syntactic generalisation that is at work in different constructions. The generalisation has no meaning in itself; rather, the construction types (Wh-Questions, Exclamatives, Relative Clauses, the Topicalisation construction, and the The X-er the Y-er) are associated with their respective meanings.

Third, Fillmore et al. identify Ellipsis constructions as syntactic generalisations that do not carry meaning. Three specific cases that they discuss are called Gapping, Stripping, and Shared Completion (also known as Right Node Raising).

(6) One sock lay on the sofa, the other one under it.
    John put the bowls in the dishwasher, and the plates, too.
    The South remains distinct from and independent of the North.

In typical examples of Gapping, two phrasal constituents are juxtaposed, and the second one is missing a verb form that is present in the first one, which is called the 'gap'. The term is motivated by the fact that the remaining parts of the phrase are still there. In the example above, the phrases *the other one* and *under it* would be called 'remnants'. The second example illustrates Stripping (Hankamer and Sag 1976), a term which is meant to convey that a full sentence is stripped of everything except one constituent. The example conveys that 'John put the plates in the dishwasher' by means of just mentioning *the plates*. Stripping can thus be seen as a more radical form of Gapping. A typical feature of Stripping is the presence of the adverbial *too* or the negative particle *not*, as in *Eric played the guitar solo, not George*. The third of the examples given above is a case of Shared Completion. It is useful to think of *distinct from* and *independent of* as two adjectival phrases that share a common ending, namely *the North*. The common ending in Shared Completion can be the noun phrase part completing a prepositional phrase, but the following examples show that other patterns are also possible.

(7) His theory is based on – but more complicated than – string theory.
    Stretching can help prevent or at least reduce soreness.

He is one of the most – if not in fact THE most – tragic figure in sports history.

Each of these examples contains a phrasal head that requires a complement: the preposition *on*, the verb *prevent*, and the determiner *one* all require a nominal complement to follow them. However, what follows these elements is a conjunction (*but, or, if*), which is followed by further linguistic material before the projected nominal structure (*string theory, soreness, tragic figure*) finally appears. Note that strings such as *prevent or at least reduce* or *one if not the most* are not syntactic constituents. Rather, it seems more appropriate to view the strings *or at least reduce* and *if not the most* as parenthetical structures that are inserted between a head and its complement. The role of PARENTHETICAL constructions in Construction Grammar is discussed in more detail in, for example, Imo (2007). To sum up, elliptical constructions such as GAPPING, STRIPPING, and SHARED COMPLETION do not lead to coercion, they do not convey meanings of their own, and they yield sentences with meanings that can be worked out by processing the meanings of the component words.

Where does this survey of 'meaningless' construction leave the idea of a construct-i-con as a repository of form–meaning pairs? Does the construct-i-con perhaps need an appendix of syntactic rules, just as the traditional view of grammar needed an appendix of idiomatic expressions? The least problematic for the Construction Grammar view, as outlined in the previous two chapters, are construction types such as the family of SUBJECT–AUXILIARY INVERSION constructions or FILLER-GAP constructions. Here, there are actually two possible routes for analysis, which are outlined by Stefanowitsch (2003: 420) in a study that addresses the different semantic relations between modifier and head in the two English GENITIVE constructions:

> There are two ways in which this issue can be approached [. . .]: by a prototype analysis that takes one of the semantic relations [between modifier and head] as basic and finds a principled way of accounting for all other relations as extensions from this basic prototype; or by a schematic analysis that finds an abstract characterization that covers all and only the relations encoded by the given construction.

We have already seen that Goldberg (2006) takes the 'schematic' approach for her analysis of SUBJECT–AUXILIARY INVERSION, looking for a common semantic core that is shared by all constructions that have this syntactic pattern. Taylor (1996: 343-7) takes the 'prototype' approach in an analysis of the English S-GENITIVE construction, trying to relate the different interpretations of that construction semantically.

Both approaches are viable in principle, as the question at what levels of abstraction speakers make generalisations is essentially an empirical one that has to be determined individually for each and every speaker and each and every grammatical phenomenon. It is further possible that schematic analyses and prototype analyses are not even mutually exclusive, as speakers may entertain several generalisations at the same time, some at lower levels, and some at higher, more abstract levels. So far then, no appendix to the construct-i-con is needed, but what about the other meaningless constructions?

The first construction type discussed by Fillmore et al. (2012), illustrated by the SUBJECT–PREDICATE construction, requires an analysis that combines the schematic approach with the prototype approach. As Fillmore et al. point out, positing a schematic meaning for all combinations of a subject with a predicate seems like a project with little hope of success. Existential and presentational constructions such as *There are no unicorns* or *There's beer in the fridge* pose difficulties for a schematic analysis. Conversely, it seems difficult to relate such an abstract meaning to the more concrete meanings that are conveyed by existential and presentational constructions. The prototype approach, as one of the solutions advocated by Stefanowitsch, is thus also of limited use. A way out of the dilemma would be a combination of the two: one could assume a schematic analysis for instances such as *John sings* and *A man walks into a bar*, while positing separate constructional schemas for sentences such as *There's beer in the fridge*. In fact, one of the foundational studies in Construction Grammar does this and presents a prototype-based analysis of English THERE constructions (Lakoff 1987). The main idea would be that specialised constructions can share selected formal and functional aspects of more general constructions, while at the same time displaying characteristics that are not shared by the more general schema. With a little goodwill, generalisations such as SUBJECT–PREDICATE and MODIFIER–HEAD can thus be brought into the fold of the construct-i-con.

What remains as a true problem, however, is the case of elliptical constructions. It seems that constructions such as SHARED COMPLETION, GAPPING, and STRIPPING have all the characteristics of traditional phrase structure rules, while not conveying any substantial meaning of their own. If we were to assign degrees of 'meaninglessness' to different constructions, these construction types would surely top the list, even when compared to SUBJECT–PREDICATE and MODIFIER–HEAD constructions. Furthermore, it is not immediately clear whether these syntactic patterns would exhibit other telltale signs of constructions, namely either idiosyncratic constraints (cf. Section 1.3.3) or collocational preferences (cf. Section 1.3.4). If all of the criteria for constructionhood fail, it would have to be conceded that these syntactic patterns do not form part of the construct-i-con, as envisioned by current practitioners of the Construction Grammar framework.

Summing up, purely formal generalisations, that is, constructions without meanings, have no natural place in the construct-i-con. In fact, if Construction Grammar is to be seen as a veritable theory of linguistic knowledge, then this theory will make the strong claim that there should not be any constructions without meanings. A scientific theory is usually considered 'good' if it makes claims that can be falsified. Construction Grammar is thus only a good theory of linguistic knowledge if it is clear what empirical observations could show that it is wrong. Hence, Construction Grammarians need to face the critical evidence of patterns such as SHARED COMPLETION, GAPPING, and STRIPPING in order either to save the current idea of the construct-i-con or to adapt the theory in an ad-hoc way to accommodate the empirical facts. As elliptical constructions are fairly frequent and productive, and as the 'problem' of meaningless constructions extends to phrasal constructions such as the VERB PHRASE construction or the PREPOSITIONAL PHRASE construction, clear answers are needed. The worst that Construction Grammarians could do would be to look the other way, towards nice meaningful patterns such as THE X-ER THE Y-ER or the WAY construction, and pretend that the problem of meaningless constructions does not exist.

3.2 The construct-i-con: a network of interlinked constructions

Up to now, the construct-i-con has been described in quite vague terms, as a large repository of form–meaning pairs that represents speakers' knowledge of language. A rather important addendum is that this repository is not a flat list or even an unordered 'bag of constructions', but instead a highly structured, hierarchical network in which constructions are interlinked. The following sections discuss how constructions are linked to one another in the construct-i-con.

3.2.1 Inheritance

A central concept in this regard is the notion of **inheritance**. Inheritance captures a relation between more abstract constructions, which are situated towards the top of the constructional network, and more specific constructions, which are found in lower levels of the constructional hierarchy. Naturally, there is no simple binary distinction between abstract constructions and concrete constructions. Rather,

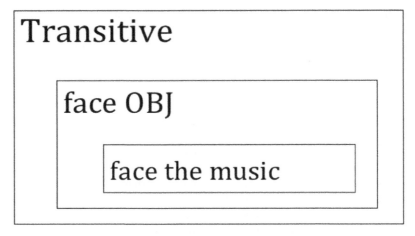

Figure 3.1 *face the music* and the constructions it instantiates

constructional generalisations are situated along a continuum from very abstract schemas down to lexically specified patterns. Concrete patterns thus instantiate more abstract patterns at increasingly schematic levels. Figure 3.1 visualises the idea that a lexically specified idiom such as *face the music* 'accept unpleasant consequences of one's actions' instantiates a number of more abstract constructions, such as the transitive use of the verb *face* and the more general TRANSITIVE construction.

Constructional characteristics, that is, characteristics of form and meaning, are inherited in a downwards direction, from higher, more schematic levels towards lower, more concrete levels. To give an example, one of the most abstract constructions we have encountered so far would be the SUBJECT–PREDICATE construction. Almost all clausal constructions in English share the formal characteristic of the verb agreeing in number and person with its subject. Specific clausal constructions thus inherit this characteristic from the SUBJECT–PREDICATE construction. Goldberg (2013) offers another example that illustrates inheritance. Consider the following set of examples.

(8) He is in prison.
     She came from school.
     John is going to university.
     They are on vacation.
     Herbert has been at sea for three years.

Each of these examples contains a sequence of a preposition and a bare count noun. Goldberg calls this pattern the PN construction.

The construction inherits a very basic formal aspect from the more general PREPOSITIONAL PHRASE construction, namely the linear order of preposition and nominal complement. Apart from this inherited formal feature, the PN construction shows several constructional idiosyncrasies: first, the construction conveys a stereotypical role in that someone can only be *in prison* as an inmate, not as a warden. Students go to university but not their lecturers, or the janitors, or the vice-chancellor. Second, unlike in regular prepositional phrases, the nominal cannot be modified with an adjective (**They are on sunny vacation*). Third, whereas regular prepositional phrases can be formed with all manner of nouns, the PN construction is clearly restricted. People may *go to bed*, but not **go to couch*. All of these idiosyncrasies are specific to the PN construction; they are not shared with prepositional phrases in general. Inheritance is thus a 'downwards' relation; more specific constructional characteristics are not projected 'upwards'.

Inheritance is not only a matter of language form, but can also be a matter of meaning. To illustrate, Michaelis and Lambrecht (1996: 237) point out that noun phrases can occasionally receive an exclamative interpretation, as in the following examples.

(9) The time he takes!
     The amount of plastic waste!
     My car payments!

What is conveyed by these examples is that the referents of the respective noun phrases represent an extreme point on a scale that has to be understood by the listener. Even for examples in decontextualised form, this is not hard to do. The first example states that someone is taking quite a long time; the second example refers to an enormous amount of waste; and the third one refers to the fact that the car payments are relatively high. Michaelis and Lambrecht call this semantic pattern the METONYMIC NP construction. The semantics of that construction is inherited by noun phrases in formally more specialised constructions, as in the following examples.

(10) I can't believe the money I spent on clothes!
      It's ridiculous the amount of plastic waste!

The first of these examples Michaelis and Lambrecht (1996: 244) identify as an instance of the NP–COMPLEMENT EXCLAMATIVE construction. The exclamative noun phrase is, in this context, an argument of the verb *believe*. The second example instantiates the NOMINAL EXTRAPOSITION construction, which consists of a predicative clause and the exclamative noun phrase. Both of these constructions thus inherit aspects of their meaning from the METONYMIC NP construction.

To summarise our first pass at the concept of inheritance, we can state that it is a relation between more abstract and more specific construction in which the more specific ones exhibit formal and functional features of the more abstract ones. Much as a squirrel is a rodent, a mammal, and an animal at the same time, an idiom such as *face the music* simultaneously instantiates a range of more abstract constructions.

3.2.2 Kinds of inheritance links

From the previous discussion it could be concluded that inheritance is more or less just a matter of organising the constructions of a language into a hierarchy: we have talked about more abstract types and more concrete instantiations of those types. While this is certainly an important part of the picture, there are several different kinds of inheritance links in the construct-i-con that deserve discussion. The basic kind of inheritance link, which was discussed above and which connects *face the music* with transitive *face* and the TRANSITIVE construction, is called an **instance link** (Goldberg 1995: 79): the idiom *face the music* is a special case of transitive *face*, which in turn is a special case of the TRANSITIVE construction.

Goldberg (1995: 75) identifies **polysemy links** as another type of inheritance link. As was discussed in Chapter 2, many argument structure constructions have several conceptually related meanings; the technical term for this is that these constructions are **polysemous**. This holds, for instance, for the DITRANSITIVE construction, which has the basic sense of 'X causes Y to receive Z', and several extended senses, such as 'X enables Y to receive Z' or 'X intends Y to receive Z in the future'. The examples below illustrate the respective senses.

(11) John gave Mary the book.
The doctor allowed me a full meal.
I promise you a rose garden.

In the construct-i-con, the central sense of the DITRANSITIVE construction would be linked to the extended senses by means of polysemy links. Note that we are not dealing with a taxonomical relation here, as an 'intended transfer' is not, strictly speaking, a type of transfer. Nonetheless, it is clear that the sense of an 'intended transfer' inherits a substantial amount of its semantics from the more general 'transfer' sense. It is useful to think of polysemy links as metonymic relations, that is, relations between a whole scenario and parts of that scenario.

Typically, the extended sense of a construction will represent a scenario that inherits central parts of the scenario that is associated with the basic sense of the construction. Another example of polysemy links can be seen in the semantic spectrum of the English *S*-Genitive construction. Taylor (1989) identifies 'possession' as the central sense, which is related to extended senses of the construction via polysemy links. Consider the following examples.

(12) John's book
       John's office
       John's train
       the country's president
       yesterday's events
       inflation's consequences

Whereas the first of these examples denotes ownership or possession, the remaining examples convey associative relations of fairly different kinds. Taylor (1989: 679) lists several features of prototypical possession, such as the possessor being animate, the possessed being a concrete object, the possessor having exclusive access to the possessed, and the possession relation being a long-term one, amongst several others. Whereas a phrase such as *John's book* may fulfil all criteria of the prototype, the remaining examples fail an increasing number of them. For instance, *John's train* 'the train John is riding on' is not owned by John and there is just a short-term relation between John and the train. These extended senses of the *S*-Genitive construction would nonetheless be connected to the central sense through polysemy links.

Constructions may further be connected through **metaphorical links**. Like the polysemy links that were discussed above, links of this kind are semantic in nature and connect a basic sense of a construction with an extended sense. The special hallmark of metaphorical links is that the two connected senses represent the source domain and the target domain of a conceptual metaphor (Lakoff and Johnson 1980). Goldberg (1995: 81) argues for a metaphorical link between the Caused Motion construction (cf. Section 2.3.2) and the Resultative construction (cf. Section 2.1). The conceptual metaphor that links the two is Change is Motion. The source domain, movement through space, is represented by the central sense of the Caused Motion construction in examples such as *John combed his hair to the side*. Interestingly, speakers commonly use exactly the same syntactic pattern to express a resultative event, as in *Anne tied her hair into a bun*. Goldberg's explanation for this observation is based on the Change is Motion metaphor, which motivates the link between these two constructional meanings.

Another example of metaphorical links between basic and extended senses of constructions can be seen in the English MODAL AUXILIARY constructions. The English core modals (*must, may, can, should*, etc.) display a systematic pattern of polysemy that has been interpreted as metaphorical. Sweetser (1990) argues that the following pairs of sentences are linked through a metaphor that has the sociophysical world as its source domain and as its target domain the world of possibility, necessity, and likelihood. The first sentences thus represent what is known as deontic modal meaning, while the second sentences convey epistemic meaning.

(13) You must be home by ten!   You must be David's brother!
      You may now kiss the bride.   He may have escaped through the
                                     window.
      I can't open the door.   That can't possibly be true.
      You should try the sushi.   Prices should go down sooner or
                                     later.

The kind of construction that we are dealing with in these examples consists of a modal auxiliary such as *must* and a non-finite verbal complement such as *be home*. The semantic difference between *You must be home by ten!* and *You must be David's brother!* is that the first is a command whereas the second is a conclusion. In the construct-i-con, deontic and epistemic uses of each MODAL AUXILIARY construction would be connected through a metaphorical link.

A fourth type of inheritance link connects constructions that show partial similarities in their respective forms or meanings. What are called **subpart links** (Goldberg 1995: 78) relate constructions that show either formal or semantic overlap, but which do not allow the classification of one construction as an instance of the other. To illustrate, the TRANSITIVE construction and the DITRANSITIVE construction have quite a few features in common: both have a subject with the role of an agent and a direct object that assumes the role of a patient or theme. Consider the following examples.

(14) John wrote a letter.
      John wrote Mary a letter.

There are clearly correspondences between these two sentences, and it would not be too unreasonable to assume that speakers' knowledge of language includes the fact that the TRANSITIVE construction and the DITRANSITIVE construction have a number of characteristics in common. Associations between constructions that share formal or semantic structures but cannot be seen as instances of one another are represented in the construct-i-con as subpart links. Trivially, every complex syntactic construction consists of a range of smaller phrasal constructions. Every instance of the TRANSITIVE construction is necessarily linked to the NOUN PHRASE construction and the VERB PHRASE construction via subpart links. The concept of subpart links is, however, more interestingly elucidated with the example of constructions that are called syntactic amalgams. The following example has been discussed by Lakoff (1974).

(15) John invited you'll never guess how many people to his party.

For want of a better label, this type of sentence will be called the MATRIX CLAUSE AS MODIFIER construction here. The sentence can be thought of as a combination of different constructions, one of which, however, only contributes a subpart of itself. In the example, one component construction would be the COMPLEMENT CLAUSE construction that is instantiated by sentences such as *You'll never guess how many people John invited to his party.* This construction is partly overlaid with the TRANSITIVE construction, which produces examples such as *John invited very many people to his party.* The string *you'll never guess how many* is a subpart of the COMPLEMENT CLAUSE construction that can stand in for the phrase *very many* in the TRANSITIVE construction, thus creating a syntactic amalgam, a mixture of constructions. The amalgamated construction would be related to the COMPLEMENT CLAUSE construction with a subpart link, and to the TRANSITIVE construction with an instance link, since it properly instantiates that construction.

The above example makes clear that constructions in the construct-i-con form a network, rather than just a hierarchy. Besides instance links, polysemy links, and metaphorical links, which relate higher and lower levels of abstraction in the construct-i-con, subpart links may connect constructions that occupy the same level of abstraction. Rather than one construction linking to just one other construction, the construct-i-con is thus a network with many-to-many links. In the Construction Grammar literature, subpart links are often discussed in connection with the phenomenon of **multiple inheritance**, which describes the way that one construction may instantiate several, successively more abstract constructions at the same time. Consider the following example.

(16) The Smiths felt it was an important enough song to put on their
       last single.

Like the previous example, this sentence can be considered a syntactic amalgam in which two constructions are interlaced. The first of these is the ATTRIBUTIVE ADJECTIVE construction, which is instantiated by noun phrases such as *an important song* or *the red ball*. The second construction is the *ENOUGH To-*INFINITIVE construction, which is further illustrated by the following examples.

(17) You're old enough to know better.
      I had trained enough to finish my first marathon in good shape.
      This fridge contains enough food to feed a small village.
      John remembered the incident clearly enough to identify the suspect.
      I was not in control enough to stop this from happening.

In its basic form, the *ENOUGH To-*INFINITIVE construction consists of a phrase in which the phrasal head is modified by the element *enough*, and that phrase is followed by a *to*-infinitive clause. Semantically, the phrase with *enough* encodes an enabling precondition that allows the event or state expressed in the *to*-infinitive clause to take place. Hence, an adjectival phrase such as *old enough* can be followed by the clause *to know better*, a verb phrase such as *had trained enough* can be followed by *to finish my first marathon in good shape*, and the noun phrase *enough food* can be followed by *to feed a small village*. If you compare this kind of structure to example (16), you will notice a syntactic difference. In the noun phrase *an important enough song*, the element *enough* modifies not the head of the phrase, but the adjective *important*. Accordingly, the noun phrase is followed by a *to*-infinitive clause that connects back semantically to the adjective. A way to deal with the structure of the example would be to analyse it as a syntactic amalgam of the two sentences shown below. As the layout suggests, the two constructions are mutually interwoven. The material of each source construction appears in full in the syntactic amalgam, which is linked to both of them via subpart links.

(18) It was an important   song.
      It was   important enough   to put on their last single.

A different example of multiple inheritance is offered by Michaelis and Lambrecht (1996). Michaelis and Lambrecht argue that the EXTRAPOSED EXCLAMATIVE construction and the METONYMIC NP construction that was discussed in the previous section can be combined into a syntactic amalgam that they call the NOMINAL EXTRAPOSITION construction. The following examples show the respective source constructions and the syntactic amalgam.

(19) It's unbelievable what he can do with the piano!
      The things he can do with the piano!
      It's unbelievable the things he can do with the piano!

The examples discussed in the previous paragraphs may give you the idea that multiple inheritance always results in syntactically quite complex structures, which is not necessarily the case. For instance, all of the cases of coercion that were discussed in Chapter 2 on argument structure constructions can be seen as cases of multiple inheritance. An example such as *Bob sliced the carrots into the salad* instantiates the CAUSED MOTION construction, but it also is connected to the TRANSITIVE construction with a subpart link, since *Bob sliced the carrots* is a typical transitive clause. In summary, subpart links are extremely pervasive in the construct-i-con, and it is the pervasiveness of these links that turns the construct-i-con into a densely woven fabric of constructions, rather than a mere hierarchy of constructions.

3.2.3 Complete inheritance vs. redundant representations

The previous section introduced the concept of instance links, describing how more specific constructions inherit characteristics from more general ones as part of their formal and functional profile. Within the Construction Grammar community, there is a broad consensus that instance links are an important structuring principle in speakers' knowledge of language. A point of divergence, however, concerns the question whether the inherited information is to be represented just once in the grammar, as associated with the most general construction, or whether this kind of information is redundantly represented across all of the constructions that share it. Put simply, if the SUBJECT–PREDICATE construction already specifies that a verb has to agree in number and person with its subject, does this information have to be associated directly with each and every construction that inherits part of its form from the SUBJECT–PREDICATE construction? It is clear that the more economical strategy would be to store information just once, so that constructions at lower levels of abstractions could be processed by 'looking up' all inherited pieces of information in the higher levels of the construct-i-con. At the same time, however, the most economical theory of linguistic knowledge need not necessarily be the most plausible theory from a psycholinguistic point of view, as will be discussed below. So, what information about language do speakers memorise, and what information do they look up in the construct-i-con? To get a sense of the point that is at issue, consider the following quote by Fillmore et al. (1988: 502).

> All of the many competing accounts of the workings of language draw a
> distinction in one way or another between what it is that speakers know

outright about their language and what it is that they have to be able to figure out. For example, speakers of English have to know what *red* means and that it is an adjective, and they have to know what *ball* means and that it is a noun. They have to know that adjectives can co-occur with nouns in a modification structure (as in a phrase like *red ball*), and they have to know the proper strategies for giving a semantic interpretation to such adjective–noun combinations. But they do not have to know separately, or to be told, what the phrase *red ball* means. That is something which what they already know enables them to figure out.

Theories of linguistic knowledge that leave a maximal amount of information to be worked out, rather than stored, endorse a view that is known as **complete inheritance**. This point of view is usually taken in branches of Construction Grammar that have the computational implementation of grammatical knowledge as their primary aim. This view assumes that inherited information is only stored once, namely with the most general construction that carries this information. A second assumption that follows from this view is that only constructional schemas are stored, not their specific instantiations. For instance, the PRESENT TENSE construction specifies that verbs in the third person carry the suffix -*s*, yielding forms such as *thinks, walks*, or *sits*. Since both form and meaning of these forms are completely transparent, a speaker would not have to memorise them. Knowing the schema is enough; the rest can be worked out. By contrast, the view that is taken in this book makes the assumption of **redundant representations**, that is, multiple memorisations of the same pieces of information across different levels of abstraction. It is assumed that besides general schemas, speakers memorise a great many concrete instantiations of those schemas. The main argument for adopting such a view is fuelled by empirical evidence for the idea that speakers retain a highly detailed record of linguistic usage events in memory (Bybee 2010). This record includes fine phonetic detail of concrete utterances, structural characteristics of utterances, and their situational context. The richness of each record of course fades with time, like any kind of memory, but it is refreshed by new usage events. Crucially, speakers do not 'strip down' the record to a more schematic representation. Gurevich et al. (2010) show that speakers retain verbatim memory of language from short stories, even when they are not explicitly asked to do so. A high level of detail is thus maintained in memory, leading to redundant representations of linguistic knowledge. There is evidence that even fully regular inflected forms are stored in memory, provided that they occur frequently enough (Stemberger and MacWhinney 1988). On this view, the construct-i-con is **usage-based**, that is, created through experience with language and continuously influenced by experience with language (Bybee 2010). This point will be further elaborated in Chapter 8 on variation and change.

3.3 'Normal syntax' in Construction Grammar

If you have taken an introductory linguistics course, the sessions on syntax will have introduced you to different word classes such as nouns, verbs, prepositions, and so on. In all likelihood, your class will also have covered how these types of words combine into phrases and sentences. Most textbooks that are currently on the market offer some discussion of syntactic schemas that allow the composition of noun phrases, verb phrases, prepositional phrases, and several others. These schemas, which are sometimes called phrase structure rules, are meant to represent knowledge of language. Speakers know that different types of words can be combined to form larger units of language, as for instance in the following examples, all of which are noun phrases.

(20) milk
     an old donkey
     the big one with the two horns
     all of my personal belongings
     my friend Amy, who recently moved to Italy

The fact that all of these examples are noun phrases can easily be demonstrated with a battery of syntactic tests. It is, for instance, possible to finish the string *Let me tell you a story about* . . . with any of the above examples. Likewise, someone could, after hearing you say that, ask *What did you want to tell me a story about?*, to which you would be answering with the respective example in its bare form. All of this strongly suggests that speakers have formed a generalisation across different kinds of noun phrases. However, having come this far in the book that you are reading, you may wonder how the phrase structure rules that you have learned for noun phrases in your introductory course fit into the picture of the construct-i-con that has been sketched in the previous sections. How does Construction Grammar handle 'normal syntax'? Is there a NOUN PHRASE construction? And is that construction just a phrase structure rule that is called something else?

The short answer to these questions is that there is in fact a NOUN PHRASE construction, but that this construction differs in many respects from phrase structure rules as they are commonly understood. One crucial difference between the two concepts is that phrase structure rules are meant to be assembly instructions, like manuals that allow you to put together a piece of furniture, whereas abstract phrasal constructions are thought of as generalisations across different linguistic structures that allow you to identify a given structure as belonging to a certain category. The NOUN PHRASE construction is thus not primary to more specific constructions such as the ATTRIBUTIVE ADJECTIVE construction (*an old donkey, the red ball*), the NOMINAL QUANTIFIER construction (*all of my personal belongings, some of the juice*), or the RELATIVE CLAUSE construction (*the man who left, the sandwich that I kept in the drawer for too long*). Rather, the NOUN PHRASE construction is an emergent phenomenon that results from speakers perceiving certain similarities across these different kinds of construction. In summary, whereas phrase structure rules would be seen as an essential tool for putting together phrases and sentences, abstract phrasal constructions are really a case of cognitive luxury: they are certainly nice to have, but nothing crucial depends on them, either in language production or in comprehension. The crucial work is done by constructions that occupy lower levels of abstraction in the construct-i-con.

Some researchers in Construction Grammar have expressed quite serious doubts about the existence of high-level syntactic generalisations such as the noun phrase, subject and object, or even part-of-speech categories such as noun or verb. For instance, Croft (2001: 55) states that 'no schematic syntactic category is ever an independent unit of grammatical representation', which means that high-level syntactic generalisations only ever become part of knowledge of language when speakers make out similarities across constructions and form a generalisation. To take a concrete example, Croft argues that there really is no overarching syntactic category of a grammatical subject. Rather, there is a certain kind of subject that occurs in the TRANSITIVE construction, there is another kind of subject that occurs in the INTRANSITIVE construction, and so on and so forth. The subject of the TRANSITIVE construction in turn is a generalisation that speakers would have made across more concrete transitive constructional schemas such as transitive *kick*, transitive *read*, transitive *eat*, and so on and so forth. Since many different constructions combine a subject constituent with a verbal constituent, speakers may perceive this similarity and arrive at a higher-order generalisation, which would correspond to the SUBJECT–PREDICATE construction, or, for that matter, to a phrase structure rule for clausal constructions. But whereas such a phrase structure rule would represent the very bedrock of grammatical knowledge in the dictionary-and-grammar model of linguistic knowledge, the SUBJECT–PREDICATE construction in usage-based Construction Grammar is nothing more than a vague idea entertained by speakers who are analytically minded enough to see similarities between different kinds of construction. Croft (2001: 57) points out that not all speakers may in fact make these high-level generalisations, so that any claim to their psychological reality would rest on shaky foundations. Importantly, Croft's arguments do not only relegate abstract syntactic schemas to a rather marginal place in the construct-i-con; they also force us to reconsider the cognitive status of word classes such as noun, verb, preposition, and determiner. In the dictionary-and-grammar model of linguistic knowledge, each lexical item that is listed in the mental dictionary has a category label that identifies it as belonging to a certain word class. Word classes are seen as the building blocks of phrases and sentences, and phrase structure rules crucially depend on them: a phrase structure rule defines a construction (say, the NOUN PHRASE construction) through parts of speech that occur in that construction. Construction Grammar stands this relation on its head: the constructions are basic, and parts of speech come into being as generalisations across different types of construction. In the construct-i-con, categories such as 'determiner' or 'preposition' thus represent generalisations at an extremely high level of abstraction, like the SUBJECT–PREDICATE construction.

Expressing a similar point of view, other researchers have stressed the importance of low-level generalisations for the overall structure of the construct-i-con. Boas (2003) offers an analysis of the RESULTATIVE construction, which he views not as a unified phenomenon, but rather as a cluster of generalisations at a slightly lower level. Importantly, the RESULTATIVE construction occurs with a wide range of verbs and resultative phrases, but there are restrictions on the kinds of elements that may occur in a given example. For instance, *Jerry danced himself to exhaustion* and *Nancy talked herself hoarse* are perfectly acceptable examples, whereas *Jerry danced himself exhausted* or *Nancy talked herself to hoarseness* are decidedly unidiomatic (Boas 2005: 449). Rather than positing a high-level argument structure construction, Boas advocates a solution that recognises several low-level generalisations, each of which may serve as the basis for further extensions. Whereas one general construction would not be able to account for the unacceptability of the above examples, the empirical facts could be explained by a cluster of 'productivity islands', that is, small-scale constructions that speakers use to form analogies.

Low-level generalisations are of course also important when it comes to the cognitive representation of word classes or even words themselves. Whereas abstract constructions would seem to suggest that when an adjective is called for, any adjective will do, this is demonstrably not the case. The ATTRIBUTIVE ADJECTIVE construction, which combines a determiner, an adjective, and a noun, yields grammatical constructs such as *the blue book*. Applied across all kinds of adjectives, it also yields ungrammatical examples such as the following.

(21)   *the awake child
       *the ready food
       *the on computer
       *the fond of children lady

Clearly, speakers' knowledge of the ATTRIBUTIVE ADJECTIVE construction includes the fact that some adjectives do not appear in that construction. This means that the construction cannot just specify that it requires an adjective, any adjective. Rather, the construction is a rich and detailed representation of speakers' experience with attributive adjectives. Adjectives such as *awake*, *ready*, or *on* are conspicuously absent from this experience, which leads to the effect of ungrammaticality in the examples above. Turning to an even finer level of detail, it has to be pointed out that even a word represents something of a generalisation. The linguistic forms *walk*, *walks*, *walked*, and *walking* all instantiate the verb *walk*, which is listed in dictionaries under the latter form only – the **lemma** *walk*. In the dictionary-and-grammar model of linguistic knowledge, it is a matter of course that only the lemma, the base form, is memorised in the mental dictionary, and the inflected forms are produced by grammatical rules. Not so in Construction Grammar, where inflected forms can be redundantly represented in the construct-i-con, and where these inflected forms may develop some independence with regard to their respective meanings. Newman and Rice (2006) compare inflected forms of the verbs *eat* and *drink*, finding that there are differences, for example, with regard to the presence or absence of an object. This means argument structure is not so much a property of a verb lemma as a property of an inflected verb form. Newman and Rice conclude that a lemma-based conception of speakers' knowledge of words is inadequate.

Summarising the paragraphs of this section, Construction Grammar handles 'normal syntax' in a way that necessitates a shift of perspective away from the common view of words, word classes, and phrase structure rules. These categories do exist in the construct-i-con, but not as building blocks and assembly manuals for syntactic structures; rather, they are generalisations at a fairly high level of abstraction. Work in Construction Grammar has furthermore stressed the importance of low-level generalisations in the representation of linguistic knowledge. Generalisations at high levels of abstraction are desirable from a theoretical point of view, as they allow the construction of 'elegant' models of linguistic knowledge. At the same time, most of the available evidence from corpora and psycholinguistic experiments points to the crucial role of low-level generalisations.

3.4 Summing up

This chapter has discussed the question how speakers' knowledge of language is organised in the construct-i-con, which has been introduced earlier as a large network of form–meaning pairings. The first section addressed the question whether the claim that constructions have meanings can in fact be maintained for all constructions, even highly abstract syntactic patterns such as the SUBJECT–PREDICATE construction or ellipsis constructions such as SHARED COMPLETION. Whereas researchers such as Goldberg (1995, 2006) maintain the idea of the construct-i-con as a repository of meaningful forms, other proponents of Construction Grammar, notably Fillmore and colleagues (2012), allow meaningless constructions into the construct-i-con. They identify three types of construction for which semantic analyses are problematic. The first type is illustrated by the SUBJECT–PREDICATE construction or the MODIFIER–HEAD construction. These constructions represent highly general formal generalisations that contribute little in the way of meaning to the utterances in which they are found. A second type of construction, illustrated by SUBJECT–AUXILIARY INVERSION or FILLER-GAP constructions, conveys a heterogeneous range of different meanings, so that a common semantic generalisation appears problematic. The third type covers ELLIPSIS constructions such as GAPPING, STRIPPING, and SHARED COMPLETION. These construction types specify particular syntactic patterns, but do not convey recognisable meanings and do not lead to coercion effects either. The chapter discussed two strategies for the analysis of these constructions as form–meaning pairs. One strategy would look for an overarching, schematic meaning whereas the second would posit a network of lower-level constructions, each of which would have a meaning of its own.

The second section of the chapter introduced the concept of inheritance, which describes links between constructions in the construct-i-con. These links concern aspects of form as well as aspects of meaning. Different kinds of inheritance links were distinguished. Instance links connect constructions in a hierarchical fashion, linking construction types with particular instances of those types. Polysemy links connect constructions that share the same form but display a variety of different senses. Examples for such constructions include the DITRANSITIVE construction and the *S*-GENITIVE construction. Metaphorical links are similar to polysemy links, since they also connect basic and extended senses of a construction. A metaphorical link is found, for instance, between the CAUSED MOTION construction and the RESULTATIVE construction. Finally, subpart links connect constructions that exhibit partial similarities in their respective forms or meanings. Subpart links establish relations between complex syntactic constructions and all those constructions that instantiate their parts. These links are largely responsible for the network-like structure of the construct-i-con. A phenomenon that was discussed in connection with subpart links is multiple inheritance, the idea that one construction may instantiate several constructions at the same time. Syntactic amalgams were examined as illustrations of multiple inheritance. The section finished with a discussion of two opposing views on how inherited information would be represented in the construct-i-con. On the view of complete inheritance, this kind of information is represented only once, namely at the most general level where it is necessary. By contrast, the view maintained in this book, and in usage-based Construction Grammar in general, is that inherited information is represented redundantly across different levels of abstraction, with every construction that shares this information.

The final section of the chapter considered the role of 'normal syntax' in Construction Grammar. In the dictionary-and-grammar model of linguistic knowledge, syntax rests on the notions of words, word classes, and phrase structure rules. It was explained that these concepts have a proper status in Construction Grammar, but that they are seen as an epiphenomenon of knowledge of constructions, rather than as the basis of syntactic knowledge.

Study questions

- Why are 'meaningless constructions' problematic for the idea of the construct-i-con?
- What types of constructions do Fillmore et al. (2012) identify as meaningless?
- What is meant by the term 'inheritance'?
- What kinds of inheritance links are there?
- What is the difference between complete inheritance and redundant representations?
- Discuss the concept of multiple inheritance with regard to the following examples.

This summer, John is travelling to I think it's the Bahamas.
That's what bothers me is that he never really listens.

• What are the similarities and differences between phrase structure rules and abstract phrasal constructions?

Further reading

The concept of inheritance, with reference to different types of inheritance links, is discussed in Goldberg (1995: ch. 3). Zeschel (2009) elaborates on the distinction of complete inheritance vs. redundant representations of linguistic knowledge. A useful discussion of abstract phrasal and clausal constructions is found in Hoffmann (2013). The question of the 'right' level of abstractness for the description of constructions is discussed in Gries (2011). Finally, Croft (2001) presents central arguments for viewing constructions as the basis for high-level generalisations such as parts of speech and categories such as subject and object.

4 Constructional morphology

4.1 More than a theory of syntax

The previous chapters have made the case that Construction Grammar is a theory of linguistic knowledge in its entirety. Everything that speakers know when they know a language is to be represented as a construct-i-con, a large network of constructions. Despite this all-encompassing commitment, most examples in this book up to now have been syntactic in nature: constructions such as the RESULTATIVE construction, the DITRANSITIVE construction, or the the *ENOUGH To*-INFINITIVE construction. In fact, most of the Construction Grammar literature that you are likely to come across deals exclusively with syntactic phenomena. However, Construction Grammar is not just a theory of syntax. This chapter turns to morphological constructions, that is, constructions that require an analysis of word-internal structures. Booij (2010, 2013) has recently developed a constructional approach to morphology, and this chapter reviews the basic ideas of that approach. What now would be examples of morphological constructions? Consider the following sentences.

(1) This is a wug. Now there is another one. There are two . . . wugs.
If you need to reach me, I'm skypable all morning.
Not quite shorts, not quite pants – shpants!
John gave me a what-the-heck-is-wrong-with-you look.

4.1.1 one wug, two wugs

The first example might be familiar to you because it comes from the famous 'wug study' (Berko Gleason 1958). In that study, young children were prompted to produce plural forms of invented words such as *wug*, *heaf*, or *gutch*. The children mastered this task, producing *wugs* with a voiced /z/, *heafs* with a voiceless /s/, and *gutches* ending in /əz/, despite the fact that they had obviously never encountered these forms before. The fact that they performed in this way indicates that the children had formed a generalisation about how the English plural is formed. This generalisation is a morpho-phonological construction. The construction is morphological because regular plural forms consist of a stem and a plural suffix, and furthermore because the form of the suffix depends on the phonological characteristics of the stem. This phenomenon is called **allomorphy**, and it is typically talked about in terms of rules. As you may already expect, the perspective from Construction Grammar recasts the idea of these rules as a construction that forms part of the construct-i-con, namely the PLURAL construction. The PLURAL construction belongs to a larger group of **inflectional** morphological constructions. Inflectional constructions mark grammatical distinctions, and there are only a limited number of them in English. Nine important ones are summarised in the following example.

(2) A group of cat*s*   the PLURAL construction
     eat*s*   the PRESENT TENSE 3RD PERSON
                                    SINGULAR construction
     John*'s* sandwich that   the S-GENITIVE construction
     he topp*ed* with cheese   the PAST TENSE construction
     produc*ed*   the PAST PARTICIPLE construction
     by graz*ing* cows   the PRESENT PARTICIPLE construction
     happi*er*   the MORPHOLOGICAL COMPARATIVE
                                    construction
     than the happi*est* clam.   the MORPHOLOGICAL SUPERLATIVE
                                    construction

As always, the whole truth is somewhat more complicated than the example suggests. Besides the PAST TENSE construction with *-ed* there are alternative ways of expressing past time reference, notably ablaut (*sing, sang, sung*) and irregular plurals (*put*). The suffix *-ing* is listed just as the PRESENT PARTICIPLE construction, but it also instantiates a part of the PROGRESSIVE construction (*He's reading*). The PAST PARTICIPLE construction is further involved in the PERFECT construction (*They have produced a lot of cheese recently*). However, as a first pass at the inflectional constructions of English, example (2) is useful enough.

4.1.2 skypable

In this chapter, the notion of morphological constructions will be exemplified chiefly with **derivational** constructions. Derivational constructions are instrumental for word formation. The word *skypable* from example (1) above illustrates the coinage of a relatively new word. There are certain parallels to the *wugs* example: even if you had never encountered the word before, you probably had little difficulty in working out what it meant. Someone who is *skypable* is 'someone who can be skyped', that is, reached over a computer-mediated channel of communication. By the same token, a fabric that is *washable* 'can be washed', a *foldable* chair 'can be folded', and so on. You can observe that speakers come up with new and original coinages of this kind, which suggests that they have not only mentally stored a long list of adjectives ending in -*able*, rather, they have stored a construction that is partially schematic, so that it allows the formation of new words such as *pigeonholeable* 'can be pigeonholed' or *cut-and-paste-able* 'can be cut-and-pasted'.

Researchers in English derivational morphology have of course studied phenomena of this kind for a long time under the heading of **word formation processes**. In approaches that associate with the dictionary-and-grammar view of linguistic knowledge, productive word formation processes are conceived of as morphological rules (e.g. Aronoff 1976; cf. also Plag 2003: 30). The core idea of constructional morphology is that speakers form generalisations that associate a schematic form with a schematic meaning. For instance, speakers are thought to generalise over sets of words such as *baker, buyer, runner, seller,* and *speaker* so that they form the schema shown in (3), which allows them to coin new words (from Booij 2010: 2).

(3) $[[x]_V \text{ er}]_N$ --- 'one who Vs'

On the face of it, morphological constructions are not very different from word formation rules. However, there are several pieces of evidence that word formation processes behave in ways that are very similar to the behaviour of syntactic constructions. These behavioural characteristics would be difficult to model as aspects of rules, but they lend themselves quite easily to a constructional account. First, word formation processes are selective with regard to the elements that they take as input. Chapter 1 discussed the HAVE LONG V-*ed* construction that licenses the expression *I have long known your father* but not **I have long read this book.* Similarly, the V-*er* construction licenses *runner* and *swimmer*, but speakers are reluctant to accept *stander* 'one who stands' or *drowner* 'one who drowns' as valid constructs. The construction is thus restricted to a specific semantic subclass of verbs; typically we find verbs that express self-controlled dynamic activities. Second, word formation processes exhibit coercion effects that have been discussed, for instance, in connection with GRINDING constructions (*There was cat all over the road*). To illustrate, the V-*able* construction typically selects transitive verbs as hosts (*washable, foldable,* and not **sleepable*), but it occasionally coerces intransitive verbs into quasi-transitive senses, thus subtly changing their meanings. Specifically, a *laughable* proposal 'can be laughed at' and a *livable* wage 'can be lived on'. These examples indicate that speakers sometimes stretch the limits of what a constructional schema typically allows, thereby creating words that are not quite prototypical of a construction, but nonetheless licensed by it. Chapter 8 will come back to this and discuss the issue of language variation in more detail.

4.1.3 shpants

Besides word formation processes that create new words through affixation, there are several morphological construction types that are called **non-concatenative**, reflecting the idea that they do not just string linguistic material together in a morpheme-by-morpheme fashion. One example is the BLEND construction, which combines parts of existing words to a new word, as in *shpants* (*shorts, pants*) or *manwich* (*man, sandwich*). Whereas it is perhaps relatively easy to see how a schema such as the V-*able* construction combines a form and a meaning, the case of blending may initially look like another case of a meaningless construction (cf. Chapter 3, Section 3.1), and thus, a potential problem case for the constructional view of linguistic knowledge.

There is compelling evidence that blending represents a formal generalisation in the minds of speakers. Blends are not formed as random combinations of two or more words, but follow a rather precise phonological pattern that Plag (2003: 123) describes as the **blending rule**: two words combine in such a way that the blend contains the first part of the first word and the second part of the second word.

(4) A B   + C D   >> A D
    motor   hotel   motel
    smoke   fog   smog
    stagnation   inflation   stagflation

Examples such as *shpants* or *guesstimate* show that sometimes blends even contain all of a component word, but in these cases too the first word has to contribute its beginning and the second word has to contribute its end.

The systematicity goes even further than that. Blending is sensitive to the syllable structure of the component words. Syllables such as *blip, couch,* or *soft* have three main parts that are called onset (the initial consonants), nucleus (the vocalic elements), and coda (any final consonants). Nucleus and coda combine to form what is called the rime of a syllable. Blend formations can combine parts of words relatively freely, but crucially, the rime of each participating syllable needs to stay intact. Consider the examples given below.

(5) linguist   magician   >>   linguician   linguagician
    dentist   torturer   >>   denturer   dentorturer
    chicken   crocodile   >>   chickodile   chickendile
    breakfast   lunch   >>   brunch   *brench
    spoon   fork   >>   spork   *spoork
    shout   yell   >>   shell   *shoull

For the first three word pairs, the BLEND construction allows speakers to form at least two possible blends: ask a few friends what a half-chicken, half-crocodile monster would be called, and the likely answers will include *chickodile, chickendile,* and perhaps a few other forms. There is thus variability; the blending rule does not completely determine the outcome of a combination of two words. However, there is not complete freedom. As the last three examples show, the rime constraint prevents formations such as *brench, *spoork, or *shoull. This is not because they might be more difficult to pronounce, but rather because these forms combine a syllable nucleus from the first word with a syllable coda from the second word. To get *spoork, you would have to take *spoo* from *spoon,* and *rk* from *fork,* dissecting the rimes of both input words. If you agree that *spoork does not feel quite right as a blend, your knowledge of English contains this idiosyncratic phonological constraint of the BLEND construction. (A puzzling exception to this generalisation is the blend *Spanglish.* If you find other exceptions, please send an email to the author of this book.)

Whereas the formal side of English blends thus clearly suggests that we are dealing with a construction, it is not so easy to find a generalisation in terms of their meaning. After all, *shpants, chunnel, brunch,* and *spork* all refer to quite different things. The most promising avenue would be to take one of the emergency strategies outlined in Chapter 3 and to posit a fairly general meaning that captures how blends always refer to a 'chimera', that is, an idea that results from the conceptual overlay of two or more previously existing ideas. This kind of meaning is motivated through **iconicity**, that is, a correspondence between form and meaning: a word that combines parts of two words also combines partial meanings of the two source words. The specifics of such an analysis will, however, not be fleshed out here.

4.1.4 a what-the-heck-is-wrong-with-you look

The fourth example of a morphological construction type illustrates what is called a PHRASAL COMPOUND. The main characteristic of phrasal compounds in English is that their non-head elements, that is, their left constituents, consist not of a word, but of a phrase. A few more examples are offered below.

(6) What really gets on my nerves are these countless 'me too' bands.
    Over the counter drugs are medicines you can buy without a prescription.
    I prefer to take a Nietzschean god-is-dead approach to life.
    The press photo shows Zuckerberg with a show-me-the-money grin.
    The army followed a don't ask don't tell policy.

A sign that these forms are in fact compounds is that their main stress lies on the rightmost edge of the non-head phrase, so that they are pronounced as *over the COUNter drugs* or *god is DEAD approach* (cf. Giegerich 2004 for a discussion of compounds and stress). This is crucial because it means that these forms, long as they are, are to be considered as single words. Phrasal compounds are difficult to explain in a dictionary-and-grammar model of linguistic knowledge that strictly separates syntactic rules and morphological rules (Sato 2010). The formation of a phrase such as *over the counter* would be the task of a syntactic component in the mental grammar, whereas word formation processes such as compounding would be handled by a morphological component. In such theories, cases of 'teamwork' require some kind of explanation, typically in the form of an interface between the different components. In Construction Grammar, no interfaces are needed because both syntactic constructions and morphological constructions are cut from the same cloth: they form part of the construct-i-con. Phrasal compounds simply represent a case of multiple inheritance where characteristics such as stress pattern and headedness are inherited from the NOUN–NOUN COMPOUND construction while the non-head inherits the structural characteristics of a general phrasal construction such as the PREPOSITIONAL PHRASE construction or the VERB PHRASE construction. Construction Grammar is usually not considered to be an elegant theory of linguistic knowledge, but in the case of phrasal compounds it provides a very straightforward account that directly follows from its main organisational principles.

Summing up the previous paragraphs, different morphological construction types show that Construction Grammar is usefully applied to issues of word structure. The following sections build on these insights and discuss a number of concepts that are crucial to the understanding of morphology from a constructionist perspective.

4.2 Morphological constructions and their properties

The preceding discussion may have left you wondering what a morphological construction really is. If there is a schema such as the V-*er* construction and if there are forms such as *baker, swimmer, smoker*, and so on, is the abstract schema a construction while its instantiations are to be seen as constructs? The view that is proposed by Booij (2010) and that is adopted here is that both the schema and its instantiations are constructions if there is evidence to suggest that they are conventionalised form–meaning pairings.

To start with the actual words, it is non-controversial to assume that speakers of English know the words *baker, teacher,* and *smoker* as parts of their active vocabulary. These items have their own firmly established representation in the construct-i-con, which makes them lexical constructions. Note also that words like *baker* and *smoker* have meanings that go beyond 'one who V-s': a *baker* is someone who bakes for a living, a *smoker* is someone who smokes habitually. The fact that speakers know this is evidence for the constructional status of these words. Evidence for the more abstract V-*er* construction comes from the fact that hearers have little trouble understanding new formations that conform to the schema. Consider the following example, which formed part of the wug study (Berko Gleason 1958). In the study, an experimenter read the example to children, showing them a picture of a man balancing a ball on his nose.

(7)   This man knows how to zib.
      What would you call a man whose job is to zib?

In order to produce the answer *zibber*, children would have to have recourse to the V-*er* construction, which most of them did. The actual word *zibber*, at that point at least, did not form part of the children's construct-i-con. Hearing a new word a few times may of course establish a new node in the construct-i-con and thus lead to the birth of a new lexical construction. To summarise the argument in a nutshell, instantiations of a word formation process are constructions if they are conventionalised form–meaning pairings; the abstract schema behind a word formation process is a construction if that schema allows speakers to produce or process new original coinages. The latter idea touches on the issue of **morphological productivity**, which we need to discuss in some more depth.

4.2.1 *Morphological productivity*

The notion of morphological productivity is not easily defined (Aronoff 1976; Mayerthaler 1981). Adopting ideas from van Marle (1985), the term is used in this book in the following way:

(8) The productivity of a schematic morphological construction describes the degree of cognitive ease with which speakers can produce or process new complex words on the basis of that construction.

This definition implies that productivity is gradient; a construction may be more or less productive. Some constructions that are very productive include the V-*er* construction (*baker, smoker*) or the ADJ-*ness* construction (*loudness, softness*); much less productive constructions are illustrated by the N-*ship* construction (*lordship, citizenship*) and the N-*eer* construction (*harpooneer, cannoneer*). For the two latter constructions, it is fairly difficult, perhaps even impossible, to generate neologisms. Some word formation processes indeed seem to be completely unproductive. A classic example is the group of English adjective-based nouns ending in -*th*, which includes *warmth, truth, depth*, and *width*. There is clearly a pattern to these nouns, but you can imagine that no wug study in the world could get children to produce nouns such as *greenth, *wrongth, or *roundth. By the same token, the V-*ment* construction (*amusement, punishment*) is also unproductive. Forms such as *emailment or *jogment are perhaps processable, but unattested. Morphological productivity shows itself in records of language use. Chapter 1 discussed the use of linguistic corpora for the analysis of constructions. With regard to the study of morphological constructions, corpora are extremely useful because they reveal two important issues that are related to productivity. First, a corpus allows the researcher to count the different instantiations of a schematic morphological construction. This measure is called the **type frequency** of a morphological construction. For instance, the ADJ-*en* construction, which is completely unproductive these days, is represented by only forty-four types in the BNC, which holds 100 million words of running text. Table 4.1 shows those types along with how often the respective forms are found in the corpus.

A type frequency of forty-four, given the large size of the BNC, is very low. Highly productive constructions such as the ADJ-*ness* construction register hundreds, sometimes thousands of types. The upper end of morphological productivity is illustrated by inflectional morphological constructions such as the PLURAL construction, which works with just about any noun in the English language (which leads second

Table 4.1 Types of the ADJ-*en* construction

Type	Tokens	Type	Tokens	Type	Tokens
weaken	322	fasten	91	toughen	34
widen	317	flatten	89	blacken	28
tighten	302	dampen	88	smarten	25
soften	283	stiffen	74	moisten	20
broaden	269	ripen	70	cheapen	14
lessen	213	awaken	70	deaden	14
loosen	162	quicken	65	redden	11
shorten	144	darken	59	deafen	8
straighten	135	thicken	58	gladden	8
sharpen	132	quieten	56	sadden	7
harden	130	waken	48	neaten	6
lighten	128	fatten	48	steepen	6
deepen	119	sweeten	43	whiten	6
brighten	109	freshen	37	madden	1
worsen	104	slacken	37		

language learners of English to make mistakes such as *informations, *evidences*, and *researches*), and the PAST TENSE construction; cf. example (2) in this chapter. The type frequencies of these constructions lie in the tens of thousands. Now, the second important issue that corpora reveal about the productivity of a morphological construction is the occurrence of low-frequency instantiations. There is a special term reserved for forms that occur only once in a given corpus; they are called **hapax legomena**, or hapaxes, for short. A look at Table 4.1 shows that only one of the forty-four types of the ADJ-*en* construction is a hapax: *madden*. A low ratio of hapaxes – and one out of forty-four is very low – indicates the absence of productivity. Clearly, speakers do not use the ADJ-*en* construction to create many neologisms. With a productive construction, corpus data will show that a substantial ratio of types occurs only once. Not all of these one-offs are neologisms: some established words simply are very rare. However, a high ratio of low-frequency instantiations still points to the fact that speakers feel free to produce new coinages, and furthermore that they expect hearers to understand forms such as *talkativeness, unexplainably*, or *applauder* without problems. The more strongly a morphological construction is represented as a node in the construct-i-con, the easier this is.

Given the premise that productivity is gradient, and given that strength of productivity correlates with the strength of mental representation in the construct-i-con, where does this leave non-productive word formation processes such as the ADJ-*en* construction? Do they deserve to be called constructions? Booij (2013: 258) argues that non-productive word formation processes should also be viewed as constructions. One of his arguments is that the suffix -*ship* is clearly identifiable in forms such as *lordship, citizenship*, and so on, so that speakers may well form a generalisation, despite the fact that *managership* or *consultantship* are words that may seem rather ad hoc, perhaps even unacceptable, to some speakers. The view that is taken in this book is that a label such as the N-*ship* construction may serve as a useful descriptor for a group of words, but if such a label is used, there needs to be evidence that speakers (and not only linguists!) do indeed generalise across the words in question and form a node in the construct-i-con, however weak that node might be. Productivity, as measured in corpus data, is one piece of evidence for that.

4.2.2 Paradigmatic organisation

Chapter 3 introduced the concept of **subpart links** (Goldberg 1995: 78), which relate constructions that partially overlap in either their form, their meaning, or typically both. An example of two syntactic constructions that share aspects of form and meaning is the case of the Transitive construction and the Ditransitive construction. Both of the examples below have a subject with the role of an agent and a direct object that has the role of a patient or theme.

(9) John wrote a letter.
John wrote Mary a letter.

Morphological constructions are heavily interlinked through subpart links. Just think of a simple lexical item such as the verb *report* and consider all the morphological constructions that are connected to it via subpart links. Some of those constructions are listed below.

(10) report-s   the Present Tense 3rd Person Singular
                   construction
report-ed   the Past Tense construction
report-er   the V-*er* construction
report-able the V-*able* construction
mis-report   the *Mis*-V construction
report   the Deverbal Noun construction

Lists of constructions that are related through subpart links by a common element are called **paradigms**. You may have come across paradigms of inflectional morphological constructions (typically constructions of different verbal tenses or different nominal case endings) in pedagogical grammars or language classes. The above list is more inclusive and also includes derivational morphological constructions. Why now are subpart links and paradigms important for the constructional view of morphology? In order to answer this question, Booij (2013: 264) presents the following list of examples.

(11) alpin-ism   alpin-ist
      commun-ism   commun-ist
      de-ism   de-ist
      fasc-ism   fasc-ist
      solips-ism   solips-ist

On the dictionary-and-grammar view of linguistic knowledge, complex morphological words are formed in such a way that an input word is fetched from the dictionary, which is then, by means of a grammatical rule, combined with an affix in the morphological component of the grammar. To form *alpinism*, a speaker may thus retrieve the adjective *alpine* from the mental lexicon and combine it with -*ism* to yield a word that means 'alpine activities, that is, sports having to do with mountains such as the Alps'. Importantly, this procedure does not seem to work equally well for all word pairs given above. There are simply no independent lexical items with the forms **de*, **fasc*, or **solips*. In order to maintain the dictionary-and-grammar view, one could assume that speakers form *fascist* by retrieving *fascism* from the mental lexicon, whereupon a grammatical rule replaces the suffix -*ism* with -*ist* (Aronoff 1976). Booij (2013: 264) points out that such deletion rules are not necessary in the constructional view of morphology. If speakers know groups of words that are interconnected through subpart links, they can form a generalisation across these word groups. In other words, speakers know that *alpine, alpinism,* and *alpinist* belong to a common paradigm that is also instantiated by *social, socialism,* and *socialist,* or *ideal, idealism,* and *idealist.* If speakers' knowledge of this paradigm is entrenched enough, hearing the word *ventriloquist* 'a performer who speaks in such a way that his voice appears to emanate from a puppet, not himself' is enough of a clue to infer that there might be a word such as *ventriloquism* for this kind of performance.

The paradigm linking words suffixed with -*ist* and -*ism* is not the only example of its kind: basically every morphological phenomenon that involves **stem allomorphy** (Plag 1999: 193) requires an analysis of this kind. Word pairs such as *summary – summarise, memory – memorise, fantasy – fantasise,* or *theory – theoretic, apology – apologetic, energy – energetic* illustrate this. Subpart links in the construct-i-con that connect these kinds of words allow speakers to 'fill in the blank' when they encounter a word they have not heard before. Knowledge of constructional paradigms further plays a major role in processes of regularisation such as the use of *weeped* instead of *wept*, and it looms large in children's overgeneralisation errors during first language acquisition. We will thus come back to this topic in later chapters of this book.

4.2.3 Non-compositional meanings

Throughout this book, we have seen examples of constructions with meanings that cannot be fully explained in terms of the meanings of the component parts. Non-compositional meanings are perhaps most easily seen in fixed idiomatic expressions such as *by and large* or *all of a sudden*. By contrast, many morphological constructions seem to be perfectly transparent, particularly inflectional morphological constructions. A construction such as the PAST TENSE construction adds a suffix to a verb stem and thereby specifies the time of an event as lying in the past, without, however, changing the meaning of the lexical verb in any way. Likewise, the derivational *Un*-ADJ construction that is used to form *unfair, unhappy*, and so on yields adjectives that express the opposite of their host adjectives. On the whole, English morphological constructions thus appear to be broadly compositional in terms of their meanings (Booij 2012: 209). Yet there are many morphological constructions that do exhibit non-compositional meanings. Consider the following examples.

(12) comparable, honourable, agreeable
      moth-eaten, husband-dominated, doctor-recommended
      moth-eating, husband-dominating, doctor-recommending
      I'll make the tuna salad and you make the salad-salad.

Non-compositional meanings are frequently seen at the level of lexical constructions, which may start out as semantically regular coinages, but which subsequently adopt more specialised meanings. This has been pointed out for *baker* and *smoker* above; it also applies to *comparable* 'roughly equal', *honourable* 'worthy of respect', and *agreeable* 'pleasant'. The second set of words in the example above illustrates a non-compositional semantic trait that is characteristic of a productive morphological construction, which is called the NOUN–PAST PARTICIPLE COMPOUND construction here. Note that the overall meanings of *moth-eaten, husband-dominated,* and *doctor-recommended* consistently portray the nominal constituent of the compound as an agent who has carried out the action that is specified by the past participle. A *doctor-recommended* procedure is one that has been recommended by doctors, not for doctors, or in a non-specific connection with doctors. Conversely, the words *moth-eating*, *husband-dominating*, and *doctor-recommending*, which instantiate the NOUN–PRESENT PARTICIPLE COMPOUND construction, convey meanings in which the nominal constituent undergoes the action specified by the verb. If you are a native or otherwise proficient speaker of English, these regularities may seem self-evident to you, but they do not automatically follow from compositional principles. There is nothing in the component words themselves that would prohibit the interpretation 'recommended for doctors' for the word *doctor-recommended*. The conventional interpretation of these words is learned as a non-compositional characteristic of the NOUN–PRESENT PARTICIPLE COMPOUND construction.

Turning to the last example, non-compositional effects can be observed in a phenomenon that will be referred to here as the CONTRASTIVE REDUPLICATION construction (Ghomeshi et al. 2004). In this construction, linguistic material is reduplicated, that is, repeated, in order to convey a particular meaning. Consider the following examples.

(13) I'm up, I'm just not up-up.
My car isn't mine-mine, it's my parent's.
They are rich, but not rich-rich, not New York City rich.

The effect that is achieved by reduplication is that the linguistic structure in question receives a prototypical or idealised interpretation, often in contrast to a less prototypical interpretation. In this way, *tuna salad* is contrasted to *salad-salad*, which typically consists of green lettuce, raw chopped vegetables, and some kind of dressing. Someone lying in bed awake after having silenced the alarm clock may claim to be *up*, though not just yet *up-up*, which would involve being in an upright position, having the eyes open, and wearing clothes. The symbolic link between a reduplicated structure and the idea of a prototype is non-compositional; knowledge of the individual words is not sufficient to work out the intended interpretation. In summary, then, the same kinds of non-compositional meanings that provide evidence for constructions in syntax also provide evidence for constructions at the level of morphology.

4.2.4 Simultaneous affixation

Word formation processes are usually thought of as applying in serial fashion, one after the other, in what is called **cyclic rule application** (Siegel 1974). According to this concept the suffix -*al* attaches to *form* to yield *formal*, and after that the suffix -*ism* attaches to *formal* to yield *formalism*. Similarly, a verb such as *deactivate* would be derived from *activate*, which in turn would be derived from *active*. Certain word formation processes may thus feed subsequent word formation processes, that is, provide input for them. Booij (2010) points out that this logic runs into trouble with the following words.

(14) caffeine   decaffeinate
     moral   demoralise
     mythology   demythologise
     nuclear   denuclearise
     Stalin   destalinise

Cyclic rule application would suggest that the verb *decaffeinate* has been formed on the basis of *caffeinate*. Perhaps unbeknownst to many people, such a verb does exist in usage (*I gotta get caffeinated!*), but common dictionaries do not list it. At any rate, an analysis that posits *caffeinate* as the input for *decaffeinate* is not very plausible because the simpler verb is much less frequent than the more complex verb. Usually, bases are more frequent than their derivatives. (The pairs *busy – business* and *govern – government* are counterexamples to this tendency.)

Now, if the cyclic model of word formation does not seem to offer a satisfactory account, how can the constructionist view of morphology handle the matter? A constructional analysis (Booij 2010: 44) would posit a morphological construction in which multiple elements attach simultaneously to a host. In other words, there is a pattern that we might call the *De-N-ate* construction that operates on nominal elements in its open slot and that yields forms such as *decarbonate*, *dehydrate*, or *decaffeinate*. Such a construction could be schematically represented as follows:

(15) [de [[x]$_N$ ate]]$_V$ --- 'to remove X'

Importantly, the *De-N-ate* construction does not require the prior existence of the verb *caffeinate*, but in its internal bracketing structure *caffeinate* forms a constituent, making such a verb a possible target of backformation. This accounts for the fact that for some speakers, *caffeinate* may be a perfectly acceptable verb, whereas others may have never heard of it. The remaining examples can receive parallel accounts, such that *demoralise* is formed by the *De-N-ise* construction, *denuclearise* is formed by the *De-ADJ-ise* construction, and so on. In some cases, it may actually be hard to decide whether simultaneous affixation or cyclic affixation yields the more plausible analysis. Consider the verbs *militarise* and *demilitarise* and their respective nominalisations. Table 4.2 lists frequencies from the BNC, including occurrences with alternative spellings (*militarize* etc.).

Table 4.2 Frequencies of *militarise* and *demilitarise*

	militar-	demilitar-
ise	4	9
ised	18	44
isation	27	56

The frequencies of *demilitarise*, *demilitarised*, and *demilitarisation* are higher, which would be suggestive of simultaneous affixation, but clearly this is not incontrovertible evidence for the *De*-N-*ise* construction. On the constructional view of morphology, the *De*-N-*ise* construction would be in evidence if and only if we found complex forms for which a corresponding simpler verb ending in -*ise* was not attested. So, if you think that the form *odorise* 'make stinky' is not a proper verb of English whereas *deodorise* 'remove stinkiness' is fine, then your knowledge of English grammar includes the *De*-N-*ise* construction.

4.3 Constructional solutions to morphological puzzles

The purpose of any morphological theory is not just to account for relatively trivial processes such as *read* and -*able* combining to form the word *readable*. A good theory should provide systematic explanations for phenomena that, at first sight, do not seem to follow any general rules. The following sections will discuss two such phenomena, namely affix ordering and compound formation, explaining how they would be analysed from a constructional perspective.

4.3.1 Affix ordering

Among the derivational morphological constructions of English, two productive constructions that can be singled out are the ADJ-*ise* construction (*generalise, specialise, stabilise*) and the V-*ive* construction (*active, collective, relative*). The ADJ-*ise* construction forms verbs; the V-*ive* construction forms adjectives. This means that theoretically, each construction should be able to occur inside the other one: it should be possible to combine ADJ-*ise* verbs with the suffix -*ive* and V-*ive* adjectives with the suffix -*ise*. Interestingly, there is an asymmetry. As the following examples show, only the latter is possible.

(16) activise
      collectivise
      relativise

*generalisive
*specialisive
*stabilisive

If you are an inquisitive person, you will probably already be thinking about possible explanations for this asymmetry. First, you might try to find counterexamples, that is, words that end in -*isive*. Good luck with that. Second, you might think of semantic or pragmatic explanations. Perhaps **generalizive* 'in a generalising way' is not a particularly useful concept to have. This may or may not be the case, but it is a fact that many rather marginal concepts are nonetheless expressible with ad-hoc morphological constructs. Third, you might explain the asymmetry with the fact that the V-*ive* construction is, after all, not as productive as we might have thought, since **discussive* 'in a discussing way' and **thinkive* 'thoughtfully' are not possible either. This is not a bad argument, but it fails to explain why native speakers of English will never, even in a jocular fashion, produce an adjective ending in -*isive*. A rather more elegant theory that has been suggested as an explanation goes by the name of the **level-ordering hypothesis** (Siegel 1974). The theory assumes that there are two levels of affixes in English. The suffix -*ive* belongs to the first level, the suffix -*ise* to the second level. Plag (2003: 168) offers the following overview:

(17)   Level 1 suffixes: -al, -ate, -ic, -ion, -ity, -ive, -ous
       Level 1 prefixes: be-, con-, de-, en-, in-, pre-, re-, sub-

       Level 2 suffixes: -able, -er, -ful, -hood, -ist, -ise, -less, -ly, -ness, -wise
       Level 2 prefixes: anti-, de-, non-, re-, sub-, un-, semi-

What the theory predicts is that words with Level 1 affixes may serve as input for words with Level 2 affixes, but not vice versa. Hence, not only **generalisive* is ruled out by the theory, but also **Mongolismian*, **atomlessity*, **pre-undress*, or **specialisic*. In other words, a single theoretical stipulation (having two levels of affixes) explains a large number of data in one fell swoop. However, the theory is not without its problems. First, the theory has nothing to say about how affixes from the same level may or may not be combined. The theory hence does not explain why *heartlessness* is fine but **darknessless* 'completely illuminated' is not. Furthermore, you may find examples that run counter to the predictions. The words *naturalistic* or *colonisation* should technically be ruled out, yet they are perfectly fine. And last, it could be objected that the theory perhaps gets most of the facts right, but does not explain why there are these two levels of affixes. Hay and Plag (2004) therefore propose a different theory based on psycholinguistic considerations and very much in line with central principles of Construction Grammar. The basic idea of that theory is the **complexity-based ordering hypothesis,** which Hay (2002: 527) expresses in the following way: 'an affix that can be easily parsed out should not occur inside an affix that cannot'. Affixes that are not easily 'parsed out', that is, distinguished from their hosts, are affixes such as *-al* or *-ate*, which Siegel (1974) classified as Level 1 affixes. Affixes that are more transparent are Level 2 affixes such as *-ness* or *-able*. How easy or hard it is cognitively to separate an affix from its host can be estimated on the basis of corpus data. Consider the frequencies from the BNC in Table 4.3.

Table 4.3 Frequencies of *government, discernment,* and their bases

	govern	discern
	568	259
-ment	59,988	56

When hearers encounter the word *government*, they are likely to process it holistically, without separating it into *govern* and *-ment*. The reason for this is that the word *government* is much more frequent than the word *govern*. Conversely, the word *discernment* is less frequent than its base *discern*, which makes it likely that hearers process the complex word by parsing it into its components. Hay and Plag (2004) analysed fifteen suffixes, determining for each one how many of its types were likely to be parsed (in the way that *discernment* is likely to be parsed). Table 4.4 shows their results, with the suffixes shown in increasing order of parsed types.

Table 4.4 Ratio of parsed types for fifteen suffixes

Suffix	Parsed types (%)	Suffix	Parsed types (%)
-ly	24	-ish	58
-th	33	-ling	62
-er	50	-ship	62
-dom	50	-hood	80
-ness	51	-less	86
-ee	53	-ful$_A$	94
-en	56	-ful$_N$	98
-ess	57		

Words such as *really* or *finally* are very frequent, even when compared to their bases *real* and *final*. Many types show this kind of distribution, so that only 24 per cent of the types ending in the suffix -*ly* are parsed. Conversely, words such as *mouthful* or *shovelful* are infrequent in comparison to their bases. If the complexity-based ordering hypothesis is right, the results from Table 4.4. mean that elements which appear later in the table should never be suffixed with elements that appear earlier in the table. To take an example, a word ending in -*ness* should never be used as input for a word ending in -*ly*. In order to test this prediction, Hay and Plag (2004) again use corpus data and retrieve all words that combine affixes from Table 4.4. Predictably, many combinations that are logically possible never appear in actual language use. Those combinations that do appear can be used to arrange the suffixes in a hierarchy that visualises the order in which suffixes may appear. This hierarchy is shown below.

(18) Corpus-based suffix hierarchy
      -th >> -en >> -er >> -ling >> -ee >> -ess >> -ly >> -dom >>
      -hood >> -ship >> -ish >> -less >> -ful$_A$ >> -ness >> -ful$_N$

The hierarchy reflects the fact that there are words such as *lengthen* (-th >> -en), *thankfulness* (-ful$_A$ >> -ness), or *leadership* (-er >> ... >> -ship). The fact that corpus data reveal a hierarchy of this kind is already a remarkable empirical observation. The crucial question for the complexity-based ordering hypothesis is whether the hierarchy is in agreement with the order of suffixes that is shown in Table 4.4. A comparison of the two lists shows a strong correlation, which is visualised in Figure 4.1.

On the whole, a strong positive correlation lends strong support to the complexity-based ordering hypothesis. Only two suffixes, -*ness* and -*ly*, stray considerably from the diagonal; the rest of the suffixes behave largely as expected. Hay and Plag thus conclude that the more easily an affix can be separated from its base in processing, the more freely it attaches to words that contain other affixes. This conclusion ties in rather nicely with the constructional view of morphology, as outlined in the earlier sections of this chapter. On this view, productivity is a characteristic of morphological constructions, such as the ADJ-*ness* construction or the N-*ful* construction. These morphological constructions will have multiple instantiations in the form of lexical constructions. To illustrate, *greatness*, *sweetness*, and *flawlessness* instantiate the ADJ-*ness* construction. These lexical constructions are connected to the overarching morphological construction via instantiation links. Now, if there are many lexical constructions with low frequencies, that means that these instantiation links are activated very often, thus strengthening the node that represents the abstract

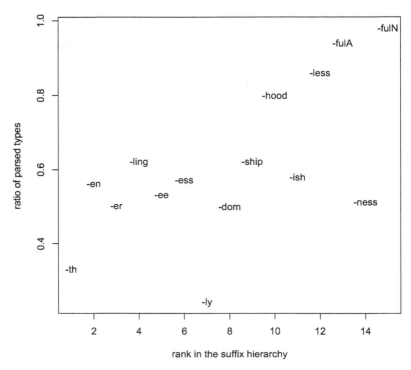

Figure 4.1 Correlation between the ratio of parsed types and rank in the suffix hierarchy

construction in the construct-i-con. Speakers are habituated to the idea that there is a pattern with an open, schematic slot. This corresponds to Hay and Plag's notion of an affix being easily parsed out: speakers know, albeit subconsciously, that there is a pattern with distinct parts. Conversely, a morphological construction that has mostly instantiations of moderately high frequency, and few low-frequency instantiations, will not receive this kind of analysis. Mid-frequency lexical constructions such as *princess* or *depth* will often not activate their respective instantiation links because their conventionalised meanings render the schema unnecessary. These words are thus interpreted directly, without recourse to the more general construction. This corresponds to the case in which an affix is difficult to parse out from its base. What follows from this is that nodes such as the N-*ess* construction or the ADJ-*th* construction barely exist in the construct-i-con. In speakers' knowledge of English, it is only vaguely represented that there is an N-*ess* construction with a slot for a noun.

To summarise the argument, what Hay and Plag (2004) discuss as parsability of base and affix is recast here as the strength with which an abstract morphological construction is represented in the construct-i-con. The technical term for this idea is **entrenchment** (cf. Bybee 2010) The more easily speakers can identify the parts of a construction, the more easily that construction will accommodate other constructions into its open slots. Coming back to the examples that this section started out with, the fact that *relativise* is a word but *specializive* is not has to do with the fact that the adjective slot in the ADJ-*ise* construction is reasonably transparent and therefore well represented in speakers' knowledge of language. By contrast, the generalisation that speakers may make across all adjectives ending in -*ive* (*active, creative, depressive,* etc.) does not yield a transparent verb slot for the V-*ive* construction, which as a consequence remains only weakly represented in the construct-i-con.

4.3.2 Compounding

On the face of it, compounding in English appears to be a highly regular process. Two independent elements, a modifier and a head, are combined to yield a form that combines their meanings in such a way that the compound refers to the kind of thing expressed by the head, bearing a relation to the kind of thing expressed by the modifier. This regularity is commonly discussed as **endocentric compounding**. Endocentric compounds such as *watchmaker, swimsuit, smartphone, angel dust,* or *contract killer* instantiate the following schema (adapted from Booij 2009: 201).

(19) [A B] – 'a kind of B that has a relation to A'

This schema, which we could call the ENDOCENTRIC COMPOUND construction, is highly general, since it does not even specify parts of speech for its component parts. Constructions such as the NOUN–NOUN COMPOUND construction (*contract killer*), the NOUN–PRESENT PARTICIPLE COMPOUND construction (*flesh-eating*), or the PHRASAL COMPOUND construction (*over the counter drug*) would be subpatterns of the general construction that are connected to it via instantiation links. The subpatterns inherit aspects of the general construction, such as prosodic stress on the non-head element and the interpretation of the rightmost element as the semantic head. Importantly, though, the subpatterns also exhibit characteristics of their own that cannot be explained through inheritance. For instance, the NOUN–NOUN

COMPOUND construction allows a certain amount of recursivity, such that existing compounds can be used as input for the formation of larger compounds. The same cannot be said of other compounding constructions. Compare the following sets of words.

(20) child language
      child language acquisition
      child language acquisition research
      child language acquisition research group
      child language acquisition research group member

      squeaky clean
      ?squeaky clean shiny, ?sterile squeaky clean
      *sterile squeaky clean shiny

      stir fry
      *stir fry simmer, *chop stir fry

Clearly, recursive compoundings works better with nouns than with adjectives or verbs, let alone prepositions. A general compounding schema would not predict this; hence constructional schemas at lower levels are needed.

These lower-level schemas impose constraints of their own and are thus productive to different degrees. As in syntactic constructions, constraints can be statistical, rather than absolute. For example, an apparent statistical constraint on the NOUN–NOUN COMPOUND construction is that the non-head can be in the plural only under certain conditions (Bauer 2006: 490). In the following examples, some compounds with plural non-heads are more acceptable than others.

(21) boy choir   boys choir
      skill development   skills development
      claim department   claims department
      reservation desk   reservations desk
      suggestion box   ?suggestions box
      citizen participation ?citizens participation
      car factory   *cars factory
      watchmaker   *watchesmaker

It is difficult to explain on semantic grounds alone why there should not be a word such as *cars factory. After all, there are many cars involved, often even several different types. To cut a long story short, the puzzle of compounds with plural non-heads is as yet unsolved, but a constructional approach at least provides a couple of leads that might be useful in a proper analysis. For instance, it is possible to identify heads such as the noun *desk*, which are particularly ready to accept plural non-heads. The compounds *reservations desk, admissions desk, communications desk, complaints desk, special orders desk*, and *IT services desk* thus illustrate a low-level construction, the PLURAL *Desk* COMPOUND construction. Hence, if it were your job to install a desk for dog licences in a local town hall, you might consider calling it the *dog licences desk* rather than the *dog licence desk*. By contrast, a head such as *factory* is heavily biased towards singular non-heads. It is instructive to look at the exceptions to this tendency: *munitions factory, arms factory*, and *plastics factory* are the three most frequent ones. The nouns *munitions* and *arms* barely have proper singulars. For all three, the plural has acquired a convention-alised meaning, so that *plastics* is not just 'several plastic materials' but rather 'industrially used plastic materials'. Hence, it is *plastics industry, manufacturing, plant*, and *company*, but *plastic bags, bottles, tubes*, and *chairs*. So, speakers know that a noun such as *factory* will predominantly combine with singular nouns, unless such a noun is unavailable. Any analysis of plural non-heads in compounding would have to resort to low-level schemas that model speakers' knowledge of individual words and their combinatorics. The construct-i-con provides a natural setting for this kind of endeavour.

A final problem case in the analysis of compounding is illustrated by forms that combine attributive adjectives with nouns referring to persons. Spencer (1988) offers examples like the following.

(22) moral philosopher
      neural scientist
      transformational grammarian
      electrical engineer
      serial composer

For ease of reference, forms like these will be called attributive compounds. What is special about these forms? It turns out that there are three characteristics that motivate the recognition of an ATTRIBUTIVE COMPOUND construction. First of all, it can be noted that these forms have meanings that deviate from ordinary combinations of attributive adjectives and nouns, such as *famous actor*. A *moral philosopher* is 'someone who studies moral philosophy', not 'a philosopher who acts morally'. Second, this kind of meaning suggests that the internal structure of *moral philosopher* is such that the adjective takes scope only over the stem of the noun, while the final nominalising suffix takes scope over the entire compound. This structure differs from the kind of structure that is usually found in the NOUN–NOUN COMPOUND construction, as illustrated by *loudspeaker*.

(23) [[moral philosoph] -er]
      [loud [speak -er]]

Third, Spencer (1988: 673) notes that his examples correspond to nominal expressions that can be viewed as compounds or at least as conventionalised set phrases, namely *moral philosophy, neural science, transformational grammar, electrical engineering,* and *serial composition.* Compare this with *famous actor* or *loudspeaker,* for which there are no corresponding expressions. Spencer therefore suggests an analysis of these compounds that is very close in spirit to the constructional analysis of paradigmatically related words such as *alpinism – alpinist* that has been proposed by Booij (2010). Specifically, Spencer proposes that speakers arrive at formations such as *transformational grammarian* or *serial composer* through correspondences between lexical items that partially instantiate one another. In the parlance of Construction Grammar, these would be subpart links. Spencer (1988: 675) proposes the following lexical networks.

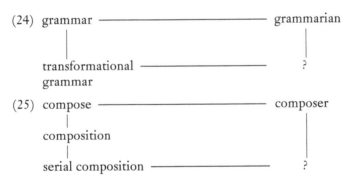

(24) grammar ———————————————— grammarian

      transformational ———————————— ?
      grammar

(25) compose ———————————————— composer

      composition

      serial composition ———————————— ?

Spencer points out that these networks can only function if the expressions in the lower left corner are in fact lexicalised, that is, in the terms of Construction Grammar, represented as lexical constructions in the construct-i-con. Consider an expression such as *secret language,* which we can assume to be a compositional phrase, rather than a compound or set expression. Someone who studies secret languages cannot be referred to as a **secret linguist,* although the structure would be exactly parallel to *moral philosopher* or *transformational grammarian.* On the constructional view of morphology, the unacceptability of **secret linguist* is expected. In order to form that expression, speakers would need to have *secret language* as an established node in the construct-i-con. Without that node, there are no subpart links that would allow the formation of **secret linguist.*

4.4 Summing up

This chapter has left the area of syntax to discuss how Construction Grammar deals with phenomena that concern morphology, as advanced by Booij (2010, 2013). Morphological constructions were defined as form–meaning pairs that require an analysis of word-internal structures. Morphological constructions can be divided into several larger groups. One such group is represented by inflectional constructions such as the PLURAL construction, the PAST TENSE construction, or the S-GENITIVE construction. These constructions mark grammatical distinctions, and there are not many of them in English. The largest group of morphological constructions in English is the one of derivational constructions, that is, constructions that are used to coin new words on the basis of existing words. Derivational constructions subsume all phenomena that other approaches to morphology describe as word formation processes or word formation rules. Many such processes involve affixation, that is, the combination of a host structure with an affix. On the constructional view of morphology, such word formation processes are represented as partially schematic constructions in the construct-i-con. The chapter discussed the V-*er* construction (*baker, smoker*) and the V-*able* construction (*foldable, washable*), among several others. Another derivational construction type is the BLEND construction (*spork, guesstimate*), which is a construction that exhibits phonological constraints at its formal pole. A large family of morphological constructions works on the basis of compounding. At the most general level, a generalisation that could be called the English ENDOCENTRIC COMPOUND construction would specify that individual words can be combined to form new words. An adequate understanding of how compounding works in English does require the analyst to posit multiple compounding constructions at lower levels of abstraction in the construct-i-con. For instance, the ENDOCENTRIC COMPOUND construction would be connected to the NOUN–NOUN COMPOUND construction (*watchmaker*), the NOUN–PRESENT PARTICIPLE COMPOUND construction (*doctor-recommended*), or the PHRASAL COMPOUND construction (*over the counter drug*) via instantiation links. At an even lower level of abstraction, the PLURAL *Desk* COMPOUND construction (*admissions desk*) connects to the NOUN–NOUN COMPOUND construction with an instantiation link.

Morphological constructions can be analysed in terms of several properties that were discussed in this chapter. A first important characteristic is morphological productivity, which was defined as the degree of cognitive ease with which speakers can produce or process new complex words on the basis of a construction. The words *flirtatiousness* and *flirtatiosity* may describe the same thing and therefore be equally fine on semantic grounds, but in all likelihood you find *flirtatiousness* easier to understand (and much easier to pronounce). This is because the ADJ-*ness* construction is highly productive, and hence strongly represented as a node in the construct-i-con, whereas a construction such as the ADJ-*ity* construction (*generality, monstrosity*) is not as productive. The productivity of a construction was shown to be related to its type frequency and to the ratio of hapax legomena in its types. The fact that speakers produce and understand newly coined words is a central piece of evidence for the idea that word formation processes are cognitive generalisations, that is, constructions. A second characteristic of morphological constructions is their paradigmatic organisation, which boils down to groups of words being strongly interconnected via subpart links. Morphological paradigms are typically discussed for inflectional constructions (as in *sing, sings, singing, sang, have sung*), but the web of subpart links that interconnects morphological constructions spreads much further than that and is just as important for an understanding of relations between derivational constructions. In particular, subpart links motivate analyses of stem allomorphy (*energy – energetic*), paradigmatically related forms such as *alpinism* and *alpinist*, and ATTRIBUTIVE COMPOUND constructions such as *moral philosopher*. In each case, processes of word formation rely on the fact that parts of words are mutually connected in the construct-i-con. A third characteristic of morphological constructions is non-compositionality in meaning. While many morphological constructions are transparent in meaning, there are examples of constructions whose meanings go beyond the meanings of their component parts. At the level of lexical constructions, a form such as *laughable* does not just mean that something 'can be laughed at': the actual meaning 'ridiculous' goes further. Also constructional patterns may convey non-compositional meanings. The CONTRASTIVE REDUPLICATION construction (*I don't want bubble tea, I want tea-tea!*) conveys the idea of a prototypical referent, which does not necessarily follow from its morphological form. The fourth characteristic of morphological constructions that was discussed in this chapter, namely simultaneous affixation, concerned forms that resist an analysis in terms of cyclic rule application. A word such as *decaffeinate* cannot be derived from either ?*caffeinate* or *decaffein*. Instead, forms like these require a constructional schema in which both affixes are attached to the base in one fell swoop.

The chapter finished with a discussion of two morphological puzzles that receive a satsifactory explanation in a constructional analysis. The first phenomenon was the one of affix ordering in English. In response to the question why, for instance, the suffixes -*ive* and -*ise* can be combined in the verb *relativise* but not in a word such as **generalizive*, one could propose a solution that groups affixes into different categories which can only combine in a fixed order. Since such a theory suffers from a number of theoretical and empirical problems, Hay and Plag (2004) propose a psycholinguistically motivated account that fits very well with the constructional view of linguistic knowledge: their proposal is that highly parsable morphological constructions will have a greater tolerance towards complex words as bases. In a highly parsable construction such as the ADJ-*ness* construction, speakers find it easy to distinguish the base adjective and the suffix -*ness*. Therefore, complex adjectives may also enter the construction to yield forms such as *flirtatiousness*. Conversely, the ADJ-*ity* construction is not as transparent, so that *flirtatiosity* remains marginal for many speakers. As a second problematic phenomenon, the chapter discussed minor compounding processes, namely compounds with plural non-heads (*claims department*) and ATTRIBUTIVE COMPOUND constructions (*urban sociologist*), which deviate both structurally and semantically from more general compounding constructions. In both cases, it was argued that low-level constructional schemas and subpart links in the construct-i-con were crucial instruments for the analysis of these phenomena.

Study questions

- What are the inflectional morphological constructions of English?
- What are non-concatenative morphological constructions?
- What is meant by the terms 'type frequency' and 'hapax legomena'?
- What can you conclude if half the types of a construction occur only once in a large corpus?
- Why are phrasal compounds (*a what-the-heck-is-wrong-with-you look*) a problem for the dictionary-and-grammar view of linguistic knowledge?
- What is remarkable about words such as *three-legged*, *curly-haired*, or *red-faced*?
- Why is *monstrosity* a word but **authoritious* not one?
- It is an empirical fact that English derivational suffixes never occur to the right of inflectional suffixes. Drawing on the findings of Hay and Plag (2004), can you explain why that is the case?

Further reading

The constructional approach to morphology is developed in Booij (2010); the summary given in Booij (2013) is an excellent primer. Plag (2003) offers a general overview of word formation in English which is highly compatible with the constructional agenda and which lays out many of the empirical phenomena that a constructional account would have to deal with. An empirical approach to the analysis of blending is offered in Gries (2004), while compounding is discussed in Bauer and Renouf (2001), Giegerich (2004), and Booij (2009). Regarding the morphological problem cases that were reviewed in this chapter, it is instructive to consult the original sources, that is, Hay and Plag (2004) on affix ordering, and Spencer (1988) on attributive compounds.

5 Information packaging constructions

5.1 The pragmatic side of Construction Grammar

If a fellow student of linguistics asked you what grammatical constructions were good for, what would you say? An answer that comes to mind, when considering examples such as the DITRANSITIVE construction or the RESULTATIVE construction, would be that grammatical constructions serve to express fundamental conceptual scenes, or very basic concepts. Chapter 2 discussed the scene encoding hypothesis (Goldberg 1995: 39), which states that basic sentence types, that is, basic syntactic constructions, encode as their central senses event types that are fundamental to human experience: acts of giving and receiving, events in which something changes, situations in which there is a cause and an effect, and so on. A related purpose of grammatical construction would be the expression of important concepts such as 'possession' (the S-GENITIVE construction) or 'difference' (the COMPARATIVE construction) and the expression of important distinctions, such as 'one vs. many' (the PLURAL construction), 'now vs. then' (the PAST TENSE construction), or 'definitely vs. maybe' (MODAL AUXILIARY constructions). Extending the scene encoding hypothesis, we could thus summarise these observations and say that grammatical constructions are good for expressing basic meanings that are fundamental to human life. But is that true of all grammatical constructions? This chapter will discuss a number of constructions that serve a different purpose, namely the purpose of relating what is being said to what has been said before. In this book, this function is called **information packaging** (Prince 1981). Consider the following list of examples.

(1) As for John, he lost his wallet.
     He lost his wallet, John.
     What happened was that John lost his wallet.
     What John did was lose his wallet.

It was John who lost his wallet.
What John lost was his wallet.
It was his wallet that John lost.
As for his wallet, John lost it.
What happened to John's wallet was that he lost it.

You will probably agree that each of the examples can be roughly paraphrased with the sentence *John lost his wallet*. This is because each of the examples is linked to the TRANSITIVE construction via a subpart link, and that construction contributes the most important semantic substance to these utterances. Yet the grammar of English affords its speakers an apparent luxury by offering a broad range of syntactic constructions to express that semantic substance in slightly different ways. Of course, rather than being a luxury, this has a purpose, namely the packaging of information.

Successful communication depends in a large measure on presenting new information in such a way that hearers can easily integrate that information with things that they already know. **Information packaging constructions**, which are sometimes also called information structure constructions, serve the function of organising and arranging meanings, relating new meanings to old meanings, rather than conveying meanings themselves. Speakers will choose a given information packaging constructions in a given situational context depending on their assumptions of what the hearer already knows, what the hearer may infer, and what is completely new to the hearer. Hence, the discussion of information packaging constructions leads us towards the pragmatic side of Construction Grammar. **Pragmatics** (Griffiths 2006) is understood in this book as the study of context-dependent meanings in linguistic utterances. If you have taken an introductory linguistics class, you will probably have heard of concepts such as indirect speech acts (such as *Could you pass me the salt?*, which is not a literal request for information) or conversational maxims (such as what is called the maxim of relevance, which asks speakers to make their contributions thematically relevant). Typically, these discussions of pragmatics have little to say about linguistic forms, that is, constructions. Rather, pragmatics is taken to be the study of those meanings that are relatively independent of linguistic forms, and conversely, dependent on the situational context. So how do Construction Grammar and pragmatics fit together?

To illustrate that relationship consider again the example *What John lost was his wallet*. This utterance instantiates a construction that is called the *WH*-CLEFT construction. Imagine the communicative situation in which this construction might be used. Clearly, not every situation is equally suitable. For instance, it is utterly unlikely that you, later today, will get a phone call from your mother that she begins with the words *Hi, it's me. What John lost was his wallet.* There is nothing syntactically odd about this utterance, but hearing it would probably make you wonder whether your mother should see a doctor. By contrast, the utterance would be perfectly in order if you had been on the phone earlier that day, and your mother had filled you in on the talk of the town, namely that your old friend John lost his mullet (that is, he finally went to the hairdresser and got rid of his embarrassing haircut). As it turns out, though, your mother had misheard. John's mullet is as mighty as ever; what he lost was in fact his wallet. Now she is calling you to correct her story. Comparing the two scenarios, three things are different in the second one. First, you and your mother had already talked about John. Second, you had already talked about John losing something. Third, there is a contrast between the lost thing that you talked about and the thing that was actually lost. These three contextual features are typical conditions for the use of a *WH*-CLEFT.

Consider the following examples, which are taken from internet sites. In each of them, the person losing something is mentioned in the prior context of the *WH*-CLEFT, as is the act of losing things, as is a lost item that contrasts with the lost item mentioned in the cleft itself.

(2) Even during the darkest years Churchill never entirely lost the affection of his countrymen; what he lost was their confidence.

When Charlie states that he lost money during the crash, but everything during the boom, he realizes that what he lost was his family and that they are important.

Rodriguez may not have lost a job or dealt with financial burdens but what he lost was his own pride of being a Mexican-American while pursuing his life dream of becoming an English Professor.

That being the case, the respondent therefore could not be said to have suffered any deprivation of the use of the money. In fact he lost no money at all. What he lost was only the opportunity to acquire a shophouse at $49,500. We therefore think that the learned trial judge was correct in awarding the interest to commence from the date of the judgment until the date of satisfaction.

In order to explain how information packaging constructions work, this chapter will first offer a definition of information packaging constructions and introduce a number of distinctions that allow us to talk about the 'context' of an utterance in more precise terms. With those distinctions in place, we will move on to a discussion of the actual constructions that speakers can use to package the information they want to get across.

5.1.1 Information packaging: the basics

The question why speakers express the same idea with different grammatical constructions under different communicative circumstances has been investigated in detail in the work of Lambrecht (1994), who defines the subject of this chapter in the following way (1994: 5).

> Information structure: That component of sentence grammar in which propositions as conceptual representations of states of affairs are paired with lexicogrammatical structures in accordance with the mental states of interlocutors who use and interpret these structures as units of information in given discourse contexts.

This dense definition needs some unpacking. To start with, Lambrecht is talking about lexicogrammatical structures: those are the information packaging constructions that will be discussed in this chapter. We have already seen one example, namely the *WH*-CLEFT construction. Then, Lambrecht views these constructions as a component of sentence grammar. This simply means that information packaging constructions typically are syntactic constructions that form entire sentences, rather than phrases or words. (We will see exceptions to this generalisation.) With the description 'propositions as conceptual representations of states of affairs' Lambrecht refers to the complex meanings that whole sentences convey. A word meaning such as 'wallet' is relatively simple in comparison to the meaning of the sentence *John lost his wallet*, which expresses a proposition (Kintsch 1998), that is, a meaningful relation between the verb *lost* and its arguments *John* and *his wallet*. In understanding that sentence, you build up a conceptual representation, a cognitive model if you like, of John having lost his wallet. The most important part of Lambrecht's definition is the phrase 'in accordance with the mental states of interlocutors'. When speakers choose a given information packaging construction, they have previously engaged in some mind-reading: their choice represents their best guess as to what it is that the hearer already knows, and what it is that is new information. Think again of your mother calling you out of the blue, saying *Hi, it's me. What John lost was his wallet*. What would worry you about this conversation opening is that your mother ventures an extremely poor guess at what you already know at this point. Keeping track of other people's minds is no hocus-pocus activity; rather, we expect this of our fellow human beings, even complete strangers, as a matter of course. Failure to do so is interpreted as being rude at best, and having mental health problems at worst.

Coming back to Lambrecht's definition of information structure, we can reuse his ideas to construct a characterisation of information packaging constructions that involves three aspects.

(3) Information packaging constructions
    are sentence-level constructions [1]
    that speakers use to express complex meanings [2]
    in a way that shows awareness of the current knowledge of the hearer. [3]

In order to apply this characterisation to the analysis of information packaging constructions, we need to flesh out its aspects, especially the second and third, in some more detail.

5.1.2 Presupposition and assertion

Lambrecht points out that propositions, that is, complex meanings, typically combine elements that are already known to the hearer with elements that are not already known (1994: 51). The information that is contained in a sentence-level construction is thus partially old and partially new. This can be illustrated with an example such as *I finally met the woman who moved in downstairs.* The speaker of such a sentence does not want to inform the hearer that there is a new female neighbour one storey below the speaker's flat. That is already taken for granted. What is new in the sentence is that the speaker has finally met that neighbour. Now you might wonder, if it is old information that there is a new female neighbour downstairs, why does the speaker bother the hearer with yesterday's news? The reason for including old information is that hearers have a much easier time processing new information when it is properly connected to things they already know. Information structure constructions thus have the purpose of making new information intelligible by connecting it to old information. Lambrecht (1994: 52) proposes the terms **pragmatic presupposition** and **pragmatic assertion** for the distinction that we have up to now discussed informally as old and new information.

(4) Pragmatic presupposition: The set of propositions lexicogrammatically evoked in a sentence which the speaker assumes the hearer already knows or is ready to take for granted at the time the sentence is uttered.

Pragmatic assertion: The proposition expressed by a sentence which the hearer is expected to know or take for granted as a result of hearing the sentence uttered.

The distinction of pragmatic presupposition and pragmatic assertion relates to linguistic forms, that is, constructions. Information packaging constructions consist of several parts, and these parts are conventionally associated with either old information or new information. This has an obvious advantage for language processing: as soon as hearers can identify a given information packaging construction, they know immediately which part of that construction will convey new information to which they should pay the most attention. Consider a construction such as the TOUGH-RAISING construction, which combines a noun phrase, a predicate adjective, and a *to*-infinitive into sentences such as *A good man is easy to kill*. Mair (1987) has studied the TOUGH-RAISING construction on the basis of corpus data, finding that the construction typically follows a recurring pattern of old and new information. A few authentic examples of the construction are offered below.

(5)   Until the last few years the paper was a modestly profitable business, but it had had structural problems for some time. Like so much else in Britain, <u>these are hard to understand</u> unless you know the history.

Pieces of nerve can be removed completely from the body and yet retain their ability to conduct nerve-impulses. Physiologists have therefore preferred to study these convenient objects, rather than the very soft brain tissue, <u>which is difficult to handle</u> and changes its characteristics when its supply of blood is interfered with.

Her part-time legal transcribing service didn't come close to providing the income she needed. <u>The Victorian she'd inherited from her grandmother was so expensive to maintain</u>, the repairs so constant, the taxes so outrageous, it took every penny she made each month just to stay ahead of her creditors.

Contrary to the initial example *A good man is easy to kill*, most authentic instances of the TOUGH-RAISING construction involve noun phrases that refer to old information. This is plainly evident in the first two examples, in which the respective noun phrases are realised pronominally. What is new is the information that is expressed in the combination of adjective and *to*-infinitive. In the third example, the noun phrase *The Victorian she'd inherited from her grandmother* exemplifies what Lambrecht describes as information that the hearer 'is ready to take for granted at the time the sentence is uttered'. At the time of the utterance, the hearer need not have known the proposition that someone (*she*) inherited a house (*The Victorian*). Note that the noun phrase is definite, rather than indefinite, which signals that the speaker expects the hearer to treat it as old information. Again, the new information in the sentence is expressed in the adjective and the *to*-infinitive: the phrase *expensive to maintain* is the new piece of information that relevantly connects to the previous sentence, elaborating on and explaining the financial difficulties of the protagonist.

5.1.3 Activation

It may have never occurred to you, but the fact that you know in what kinds of situation you may use a WH-CLEFT construction (*What John needs now is a double espresso*), a TOUGH-RAISING construction (*That is hard to believe!*), or a RESTRICTIVE RELATIVE CLAUSE construction (*I finally met the woman who moved in downstairs*) is evidence that during ordinary conversation, you continuously simulate the cognitive model of the current situation that your interlocutor entertains. Furthermore, you structure your speech accordingly, by using constructions that present some pieces of information as new, and others as old, in accordance with what is going on in the hearer's cognitive model. But that is not all. Crucially, you simulate not only the hearer's knowledge, but, as Lambrecht points out (1994: 53), also the hearer's consciousness and awareness of things in the current situation.

Consider the following example; again, let us assume that it is uttered by your mother during a telephone conversation.

(6) John speaks excellent Finnish although he never lived there.

You probably did not have any difficulty understanding that the little word *there* refers to Finland. This is remarkable, as the word *Finland* is not mentioned once, and has not been mentioned before during your conversation. Hearing the first part of the example, *John speaks excellent Finnish*, would lead you to construct a cognitive model in which John has the skill of speaking Finnish. That would be the proposition that your mother could expect you to know as a result of hearing that part of her utterance. In addition, however, the word *Finnish* brings a number of associations into play, among them, quite trivially, the country where Finnish is spoken. In your mother's simulation of your cognitive model of the speech situation (you see that this is getting a little complicated), she assumes that you are to some degree conscious of the idea 'Finland'.

That being the case, she can refer to that idea with the pronoun *there*, rather than with a full lexical item. In this way, your mother is treating 'Finland' as old information that need not be formally introduced. And in assuming that 'Finland' is old information to you, she's of course right, as always.

A term that has been established for the ideas that are more or less present in the hearer's consciousness is **activation**. The metaphor here is of ideas being more or less activated in the hearer's mind. In the example above, your mother correctly estimated that the idea 'Finland' would be activated in your mind, which led her to choose a pronoun for its linguistic expression. The relation between activation and linguistic expression is explained by Chafe (1987: 26) in the following way.

> Those concepts which are already active for the speaker, and which the speaker judges to be active for the hearer as well, are verbalized in a special way, having properties which have often been discussed in terms of 'old' or 'given' information. The general thing to say is that given concepts are spoken with an attenuated pronunciation. The attenuation involves, at the very least, weak stress. Typically, though not always, it involves either pronominalization or omission from verbalization altogether.

Besides pronominal coding, which is perhaps the clearest evidence that the speaker assumes an idea to be active, the grammatical category of definiteness should also be mentioned. In order to capture the idea that there are degrees of activation, Chafe (1987: 25) not only distinguishes active and inactive referents, but adds a third category, namely that of semi-active referents, which are also called accessible referents. Referents become semi-active in the hearer's mind through associations that are sparked by an utterance. For instance, let us imagine that your mother surprises you with yet another phone call and says *Hi, it's me. Mary is pregnant again.* This opening causes a number of ideas to become semi-active referents in your mind, most obviously perhaps the ideas that there is a baby and a father, but also several others. Semi-active referents can be expressed in the subsequent discourse with definite noun phrases, or even pronouns. Hence, your mother can continue her story by telling you that *The doctor saw on the ultrasound that it's a boy*, bringing no fewer than three previously semi-active ideas (an obstetrician, ultrasound examinations, the baby's gender) to the centre of attention. The activation status of a given referent is transient: as the conversation goes on, active referents that are not further discussed gradually fade back into a state of being semi-active, and ultimately inactive.

5.1.4 Topic and focus

A further distinction that is crucial for the analysis of information packaging constructions is the contrast between the notions of topic and focus. These terms are problematic because they are used with several meanings in everyday language and in different linguistic frameworks, which necessitates a clarification. In an everyday understanding of the term, a topic is a characteristic of texts or conversations. A news article might report on the topic of an election, or a public meeting might be held on the topic of, say, the construction of a new sports stadium. Lambrecht (1994: 118) uses the term 'topic' not on the level of texts or conversations, but exclusively on the level of sentences. A topic, as understood in this chapter, is the subject matter of a sentence, that is, that which a sentence is about. In conversation, the topic of a given sentence is thus a matter of current interest, and the pragmatic assertion that is made in that sentence is informative for the hearer by virtue of making a statement that is relevant with respect to the topic. Lambrecht points out that it is not always possible to identify a particular constituent of a sentence as its topic: the topic itself need not even be mentioned in the sentence as long as it is understood as the relevant background. This means that the topic of a sentence and its pragmatic presupposition (i.e. that which the hearer is expected to know already or to take for granted) do not necessarily coincide. Consider the following example.

(7) Personally, I don't even eat chicken; I prefer my protein to come from eggs, fish, and cheese.

What is the topic of the second sentence, which begins after the semicolon? If you had to answer what the sentence is about you would be likely to agree that it is about eating habits, which, however, is not explicitly mentioned in the sentence itself. The pragmatic presupposition of the sentence invites the hearer to take for granted that the speaker, and humans in general, rely on proteins for their diet, and the pragmatic assertion is that the speaker prefers certain kinds of proteins. The crucial distinction here is that proteins are not the topic: the sentence is not about proteins, it is about eating habits.

While the topic of a sentence may thus occasionally be difficult to pin down to a particular form, we will see that there are certain information packaging constructions in which a given part of the construction is conventionally used to express the topic. The following examples illustrate three of them.

(8) As for John, he lost his wallet.

The coolest guitar I own, it's a black US stratocaster from the 80s. Most heavy metal I don't really like.

These sentences instantiate different **topicalisation constructions**, which have syntactic parts that are reserved for the expression of topics. In the AS-FOR-TOPICALISATION construction, the constituent that is being introduced by *as for* sets up a topic, simultaneously raising the expectation that the rest of the sentence will offer a proposition that conveys relevant new information about that topic. The second example instantiates the LEFT-DISLOCATION construction. Again, the topical constituent appears initially, and the subsequent full sentence offers a relevant elaboration. The third example is commonly talked about as the TOPICALISATION construction, despite the fact that other constructions also serve this function. The reason that the TOPICALISATION construction enjoys this privileged status is that it merely rearranges the word order of the TRANSITIVE construction such that the topicalised object constituent appears initially.

Given the notion of a topic, as introduced in the previous paragraphs, it may be tempting to think of the focus of a sentence as 'that which is not the topic' or 'the new information that is offered about the topic'. The latter idea would be identical with the pragmatic assertion of a sentence, as defined above. As you may expect, Lambrecht views the notion of focus as something more specific than that. Just as the topic relates to the pragmatic presupposition of a sentence without being the same thing, the idea of focus only relates to the pragmatic assertion of a sentence. Specifically, the focus of a sentence forms the most important part of the pragmatic assertion. Lambrecht (1994: 207) defines it as 'the element of information whereby the presupposition and the assertion differ from each other'. Lambrecht offers the following example to elaborate on that definition.

(9) Q: Where did you go last night?
     A: I went to the movies.

Clearly, the presupposition of the answer is that the speaker went somewhere last night, and the assertion differs from that preposition in specifying a certain place where the speaker went, namely the movies. Lambrecht (1994: 209) is, however, careful to point out that the word *movies* conveys focal information only by virtue of its relation to the proposition that the speaker went somewhere, which is what Lambrecht calls a **focus relation**. It is this relation that ultimately constitutes new information. Reconsider the above example, with the slight difference that the question would be phrased as *Where did you go last night, to the* *restaurant or to the movies?* After that question, the word *movies* in the answer does not constitute new information, but what is new is the identification of the movies with the place that the speaker went to.

Concerning the formal realisation of focus, Lambrecht (1994: 213) points out that there is often no conventionalised correspondence of pragmatic meaning and syntactic form, not least because sentential prosody, that is, the placement of sentence accent, can heavily modulate the interpretation of what the focus of a given sentence is. Depending on different sentence accents, the same sentences may differ with regard to their focal information, and so may serve as answers to different questions. Imagine that you overhear the following three mini-dialogues.

(10) Q: What happened to your car?
       A: My car broke down.

       Q: I heard your motorcycle broke down?
       A: My car broke down.

       Q: Why are you late?
       A: My car broke down.

In your imagination, the three answers will probably have sounded a little different, with the sentence accent placed differently in each answer. Lambrecht (1994: 223) uses the term **predicate focus** for the first kind of answer, which conveys focal information that is expressed by the entire verb phrase *broke down*. The second answer carries **argument focus**, which means that an argument of the verb, here the subject *my car*, represents the focus. Lastly, the third answer is said to carry **sentence focus** because all of the information conveyed by the answer differs from what is pragmatically presupposed. With these distinctions in place, we can move on to a discussion of how information packaging is conventionally associated with grammatical form.

5.2 Information packaging and grammar

In ordinary conversation, speakers are facing common communicative tasks with regard to information packaging. For instance, a speaker might want to make a point about something that has not as yet been part of the conversation. In order to do that, she needs to establish the new topic in such a way that the hearer recognises it. Another common task would be to clear up a misunderstanding. The hearer may have understood one half of a message correctly while misunderstanding the other half. The speaker's job now is to clarify which half is which. If situations of this kind are recurrent enough, linguistic forms will establish themselves as conventionalised means to deal with these situations. The following sections will discuss several information packaging constructions that pair a syntactic or morphosyntactic form with a particular arrangement of information.

5.2.1 Cleft constructions

An important family of information packaging constructions in English is the family of CLEFT constructions (Lambrecht 2001a). The main characteristic that distinguishes cleft constructions from other complex syntactic constructions is that clefts are bi-clausal constructions that tend to have a simple monoclausal counterpart, as illustrated in the examples below.

(11) It is the wife who decides.   The wife decides.
      What I want is a gin and tonic.   I want a gin and tonic.
      That's what I'm talking about.   I'm talking about that.

Different cleft construction types serve to package information in different ways, but it is nonetheless useful to consider the syntactic and pragmatic aspects that these construction types have in common. Lambrecht (2001a: 467) offers the following definition as a generalisation across cleft constructions.

> A cleft construction is a complex sentence structure consisting of a matrix clause headed by a copula and a relative or relative-like clause whose relativized argument is coindexed with the predicative argument of the copula. Taken together, the matrix and the relative express a logically simple proposition, which can also be expressed in the form of a single clause without a change in truth conditions.

Unpacking this definition, we can state that at the basis of cleft constructions we have a PREDICATIVE construction of the form 'X is Y'. This construction instantiates what Lambrecht calls the matrix clause. The principal parts of that matrix clause, X and Y, are connected by a copula, that is, a form of the verb *to be* or a functionally equivalent verb. Now, one of the principal parts either instantiates or connects to a RELATIVE CLAUSE construction. Consider the sentence *It is the wife who decides*. The relative clause in this sentence is *who decides*, which connects to *the wife*. The relativised argument of that relative clause, expressed by the relative pronoun *who*, refers to *the wife*, which is captured by Lambrecht's requirement that the relativised argument should be co-indexed with the predicative argument of the copula (which could be formally rendered as *It is the wife$_i$ who$_i$ decides*). The second part of Lambrecht's definition states that a sentence such as *It is the wife who decides* expresses a meaning that is, from a purely logical standpoint, identical to the meaning of *The wife decides*. This definition captures aspects of form and meaning that are shared by the three cleft construction types that were used as examples above, and which are given their proper labels below.

(12) It is the wife who decides.   *IT*-CLEFT construction
      What I want is a gin and tonic. *WH*-CLEFT construction
      That's what I'm talking about.   REVERSE *WH*-CLEFT construction

What now are the conventionalised characteristics of cleft constructions with regard to information packaging? In order to answer this question, we need to apply the analytical tools that were developed in the previous sections. Lambrecht (2001a: 475) uses the following example to analyse the information packaging in *WH*-CLEFTS.

(13) Q: What do you need?
      A: What I need is a sheet of paper and a pencil.

      Pragmatic presupposition: 'the speaker needs X'
      Pragmatic assertion: 'X is a sheet of paper and a pencil'
      Focus: 'a sheet of paper and a pencil'

The different pieces of information that are listed above map onto the structure of a *WH*-CLEFT in a systematic way. The pragmatic presupposition ('the speaker needs X') is expressed in the initial relative clause *What I need*. The copula links that relative clause with the predicative argument of the *WH*-CLEFT, which expresses the focus ('a sheet of paper and a pencil'). The predicative argument of a *WH*-CLEFT is therefore also called the **focus phrase**.

Lambrecht points out that a pragmatic presupposition such as 'the speaker needs X' is strictly speaking not a sufficient condition for the use of a *WH*-CLEFT. Let me illustrate this point with a personal anecdote. At the time I'm writing this, my 5-year-old son is a big fan of Star Wars. He has repeatedly asked for a toy light sabre for his sixth birthday, so I know that he wants a light sabre, and he knows that I know that he wants a light sabre. (He frequently checks that I have not forgotten.) But crucially, despite this mutual knowledge it would be odd for him to come up to me and specify his wish with a *WH*-CLEFT such as *What I want is a green light sabre*. Lambrecht (2001a: 476) offers an explanation for why this is the case. In order for a speaker to use a *WH*-CLEFT, it is not enough to have mutual knowledge with the hearer. Crucially, the speaker must be sure that this knowledge is currently active in the hearer's mind (cf. Section 5.1.3), and the speaker must be sure that the hearer considers it to be a matter of current interest, that is, a topic (cf. Section 5.1.4). The comparison of IT-CLEFTS, WH-CLEFTS, and REVERSE WH-CLEFTS in the following examples shows that these criteria are identical across the three construction types.

(14) It's the use of clefts that he wants to explain. IT-CLEFT
What he wants to explain is the use of clefts. WH-CLEFT
The use of clefts is what he wants to explain. REVERSE WH-CLEFT

Pragmatic presupposition: 'he wants to explain X'
Pragmatic assertion: 'X is the use of clefts'
Focus: 'the use of clefts'

Given these similarities between the constructions, you may wonder what the differences are that motivate speakers to choose one construction type over the other two in a particular speech situation. Lambrecht (2001a: 497) discusses four factors that affect speakers' choices between different cleft constructions.

The first factor concerns the relative length of the focus phrase and the relative clause. As a general rule of thumb, speakers will try to organise their utterances in such a way that long (or 'heavy') constituents are placed towards the end. This tendency, which is known as the **end-weight principle** (Behaghel 1932; Quirk et al 1985), can be explained in terms of processing ease. Compare the following two examples.

(15) It's the use of clefts in English medical writings from the sixteenth to the eighteenth century that he wants to explain.
What he wants to explain is the use of clefts in English medical writings from the sixteenth to the eighteenth century.

The chances are that you found the second sentence much easier to read and understand. In order to process the IT-CLEFT, you have to keep in mind the entire noun phrase (*the use of clefts in English medical writings from the sixteenth to the eighteenth century*) before the final relative clause allows you to understand its syntactic role in the sentence. In a WH-CLEFT, there are no such difficulties. The initial relative clause, followed by the copula (*What he wants to explain is*) already tells you that what follows is a noun phrase that has the function of a subject complement. As will be discussed in subsequent sections of this chapter, the end-weight principle not only affects the choice of cleft constructions. It influences speakers' syntactic choices across many pairs of constructions, including the DITRANSITIVE and the PREPOSITIONAL DATIVE construction, as well as the S-GENITIVE and the OF-GENITIVE construction.

The second factor that distinguishes the three cleft constructions concerns the activation of the pragmatic presupposition in the relative clause. As was discussed above, ideas can be more or less active in a given speech situation. The speaker keeps a continuous record of what ideas are currently active, semi-active, or probably inactive in the hearer's mind, choosing information packaging constructions accordingly. Imagine that you are taking a trip to London where you would like to visit the British Museum. After leaving the Underground at Tottenham Court Road, you wonder where to turn. Armed with a map, but unable to work out where to go, you approach someone. Which of the sentences below would you choose?

(16) Excuse me, I'm looking for the British Museum.
      Excuse me, what I'm looking for is the British Museum.
      Excuse me, it's the British Museum that I'm looking for.

Clearly, the first option is the most appropriate one, since it does not make any pragmatic presupposition. But what about the second and third examples? Both of those would signal to the hearer that 'I am looking for X' is a shared piece of knowledge, which might be a reasonable guess, given that you are confusedly waving a map of London and perhaps have a camera dangling across your chest. Still, you will probably agree that the WH-CLEFT is somewhat more appropriate than the IT-CLEFT. This is because IT-CLEFTS are restricted to contexts in which the pragmatic presupposition is strongly activated. By contrast, WH-CLEFTS tolerate pragmatic presuppositions that are only semi-active at the time of the utterance.

Topicality is the third factor that plays a role in the use of clefts. Both IT-CLEFTS and WH-CLEFTS are usable in contexts where the relative clause expresses an established topic. To illustrate this point, in the example below, a question can be answered with either an IT-CLEFT or a WH-CLEFT. In both cases, the relative clause reiterates the topic that has been set up by the question.

(17) Q: Where did you meet your wife?
      A: It was in Paris that I met my wife.
      A: Where I met my wife was in Paris.

If we alter the question so that 'meeting one's wife' is no longer an established topic, a difference in the acceptability of the two answers emerges. Specifically, the IT-CLEFT still constitutes an appropriate answer, whereas the WH-CLEFT sounds out of place.

(18) Q: Why are you so interested in Paris?
      A: It was in Paris that I met my wife.
      A: ?Where I met my wife was in Paris.

The difference between *It*-Clefts and *Wh*-Clefts revealed by the two answers is that *It*-Clefts tolerate non-topical relative clauses whereas *Wh*-Clefts do not. This tolerance of *It*-Clefts is sometimes used for rhetorical purposes in examples such as the following, which may introduce lectures or newspaper articles.

(19) It was Cicero who once said that the greatest of all virtues is gratitude.
      It was just about 50 years ago that Henry Ford gave us the weekend.
      It is a truism that almost any sect, cult, or religion will legislate its creed into law if it acquires the political power to do so.

Lambrecht analyses examples such as these, which are also called **informative presupposition clefts** (Prince 1978), as rhetorical exploitations of the information packaging that *It*-Clefts conventionally evoke. The speakers of the above examples in no way assume that their hearers already have the information that is expressed in the respective relative clauses. However, they invite their hearers to take this information as something that is not to be challenged. The term that Lambrecht (2001a: 485) uses to label this phenomenon is **pragmatic accommodation**.

   The fourth and final factor concerns restrictions that result from more general morphosyntactic characteristics of English. For instance, the use of *Wh*-Clefts is naturally restricted by the range of *wh*-words that exist in English: *what, who, where, when, why*, and *how*. Two issues are worth noting. First, whereas *what* and *who* are freely usable for the construction of *Wh*-Clefts, the remaining ones are less felicitous, as the following examples illustrate.

(20) It is champagne that I like.
      What I like is champagne.

      It was John who we saw.
      Who we saw was John.

      It was behind the books that I hid it.
      ?Where I hid it was behind the books.

      It is in ten minutes that the train will depart.
      ?When the train will depart is in ten minutes.

It was for personal reasons that he left.
??Why he left was for personal reasons.

It was with relief that she heard the door close.
??How she heard the door close was with relief.

Second, IT-CLEFTS commonly occur with focus phrases that do not match an existing *wh*-word in English. A focus phrase such as *It is champagne* clearly matches *what*, the focus phrase *It was John* clearly matches *who*, but how about the focus phrases in the following examples?

(21) It was <u>under protest</u> that the kids ate their vegetables.
It was <u>in no time</u> that they had finished their ice creams.
It was <u>despite his best efforts</u> that things took a turn for the worse.

The English lexicon does not contain *wh*-words with the meanings 'while doing what', 'how fast', or 'despite what'. Hence, the IT-CLEFTS in the examples above do not have WH-CLEFT counterparts in the way that *It was John we saw* matches *Who we saw was John*.

Summing up, how do speakers select one particular cleft constructions when several choices are available in the grammar of English? The choice of an information packaging constructions is first of all influenced by the assumptions that the speaker makes about the current knowledge of the hearer. Beyond that, influences include processing-related factors such as the end-weight principle, constraints relating to other construction in the grammar, such as the availability of a *wh*-word, and construction-specific constraints, such as the tolerance for non-topical ideas or ideas that have only a low degree of current activation.

5.2.2 *Dislocation and related constructions*

A second important family of information packaging constructions in English goes by the name of dislocation constructions. Two major constructions that have been discussed in the literature are the LEFT-DISLOCATION construction and the RIGHT-DISLOCATION construction, which are illustrated below. As is shown in the respective corresponding examples, both constructions can be paraphrased by canonical declarative sentences.

(22) My brother, he rarely calls me these days.   LEFT-DISLOCATION
My brother rarely calls me these days.

I love that, being a father.   RIGHT-DISLOCATION
I love being a father.

Again, one might wonder why the grammar of English provides speakers with different syntactic constructions for the expression of largely identical meanings. By now, you are trained to notice that what is different between the members of each pair is how new information is integrated into previously shared information. You would perhaps point out that the notion of topicality plays a role. An analysis of the LEFT-DISLOCATION construction would have to address how the initial, left-dislocated constituent (here: *my brother*) sets up a topic, so that the subsequent clause can provide relevant information about that topic (*he rarely calls me these days*). The example of the RIGHT-DISLOCATION construction that is given above differs from the canonical clause in such a way that we know that the idea 'fatherhood' must have figured somehow as a topic in the previous context. Hence, the speaker initially opts for the pronominal form *that*, but as the idea might only be semi-active in the hearer's mind, the speaker backs up and adds the phrase *being a father*.

Dislocation constructions have been analysed in the Construction Grammar literature not only in contrast to canonical sentence patterns, but crucially also in contrast to other information packaging constructions that superficially look very similar. Consider the following pairs of examples.

(23) Their cat, they feed it steak tartare.   LEFT-DISLOCATION
      Their cat they feed steak tartare.   TOPICALISATION

Whereas the difference between a dislocation construction and a canonical sentence may be relatively straightforward to determine, contrasts such as the one illustrated above are more intricate. Gregory and Michaelis (2001) investigate the functional contrast between the LEFT-DISLOCATION construction and the TOPICALISATION construction, which are formally and functionally very similar: First, both can be characterised as fronting constructions, since they differ from canonical sentences with regard to their initial constituent. Second, the constructions share similar prosodic characteristics. In both of the examples above, the words *cat* and *steak tartare* form prosodic peaks. Third, in both constructions the focus is associated with the second prosodic peak. A formal difference concerns the fact that the preclausal noun phrase (*their cat*) corresponds to a pronominal expression (*it*) in the LEFT-DISLOCATION construction, whereas there is no such correspondence in the TOPICALISATION construction. This means that the TOPICALISATION construction is restricted to preclausal noun phrases that instantiate an object of the main verb – the subject of a canonical sentence such as *Their cat eats steak tartare* is already located sentence-initially. Another formal difference is that the LEFT-DISLOCATION construction allows coreference across what are called **long-distance dependencies** (cf. Sag et al. 2003; Sag 2010), whereas the TOPICALISATION construction is more heavily restricted in this regard (Gregory and Michaelis 2001: 1668). This observation relates to the phenomenon of **island constraints** (Ambridge and Goldberg 2008), which will be discussed in the final section of this chapter. In the following examples, LEFT-DISLOCATION is acceptable whereas the TOPICALISATION construction yields an ungrammatical sentence.

(24) Their cat, you will hear fantastic stories what stuff they feed it.
      *Their cat you will hear fantastic stories what stuff they feed.

A functional difference that Gregory and Michaelis make out is that TOPICALISATION frequently involves anaphoric pronouns as preclausal noun phrases. In such contexts, LEFT-DISLOCATION is unacceptable.

(25) A: You are such a gifted singer, you should make a career of it!
      B: That I'm not so sure about.
      B: *That, I'm not so sure about it.

In order to find out more about the conditions under which speakers use the two constructions in ordinary conversation, Gregory and Michaelis turn to corpus data of telephone conversations, retrieve examples of the two constructions, and annotate them for several characteristics, which reveals two contrasts (2001: 1695). First, the referents of preclausal noun phrases in LEFT-DISLOCATION constructions are rarely topical or active, whereas this is typically the case in TOPICALISATION. This is consistent with the proposal that the main function of LEFT-DISLOCATION is to assign topical status to a discourse-new referent (Lambrecht 1994). Second, the referents that are highlighted in the preclausal noun phrases of LEFT-DISLOCATION constructions tend to persist longer as topics in the conversation than do the preclausal noun phrases in TOPICALISATION. In other words, if a speaker utters a sentence such as *Their cat, they feed it steak tartare*, you can be fairly certain that there is more cat-related information coming up. The cat is likely to be mentioned again at least once or twice in the following conversation. By contrast, *Their cat they feed steak tartare* does not warrant an expectation of this kind. This contrast with regard to topic persistence illuminates an aspect of information packaging constructions that up to now has escaped the discussion in this chapter: information packaging constructions are not only good for organising meanings in a way that facilitates the integration of old and new information, but crucially also set up expectations in the hearer about what will be coming up in the immediate future. Speakers use these constructions to signal whether they are going to elaborate on a topic or whether the current topic is a mere sidetrack to something else that they want to communicate. This function of constructions has been discussed under the heading of **projection** (Auer 2005). A phenomenon that you will frequently encounter in everyday conversation is that speakers finish each other's sentences, often very accurately expressing what their interlocutors had in mind. The fact that this is so commonplace, even between speakers that do not know each other extremely well, suggests that projection is a function that is fundamental to a wide range of grammatical constructions.

Let us consider another pair of contrasting information packaging constructions. Michaelis and Lambrecht (1996) study a construction that they call NOMINAL EXTRAPOSITION. This construction shares structural and functional characteristics with the RIGHT-DISLOCATION construction, but there are also clear differences that suggest that both constructions are separately represented in speakers' knowledge of language. The following examples illustrate the two constructions.

(26) It's amazing, the things children say.   NOMINAL EXTRAPOSITION
      They're amazing, the things children   RIGHT-DISLOCATION
      say.

Both examples above consist of an initial PREDICATIVE construction (*it's amazing, they're amazing*) and an extraposed or dislocated post-clausal noun phrase (*the things children say*). This structural similarity is, however, only superficial: whereas in RIGHT-DISLOCATION the dislocated nominal must be coreferential with the subject of the PREDICATIVE construction (*they* = *the things children say*), this is not the case with NOMINAL EXTRAPOSITION. As the above example shows, the initial subject (*it*) and the extraposed nominal (*the things children say*) differ in number, one being in the singular, the other in the plural. Michaelis and Lambrecht (1996: 222) thus bring out a first important characteristic of the NOMINAL EXTRAPOSITION construction: its clausal subject is non-referential, as in constructions such as *It seems you're right* or *It is important to wash your hands*. Another difference concerns the conventional prosody of the two constructions. Whereas the dislocated noun phrases in RIGHT-DISLOCATION tend to receive a low and flat intonation, the extraposed noun phrase in NOMINAL EXTRAPOSITION must be stressed and pronounced with a rising and falling intonation. This prosodic difference reflects the fact that the two constructions differ with regard to information packaging. Specifically, in RIGHT-DISLOCATION, the dislocated nominal is not involved in the presentation of new, focal information. Section 5.1.4 above introduced the term 'focus relation' to capture how newly offered information is made informative. In the NOMINAL EXTRAPOSITION construction, the speaker establishes a focus relation between the adjective in the PREDICATIVE construction and the focal part of the extraposed noun phrase. Both of these constituents tend to receive stressed pronunciation. The following examples illustrate that idea.

(27) It's UNBELIEVABLE the money she spends on DOG FOOD.
      It's IMMEASURABLE the TOLL it has taken on him.
      It's STAGGERING the number of BOOKS that pile up.

Yet another syntactic difference between the two constructions is that RIGHT-DISLOCATION may appear in syntactically subordinate contexts whereas NOMINAL EXTRAPOSITION is restricted to main clauses. The examples below show that a right-dislocated noun phrase may meaningfully complement an adverbial clause with *although*. By contrast, if there is a secondary stress that identifies the sentence as an example of the NOMINAL EXTRAPOSITION construction, the example becomes essentially uninterpretable.

(28) Although it's AMAZING, the movie he did with Pacino, they
      never collaborated again.
      *Although it's AMAZING, the movie he did with PACINO, they
      never collaborated again.

Michaelis and Lambrecht (1996: 224) explain this contrast with reference to the pragmatic function of the construction. NOMINAL EXTRAPOSITION is an **exclamative construction,** and like utterances such as *How cool!, What a ridiculous idea!,* or *That's insane!,* it serves the function of presenting focal information, which clashes pragmatically with the typical function of subordinate clauses, which is to flesh out topical information. This then appears to be the primary distinction between RIGHT-DISLOCATION and NOMINAL EXTRAPOSITION: Whereas the postclausal noun phrase has to be at least semi-active for the use of either construction, the noun phrase is topical in RIGHT-DISLOCATION but contains focal information in the NOMINAL EXTRAPOSITION construction.

Using the conceptual distinctions introduced by Lambrecht (1994), we can now dissect the information packaging characteristics of an authentic example of the NOMINAL EXTRAPOSITION construction.

(29) Pilar Sander's baby girl is showing her face to the world. The
      actress revealed little Sharon at LAX on Tuesday, carrying her
      in her arms as she walked through the airport. Sander previously
      covered her daughter with a towel for trips around town,

ensuring no photographers or onlookers caught a glimpse of her baby girl. The 36-year-old Oscar winner adopted Sharon in April. In a recent interview on ABC she said her life's 'changed a tiny bit' since becoming a mom. 'I now travel with a lot of luggage – diapers, bottles, toys, you name it.' 'Look, **it's been amazing the amount of emails and congratulations**,' she added. 'Everyone's just been so lovely.'

Pragmatic presuppositions:	1: 'Pilar and her new baby are topical'
	2: 'new parents receive congratulations'
	3: '2 is semi-active in the hearer's mind'
Pragmatic assertion:	'the amount of congratulations has been high'
Focus:	'the amount of congratulations has been high'

Lambrecht and Michaelis (1996: 234) point out that in NOMINAL EXTRAPOSITION the pragmatic assertion and the focus are identical. Remember that the focus is defined as the difference between what is pragmatically presupposed and what is pragmatically asserted. In the example above, the pragmatic presupposition does not contain any information about the amount of congratulations that new parents commonly receive. Hence, the focus contains two ideas: first, that there is a scale of how many congratulations are typically received, and second, that Pilar's reception of congratulations has ranked high on that scale.

Summing up the discussion of dislocation constructions and related information packaging constructions, we can take away the following points. First, even pairs of constructions that may look rather similar in terms of their structure may exhibit functionally motivated differences with regard to information packaging. Second, the contrasts between pragmatically presupposed and pragmatically asserted, between topic and focus, and between active, semi-active, and inactive are instrumental in working out the conditions under which speakers use these constructions. And third, the intricate relations between form and pragmatic meaning show that pragmatics must be more than a set of general guidelines for communication. A conception of pragmatics that continues to be popular is the idea that speakers follow conversational maxims (Grice 1975), so that they say things that are true and relevant and present information in an orderly fashion. Ordinary conversation can certainly be interpreted as showing the effects of such maxims, but at the same time, the maxims are not specific enough to predict any difference between two constructions such as RIGHT-DISLOCATION and NOMINAL EXTRAPOSITION. It is therefore necessary to assume that speakers mentally represent syntactic constructions not only together with their constructional semantics, but also with their pragmatic characteristics.

5.3 Island constraints

Imagine once more that you are on the phone talking to your mother. This time she tells you a story about John and his girlfriend Mary. Mary, as you will remember from a previous conversation, is pregnant again, so the smell of certain foods give her terrible nausea attacks. In the middle of her episode, your mother says *The smell of the scrambled eggs already made her a little queasy. And then, she had to run out of the kitchen because John was starting to fry* – when the phone line is suddenly crackling. What was it that John was frying? What was it that made Mary run out of the kitchen? Interestingly, the grammar of English does not seem to allow you to ask for a specific clarification. The following question is clearly ungrammatical.

(30)   *What did Mary run out of the kitchen because John was starting to fry?

Syntacticians have for a long time been troubled by the question why examples such as the one above should be impossible. An explanation that you might consider is that perhaps the length of the sentence plays a role. There is a considerable distance between the *wh*-word *what* and the verb *fry*, which is crucial here because the thing that we are questioning with *what* is an argument of the verb *fry*, namely its object. Perhaps it might also play a role that between *what* and *fry* we have an entire clausal structure that intervenes, namely *did Mary run out of the kitchen*. These are valid concerns, but there are examples of comparable length and complexity that nonetheless seem to be much more acceptable. Consider the following question.

(31)   What did your mother say that Mary's boyfriend John was starting to fry?

It appears that the distance between *what* and *fry* is roughly the same, and we also have an intervening clause, namely *did your mother say*. Ambridge and Goldberg (2008) suggest an explanation for the unacceptability of the first example, and as you may already guess, that explanation has to do with information packaging.

Before we go into the details of that explanation, we first need to discuss the overall phenomenon a little more thoroughly. What we are dealing with goes by the name of **island constraints** in the syntactic

literature. The term goes back to Ross (1967), who coined it as a metaphor: the formation of a *WH*-QUESTION construction requires that the
thing that is questioned 'moves' from its canonical position into the
position of the *wh*-word. So, in order to form the question *What did John
start to fry?*, speakers were thought to transform the canonical sentence
John started to fry XY by replacing XY, the 'gap', with the *wh*-word and
moving that *wh*-word to the front of the sentence, with *do*-support
(Huddleston and Pullum 2002: 93) as an attendant procedure. Now,
the fact that some questions are ungrammatical can be interpreted in
such a way that the gap is in a place from where it 'cannot move'. Such
places Ross called syntactic islands, presumably because words cannot
swim. Syntactic prisons or syntactic mousetraps might have been
equally appropriate terms, but admittedly the idea of an island is more
pleasurable. Several phrase types are syntactic islands in English. The
following examples illustrate them through comparisons of canonical
sentences with 'failed' questions.

(32) Complex object noun phrases
        She saw [the documentary that was about <u>Churchill</u>]$_{NP}$.
        *<u>Who</u> did she see [the documentary that was about __]$_{NP}$?

      Complex subject noun phrases
        [That he kept smoking <u>marijuana</u>]$_{NP}$ bothered her.
        *<u>What</u> did [that he kept smoking __]$_{NP}$ bother her?

      Adverbial clauses
        She left the room [because John started to fry <u>bacon</u>]$_{AdvCl}$.
        *<u>What</u> did she leave the room [because John started to
        fry __]$_{AdvCl}$?

      Complement clauses of factive verbs
        He regretted [that he didn't bring <u>an umbrella</u>]$_{ThatCl}$.
        *<u>What</u> did he regret [that he didn't bring __]$_{ThatCl}$?

      Complement clauses of manner-of-speaking verbs
        He muttered [that he didn't bring <u>an umbrella</u>]$_{ThatCl}$.
        *<u>What</u> did he mutter [that he didn't bring __]$_{ThatCl}$?

The traditional explanation of why these phrase types are syntactic
islands and hence cannot contain the gap is not too far off the consideration that was initially proposed above: if certain kinds of phrases
intervene between the *wh*-word and the gap, those phrases act as
boundaries that are impossible to overcome. (The metaphor of a syntactic prison might have been more consistent after all.) Noun phrases
and clauses in particular have been seen as such boundaries. However,

this explanation faces a problem. There is an apparent difference in acceptability between manner-of-speaking verbs and regular speaking verbs such as *say*. Despite identical syntax, the second example below is fully acceptable.

(33) *<u>What</u> did he mutter [that he didn't bring __]$_{\text{ThatCl}}$?
       <u>What</u> did he say [that he didn't bring __]$_{\text{ThatCl}}$?

The explanation that Ambridge and Goldberg (2008: 356) offer to account for the behaviour of syntactic islands takes the shape of a hypothesis, which they call the **backgrounded constructions are islands** hypothesis, or BCI for short. What this hypothesis boils down to is the following. The previous sections have established that information packaging constructions have parts, some of which express old, pragmatically presupposed information, whereas others express new, pragmatically asserted information. Now, when information packaging constructions are used to form part of a WH-QUESTION, via multiple inheritance and subpart links (cf. Chapter 3), there is one fundamental constraint. The thing that is asked for in WH-QUESTIONS, the gap, must not be situated in a part of a construction that is conventionally associated with pragmatically presupposed information.

Let us illustrate this with a concrete example. Section 5.2.1 has discussed the use of IT-CLEFTS, which present focal information in the initial PREDICATIVE construction and topical information in the final RELATIVE CLAUSE. Consider the following example.

(34) It is the smell of bacon that bothers Mary.

If you would like to question a particular part of the IT-CLEFT, your knowledge of English grammar, as represented in the construct-i-con, allows you to combine the IT-CLEFT with the WH-QUESTION construction. However, what the BCI hypothesis predicts is that this kind of combination will only work if the questioned element coincides with that part of the IT-CLEFT that encodes focal information, not with parts that encode topical information. As the following examples show, this is indeed the case. You can question *the smell of bacon*, but not *Mary*.

(35) What is it that bothers Mary?
       *Who is it the smell of bacon that bothers?

Ambridge and Goldberg (2008: 358) propose a reason for this: the *wh*-word in a WH-QUESTION construction is its primary focus. If that WH-QUESTION is combined with an information packaging construction that presents the gap as backgrounded information, the result will be a mixed message: a piece of information is presented as new and old at the same time. This, Ambridge and Goldberg suggest, is communicatively dysfunctional and hence does not occur.

The phrase types that have been identified as syntactic islands all have in common that they express backgrounded information. But, you may wonder, what about the difference between complement clauses of *mutter* and *say*? Here, the syntax is identical and yet there is a difference with regard to island status. Ambridge and Goldberg (2008: 357) point out that verbs such as *mutter*, *shout*, or *mumble* tend to be used primarily in contexts where the manner of speaking constitutes focal information whereas the content of what is spoken constitutes pragmatically presupposed information. This is not the case with the verb *say*. Consider the following two examples.

(36)   I wasn't saying that you should apologise. I merely suggested that you leave her alone for a while.
I wasn't mumbling that you should apologise. I said that loud and clear.

This difference between *say* and manner-of-speaking verbs brings the latter into the fold of the BCI hypothesis.

To conclude, the fact that backgrounded constructions disallow questioning of their parts receives an explanation that is pragmatic and syntactic at the same time. The explanation is pragmatic because information packaging reflects the knowledge and consciousness of interlocutors in the speech situation. It is also syntactic because speakers' knowledge of constructions includes knowledge about what kind of information can be expressed with what kind of syntactic structure.

5.4 Summing up

This chapter has introduced information packaging constructions, which are sentence-level constructions that serve the purpose of organising and presenting information in such a way that hearers can successfully connect pieces of new information to already shared pieces of information. Speakers choose a given information packaging construction on the basis of assumptions about the hearer's knowledge. In order to make an adequate and communicatively successful choice, speakers have to keep close track of what it is that the hearer knows and what it is that the hearer will be able to work out.

The first sections of the chapter introduced theoretical notions that Lambrecht (1994) develops for the analysis of information packaging constructions. The notions of pragmatic presupposition and pragmatic assertion largely map onto what can informally be called old and new information. The former terms are, however, somewhat more inclusive. Pragmatically presupposed information also includes ideas that the hearer is merely invited to take for granted from previous utterances, and pragmatically asserted information includes those ideas that are merely evoked, not necessarily expressed, by the current utterance. A second distinction that is crucial for information packaging is the contrast between active, semi-active, and inactive referents. Referents that are currently talked about are active, related ideas are semi-active, and unrelated ideas are inactive. As the subject matter of a conversation changes, so does the activation status of the referents. Lambrecht (1994) further offers definitions of the terms 'topic' and 'focus', which he views as characteristics of sentences, not texts. In the simplest of terms, a topic is what a sentence is about. The focus of a sentence is defined technically as the difference between the pragmatic presupposition and the pragmatic assertion. Often, these two overlap in multiple elements. The set of non-overlapping elements constitutes the focus. If there is no conceptual overlap between pragmatic presupposition and pragmatic assertion, then the focus is identical to the pragmatic assertion. Lambrecht distinguishes between predicate focus, argument focus, and sentence focus to account for these respective possibilities.

The main point of the chapter was to illustrate how syntactic constructions are conventionally associated with specific information packaging characteristics. Speakers' knowledge of English grammar thus includes knowledge of syntactic constructions that have the main purpose of managing information, packaging it in ways that facilitate processing by the hearer, and signalling that the speaker is aware of the current knowledge of the hearer. A family of constructions that does just that is the family of English cleft constructions. The chapter distinguished IT-CLEFTS, WH-CLEFTS, and REVERSE WH-CLEFTS, discussing similarities and differences between these constructions. It was shown that IT-CLEFTS and WH-CLEFTS are similar with regard to pragmatic presupposition and pragmatic assertion, but that they differ, for instance, with regard to the issues of topicality and activation. The end-weight principle was identified as another factor influencing the choices between cleft constructions. A second group of constructions discussed in the chapter was that of the LEFT-DISLOCATION construction and the RIGHT-DISLOCATION construction, which were contrasted with superficially similar constructions. LEFT-DISLOCATION and TOPICALISATION share syntactic and prosodic features but differ with regard to topicality: the topic of the LEFT-DISLOCATION construction has a greater tendency to persist in the following discourse. RIGHT-DISLOCATION and NOMINAL EXTRAPOSITION differ with regard to their respective postclausal noun phrases. It is only in the NOMINAL EXTRAPOSITION construction that this constituent conveys focal information.

The third section of the chapter examined the classic problem of syntactic island constraints. Syntactic islands are phrase types whose parts cannot be questioned in a *WH*-QUESTION construction. Whereas previous explanations of island constraints have been syntactic, identifying specific syntactic phrase types as obstacles to question formation, Ambridge and Goldberg (2008) suggest an explanation in terms of information packaging. Specifically, they argue that backgrounded constructions are islands. If a part of an information packaging construction is conventionally associated with the expression of pragmatically presupposed information, the parts of that construction are not available for questioning.

Study questions

- What are information packaging constructions and what is their purpose?
- Define pragmatic presupposition, pragmatic assertion, and focus.
- How can an idea become semi-active in the hearer's mind?
- What kinds of CLEFT constructions do you know and how do they differ?
- What is the end-weight principle and how would you explain it?
- What is meant by the term 'pragmatic accommodation'?
- Which answer to the following question do you prefer and why?

  Q: Why do you like surfing so much?
  A: It is surfing that my father taught me when I was young.
  A: What my father taught me when I was young was surfing.

- Discuss the structural and functional differences between LEFT-DISLOCATION and RIGHT-DISLOCATION.
- What are syntactic islands?
- Discuss how Ambridge and Goldberg's BCI hypothesis differs from previous accounts of island constraints.

Further reading

For a first overview of information packaging constructions, Leino (2013) is a good place to start. The cornerstone reference for this topic is Lambrecht (1994), which is useful furthermore because it explains in detail how the constructional approach to information packaging differs from earlier approaches. Classic treatments of information packaging, which prefigure much of what has been discussed in this chapter, include Halliday (1967), Chafe (1976), and Prince (1981). Besides the studies on information packaging constructions that were covered in the text of this chapter (Ambridge and Goldberg 2008; Gregory and Michaelis 2001; Lambrecht 2001b; Michaelis and Lambrecht 1996), important constructional studies of information packaging in English include Goldberg (2001) on CAUSATIVE constructions, Goldberg and Ackerman (2001) on obligatory adjuncts, and Wasow and Arnold (2003) on postverbal constituent ordering. A paper that proposes a cognitive-linguistic explanation of island constraints that differs from the one given by Ambridge and Goldberg (2008) is Dąbrowska (2008).

6 Constructions and language processing

6.1 The quest for behavioural evidence

If you are reading this sentence, that could mean one of two things. Either you found the preceding chapters on constructions and their properties convincing enough to read on, or you were so enraged by them that you have to keep reading in order to find out what nonsense comes next. This chapter has been written with the second type of reader in mind, a reader who remains sceptical about Construction Grammar as a useful theory of linguistic knowledge. If someone like that asked you to list the two or three strongest arguments for Construction Grammar, what would you say? Armed with what you have read in the preceding five chapters, you could come up with the following talking points:

- Speakers must know constructions: ordinary language contains a large number of idiomatic expressions (*by and large, all of a sudden*, etc.) that show formal peculiarities and/or non-compositional meanings. It is a useful assumption that these patterns are stored in a large network, the construct-i-con.
- There are coercion effects: constructional patterns can override lexical meanings, for instance when count nouns are used in mass noun contexts (*Could I have a little more kangaroo, please?*) Viewing constructions as schematic form–meaning pairs elegantly explains effects of this kind.
- Even general syntactic patterns have idiosyncratic constraints: a pattern such as the DITRANSITIVE construction must be endowed with meaning, as is evidenced by failed examples such as **I brought the table a glass of water*. Modelling this with syntactic rules is difficult; a constructional approach accounts naturally for it.

A sceptic might listen to those points, nod at regular intervals, and then put on a sly smile, saying *So all of your best arguments are based on anecdotal observations?* There is nothing wrong in principle with a theory

130

that is based on careful considerations of individual linguistic examples. However, someone who is not convinced by three such examples is unlikely to change their mind after the fourth, fifth, or sixth example. What is needed is a different sort of empirical evidence, namely **behavioural evidence** that is gathered in reproducible ways under controlled laboratory conditions. The fundamental difference between evidence from casual observation and evidence from experimentation is that in gathering the latter the researcher actively manipulates the factors that are hypothesised to be at work. To offer an analogy, say that you want to know what foods are good for people's health. One way to do this would be to choose a group of your friends, take note of what they eat during a given week, and then look whether differences in food consumption correspond in some ways to your friends' health, as measured by body mass index, pulse at rest, performance in a 100-metre sprint, a self-assessment of how healthy they feel, or some other measure of your choice. Now imagine that you present your results to a friend who has a job doing clinical studies for a pharmaceutical company. The chances are that this friend would shake her head in disbelief. The way to find out whether some food makes a difference, she would explain to you, is to have two groups of subjects, and to feed them different things. If you are interested in finding out something about the factor 'food', you need to manipulate that factor. Have two groups of friends, feed one group broccoli and the other lasagne, and see if after a month there are reliable differences in the results of the 100-metre sprint. In a way, the evidence for Construction Grammar that this book has presented up to now has been gathered with an approach that resembles the first way of analysing food and health more than the second. We have been collecting observations, individual pieces of evidence, and taken together, those pieces of evidence appear to be largely compatible with the idea of a construct-i-con that represents speakers' knowledge of language. An inherent danger in this approach is that we unconsciously turn towards such pieces of evidence as conform to our theory, and disregard other, more problematic pieces. Counterintuitive as it may seem, what we would need to do in order to find support for Construction Grammar is to try to prove it wrong. Scientific advances can only be made if we try to disprove our current theories, finding out in the process what ideas we need to revise and what other ideas might replace them. If we fail to find counterevidence, we should still view our theory critically, but we are entitled to the conclusion that no better alternatives are currently available.

As the following sections will discuss, there is actually a substantial body of psycholinguistic work that has been carried out with the express purpose of trying to test Construction Grammar as a theory. Psycholinguistics is usually thought of as covering the areas of language comprehension, language production, and language acquisition. This chapter will focus on work that has examined aspects of language comprehension and production; the topic of language acquisition will be dealt with separately in Chapter 7. The main purpose of this chapter will be to bundle together those pieces of behavioural evidence that would allow you to respond to the critic's question, saying *Well, since you're asking, the illustrating examples that I have given you are backed up by several types of behavioural evidence, both in language comprehension and in language production. For example, it has been shown that* . . .

6.2 Evidence from language comprehension

6.2.1 Constructions explain how hearers understand novel denominal verbs

English is notorious for its highly productive use of morphological **conversion**, that is, the use of nouns as verbs (*water a plant*), verbs as nouns (*have a drink*), or adjectives as verbs (*calm the baby*). The fact that speakers use conversion productively means that you are likely to come across examples that you have never encountered before, which raises the question how you understand these examples. To take an instance, how do you interpret an innovative denominal verb such as *to monk*? Looking at the verb in isolation, several interpretations seem possible, for instance 'turn someone into a monk', 'behave like a monk', or 'populate some place with monks'; depending on how imaginative you are, you might come up with further meanings. A commonsensical approach to the question how denominal verbs are understood would be that it is the immediate linguistic context that determines the interpretation. More specifically, the constructional view of linguistic knowledge would predict that in cases where there is no established verb meaning, it is the morphosyntactic form of the construction in which it appears, that is, the linguistic context of the verb, that lends its meaning to the verb via the principle of coercion.

Consider the following examples.

(1)   It was not before his twenty-fourth birthday that Luther was monked.
      Hey hey we're the monks. We're just monking around.
      In the thirteenth century the Catholic church started to monk Northern Europe.

What the constructional approach would have to say about these examples is that the respective differences in the interpretations of *to monk* are influenced by the PASSIVE construction, the PROGRESSIVE construction, and the TRANSITIVE construction. This, however, is a claim that does not follow as a matter of course. An alternative explanation might be that the interpretations are determined by lexical elements in the context and general world knowledge. So, a hearer might know that Luther was a German Augustinian monk who hence must have been 'monked' at some point. By the same token, if a hearer triangulates the ideas 'Catholic church', 'Northern Europe', and 'monk', there remain few other interpretations than the one that implies sending out missionaries. In keeping with the aim of trying to test Construction Grammar, what kind of evidence could we gather to decide between these two possibilities?

Kaschak and Glenberg (2000) devised a series of experiments to test whether constructions measurably influence the interpretation of denominal verbs. In particular, these authors intended to answer the question whether or not adult speakers of English are sensitive to the relationship between abstract syntactic forms and basic conceptual scenes that is posited by Goldberg (1995) as the scene encoding hypothesis (cf. Chapter 2). In a first experiment, participants were exposed to pairs of sentences such as the following.

(2) Lyn crutched Tom the apple so he wouldn't starve.
    Lyn crutched the apple so Tom wouldn't starve.

In terms of the lexical material, the two sentences are identical. In terms of the syntax of their main clauses, they differ: the first instantiates the DITRANSITIVE construction, while the second is an example of the TRANSITIVE construction. The presentation of the two sentences was followed by what is called an inference task. Participants were shown a sentence such as *Tom got the apple* or *Lyn acted on the apple* and were asked to indicate which of the original sentences would be semantically consistent with the test sentence. As you may expect, the sentence *Tom got the apple* was matched most often with the DITRANSITIVE construction whereas speakers paired *Lyn acted on the apple* with the TRANSITIVE construction. This demonstrates an effect of syntax and hence of constructions.

In a second experiment, Kaschak and Glenberg tested whether this effect would also be apparent when participants were asked to give definitions of novel denominal verbs. Participants were exposed to short stories that ended in a critical sentence with a verb such as *crutch*. Crucially, the syntactic form of that sentence was varied across groups of participants. Consider the following text.

(3) Tom and Lyn competed on different baseball teams. After the game, Tom was teasing Lyn about striking out three times. Lyn said: 'I was just distracted by your ugly face. I can hit anything to any field using anything!' To prove it, she took an apple that she had brought as a snack, and a crutch that belonged to the baseball club's infirmary.

Lyn crutched Tom her apple to prove her point.
Lyn crutched her apple to prove her point to Tom.

Participants were asked to define the denominal verb in the critical sentence. Kaschak and Glenberg determined whether the participants explicitly attributed the idea of a transfer to the verb meaning. If someone wrote 'to crutch means to hit something to someone using a crutch', that response was counted as referring to a transfer. Definitions such as 'to crutch means to make something move by hitting it with a crutch' were counted as non-transfer responses. The central question was whether the constructional form of the critical sentences has an impact on participants' responses. Indeed, Kaschak and Glenberg found that transfer definitions are significantly more frequent when the critical sentence instantiates the DITRANSITIVE construction. Taken together, the results of the two experiments show that the syntactic form of constructions guides the comprehension of newly coined words. This result does not preclude the possibility that world knowledge and lexical items in the immediate context also have an influence; indeed, this is very likely to be the case. But besides these, constructional form is a force to be reckoned with in language comprehension.

6.2.2 Constructional meanings are routinely accessed in sentence comprehension

One of the core ideas presented in this book is the notion that constructions are symbolic units that pair a morphosyntactic form with a meaning. That meaning may concern the semantic integration of the formal parts (as in the NOUN–NOUN COMPOUND construction), it may represent a basic situation type (as in the CAUSED MOTION construction), or it may assign the status of new or old information to the formal parts (as in the WH-CLEFT construction). What unites these different kinds of meanings is that they are independent of the lexical material that enters the specific constructs, that is, the concrete instantiations of those constructions. The claim that there are these constructional, lexis-independent meanings can be pitted against the hypothesis that hearers build up the meaning of a sentence by accessing the meanings of the component lexical items and bringing those meanings into a coherent configuration.

To take a concrete example, the sentence *John eats a cookie* would, on that theory, be understood in such a way that hearers access the lexical meaning of *eat*, which involves two arguments, an animate agent who eats and a patient argument that is eaten, the first of which is assigned to the subject *John* and the latter to the object *a cookie*. Let us refer to this hypothesis as the **verb-centred view of sentence comprehension**. On this view, it is the verb that is the main determinant of sentence meaning. This is a very reasonable idea, given that verbs express meanings that are intrinsically relational by involving several participants. There is, furthermore, psycholinguistic evidence for the primacy of verb meaning over other determinants of sentence meaning. Healy and Miller (1970) presented speakers of English with a list of sentences, asking them to sort those sentences into sensible categories. Given this task, the participants were more likely to sort sentences according to their main verbs than according to the subject argument. However, the verb-centred view may not be the whole story. Bencini and Goldberg (2000: 641) point out two problematic issues. First, it is an empirical fact that verbs are usually not restricted to a single pattern of argument structure. As is shown below, even a verb such as *kick*, which might be considered a rather typical transitive verb, is not restricted to the TRANSITIVE construction.

(4) Pat kicked the ball.
    Pat kicked at the ball.
    Pat kicked the ball out of the stadium.
    Pat kicked Bob the ball.
    Pat kicked and kicked.
    Pat kicked his way into the Champions League.

A second problem relates to the observation that different argument structure patterns impose different constraints on the kinds of arguments that a given verb can take. As the examples below illustrate, the DITRANSITIVE construction is restricted to animate recipients whereas the PREPOSITIONAL DATIVE construction takes animate and inanimate goal arguments.

(5) I brought the patient a glass of water.   DITRANSITIVE
    I brought a glass of water to the patient.   PREPOSITIONAL DATIVE

    *I brought the table a glass of water.   DITRANSITIVE
    I brought a glass of water to the table.   PREPOSITIONAL DATIVE

On the verb-centred view of sentence comprehension, the only way to account for this would be to posit two different senses of the verb *bring*, one with a theme and a recipient argument and a second one with a theme and a goal argument. The main arguments against such a multiple-sense approach is that there is no independent reason for adopting it apart from preserving the idea of one-to-one mappings between verb senses and argument structure patterns (Goldberg 1995; cf. also the discussion in Chapter 2). The **constructional view of sentence comprehension** thus suggests itself as an alternative.

But how can it be empirically tested whether or not the meaning of argument structure constructions plays a role in sentence comprehension? Bencini and Goldberg (2000) adopt the same methodology that Healy and Miller (1970) used to uncover the importance of verb meanings for sentence comprehension, but they extend it with another variable, namely the variable of constructional form. Again, the task that participants had to accomplish was to sort sentences into sensible categories, according to overall sentence meanings. Bencini and Goldberg designed sixteen sentences with four different main verbs, namely *throw*, *take*, *get*, and *slice*. The crucial twist to the methodology is that each of these verbs appeared in four sentences that represented four different constructions, namely the TRANSITIVE construction, the DITRANSITIVE construction, the CAUSED MOTION construction, and the RESULTATIVE construction. This design creates a tension: it gives participants the option to sort by verb, but also by syntactic form. Table 6.1 shows the stimuli that Bencini and Goldberg used.

Table 6.1 Sentences used by Bencini and Goldberg (2000: 650)

	Construction			
Verb	TRANSITIVE	DITRANSITIVE	CAUSED MOTION	RESULTATIVE
throw	Anita threw the hammer.	Chris threw Linda the ball.	Pat threw the keys onto the roof.	Lyn threw the box apart.
get	Michelle got the book.	Beth got Lyn an invitation.	Laura got the ball into the net.	Dana got the mattress inflated.
slice	Barbara sliced the bread.	Jennifer sliced Terry an apple.	Meg sliced the ham onto the plate.	Nancy sliced the tyre open.
take	Audrey took the watch.	Paula took Sue a message.	Kim took the rose into the house.	Rachel took the wall down.

You will notice that the sentences in the columns share the same syntax, but not at all the same semantic content. Their similarity is abstract and relational, rather than lexical. At the same time, the sentences in the rows differ in everything except the verb. Bencini and Goldberg have thus made sure that the variables that participants could rely on are narrowly defined as either the lexical verbs or the argument structure constructions. Bencini and Goldberg (2000: 644) administered the task of sorting the sentences to seventeen participants, who were asked to produce four categories. Seven participants produced perfect constructional sortings, the remaining ten produced mixed sortings, and no participant sorted after the verbs. An analysis of the mixed sortings revealed that these were closer to a constructional sorting than to a verbal sorting: Bencini and Goldberg determined this by counting the number of changes that were necessary to transform a mixed sorting into either a constructional or a verbal sorting. These results suggest that sentence comprehension is not entirely driven by the verb, but there are other factors at play. Constructional meaning is one of those factors. Bencini and Goldberg (2000: 645) consider the possibility that perhaps the verbs that were chosen in the task were highly general, so that the participants did not recognise them as powerful clues to sentence meaning. However, this only applies to the verbs *take* and *get*, and not to *throw* and *slice*. The results do not reveal any more verbal sortings with the latter than with the former. Bencini and Goldberg therefore conclude that constructional meanings are routinely accessed during sentence comprehension.

6.2.3 Constructions explain knowledge of grammatical unacceptability

Speakers' knowledge of language includes the ability to judge whether or not a given utterance is part of that language. Many approaches to linguistic analysis exploit this and rest on the analyst's ability to distinguish acceptable and unacceptable sentences. Current work on syntax is highly critical of using acceptability judgements of the analyst as the sole source of evidence (Schütze 1996; Dąbrowska 2010; Gibson and Fedorenko 2010). The problems are manifold. First, the researcher's awareness of the research question may introduce a certain bias. Second, individual constructed sentences may be unacceptable for a wide range of reasons, which are usually not properly controlled for. Third, there is considerable variation in the acceptability judgements. The same analyst will judge the same example in different ways at different times. Furthermore, some acceptability judgements are hard to validate for non-native English linguists. Still, it will not have escaped your notice that this book has been making rather generous use of starred examples, including the following.

(6)   *What did Mary run out of the room because John started to fry?
      *The magician vanished Mary.
      *Mary explained him the news.
      *Mary considered to go to the store.
      *Mary guitared a song.

As a suggestion for best practice, Chapter 1 encouraged the use of unacceptable examples as a heuristic: it is fine to use them as 'educated guesses' about how a construction may be constrained. The crucial issue is that these guesses should be followed up by corpus-based or experimental validation.

However, regardless of whether and how acceptability judgements are used, the fact remains that speakers have intuitions that reflect constraints on constructions. Construction Grammar, as a theory of linguistic knowledge, needs to account for those intuitions. Phrasing this in more concrete terms, we have to find out how speakers know what not to say. A possible explanation would be that speakers, especially at a young age, are corrected when they say something that does not conform to conventional norms. This explanation is easily refuted on empirical grounds, since direct negative evidence is very sparse in language use. Another explanation would be that speakers are creatures of habit and are thus critical of utterances that they have not heard before. Again, the empirical evidence refutes this. There are creative uses of language that are even recognised as such but that are judged as fully acceptable. If you read in a children's book that *The dinosaur swam his friends to the mainland* you recognise that the verb *swim* is used in a somewhat creative way, but you will not write to the publisher to say that you found a grammatical error in the book. Boyd and Goldberg (2011) propose a third explanation that is in line with the constructional view of linguistic knowledge and that is amenable to empirical testing. Their explanation rests on a concept that they call **statistical pre-emption**. The basic premise of statistical pre-emption is that speakers unconsciously accomplish two things.

First, speakers form generalisations over sets of constructions that are comparable with regard to their meanings, as for instance the following pairs of constructions.

(7)   John gave Mary a book.   DITRANSITIVE
      John gave a book to Mary   PREPOSITIONAL DATIVE

the blue book	ATTRIBUTIVE ADJECTIVE
the book that is blue	RELATIVE CLAUSE
The chef melted the cheese.	TRANSITIVE
The chef made the cheese melt.	*MAKE*-CAUSATIVE
It is difficult to catch trout.	*IT*-EXTRAPOSITION
Trout are difficult to catch.	*TOUGH*-RAISING

Second, it is assumed that speakers keep a detailed record of the lexical elements that they hear in these constructions. More specifically, for any given lexical element, they will keep track of its absolute text frequency and of its relative frequencies in each member of the construction pair. Take, for instance, the verb *recommend*. If you were to guess the text frequency of *recommend* on a scale from one (very rare) to seven (extremely frequent), the chances are that you would give it a three or four, feeling that it is reasonably frequent – less frequent than *give*, but more frequent than *assign*. You know furthermore that *recommend* is commonly used in the PREPOSITIONAL DATIVE construction (*John recommended the book to Mary*) while you do not easily recall hearing it used in the DITRANSITIVE construction. Or do you? What do you think of the following examples? (Spoiler alert: they are in fact attested.)

(8) He wondered what to order, I recommended him the steak tartare.
App Man is here to recommend you the best apps of the week.
John complained that I should have recommended him the book earlier.

Maybe you are warming up to the idea that *recommend* can, on certain occasions, be used ditransitively, but for many speakers of English, this is completely out of the question. According to the idea of statistical pre-emption, speakers staunchly reject ditransitive *recommend* because given its overall text frequency, and given its frequency in the PREPOSITIONAL DATIVE construction, *recommend* is astonishingly infrequent in the DITRANSITIVE construction. In their mental record of the two constructions, speakers perceive a statistical imbalance, and they interpret that imbalance as meaningful: if a lexical item rarely or never appears where it would be expected with a certain base frequency, then it is absent because of a constructional constraint.

In order to test whether speakers rely on statistical pre-emption when they learn constructional constraints, Boyd and Goldberg (2011) designed a series of experiments that involved English *A*-ADJECTIVES such as *afraid, afloat,* and *alive*. A special characteristic of these adjectives is that they cannot be used attributively (*the afraid child, *the alive fox). This constraint is not motivated by semantic characteristics (the scared child, the living fox) or by phonological characteristics (the adult male, the astute remark); A-ADJECTIVES thus pose something of a challenge to language users. How do speakers acquire the knowledge that some adjectives are for predicative use only? Boyd and Goldberg presented participants with visual scenes on a computer screen. The scene showed three elements, namely two identical animals in the lower half of the screen and a star at the top of the screen. Each scene was described with a short sentence, such as Here are two cows. In the experimental trials, one of the animals moved across the screen, towards the star. Both animals were labelled with a word, for instance an adjective such as vigilant or sleepy. The task that speakers had to accomplish was to identify verbally which of the two animals had moved. The grammar of English holds two basic possibilities for doing this: speakers could use an ATTRIBUTIVE ADJECTIVE construction and say The sleepy cow moved to the star or they could use a RELATIVE CLAUSE construction to say The cow that is sleepy moved to the star. Both variants were used in a short training phase that familiarised participants with the experimental procedure. In order to elicit both construction types, Boyd and Goldberg included filler trials of two kinds. In the first kind, animals were labelled with verbal attributes such as smokes or gambles. Faced with such an attribute, participants had to resort to the RELATIVE CLAUSE construction and respond The cow that gambles moved to the star. The second kind consisted of very frequent adjectival attributes such as slow or fast. These adjectives have a natural disposition to occur prenominally, so that speakers would be biased towards using the ATTRIBUTIVE ADJECTIVE construction.

In a first experiment, Boyd and Goldberg investigated whether speaker would avoid attributive uses of common A-ADJECTIVES such as asleep or afraid, and more importantly, whether they would treat novel A-ADJECTIVES, that is, coinages such as ablim or adax, in the same way. The results showed the expected effect for known A-ADJECTIVES: the participants used the RELATIVE CLAUSE construction in the large majority of cases. A significant effect, albeit weaker, was also observed with novel A-ADJECTIVES. This observation is evidence that speakers of English entertain a generalisation, the A-ADJECTIVE construction, and that they will consider novel adjectives such as adax as falling under that generalisation. However, the weaker preference of novel A-ADJECTIVES for the RELATIVE CLAUSE construction suggests that some speakers were uncertain whether or not to view the novel stimuli as A-ADJECTIVES. After all, there are forms such as adult or astute that are not A-ADJECTIVES.

To solidify these insights, Boyd and Goldberg implemented a second experiment that was identical in procedure to the first one, but which differed in how participants were trained for the experimental task. In the explanation of the experimental procedure, participants were given examples that included novel *A*-ADJECTIVES, for which the experimenter offered the RELATIVE CLAUSE construction as a description. Hence, participants saw screens with animals and heard the experimenter say *The lizard that is adax moved to the star.* Does an exposure of this kind alter the subsequent responses to previously unheard *A*-ADJECTIVES? The responses that Boyd and Goldberg obtained show that participants were quick to generalise from one attested novel *A*-ADJECTIVE to other potential *A*-ADJECTIVES. Whereas the first experiment showed a substantial difference between common and novel *A*-ADJECTIVES, that difference disappeared in the second experiment. What encourages hearers to treat novel *A*-ADJECTIVES as such is the process of statistical pre-emption: hearing a novel *A*-ADJECTIVE in a RELATIVE CLAUSE construction, where an ATTRIBUTIVE ADJECTIVE construction would be expected as a default, leads hearers to infer the presence of a constraint. The RELATIVE CLAUSE construction serves as a cue for this, and Boyd and Goldberg call this cue the **pre-emptive context**.

If you think about it, identifying a construction as a pre-emptive context is not trivial; it involves quite sophisticated counterfactual reasoning. The hearer observes the speaker choose a construction, the hearer knows that there are other constructions that serve similar functions, and depending on the relative frequencies of the alternative constructions the hearer constructs an explanation for why the speaker would not have chosen a more frequent construction. The activity of mind-reading, which informed much of the discussion in Chapter 5 on information packaging, is again visible in this kind of reasoning. To investigate this process more closely, Boyd and Goldberg carried out a third experiment that introduced another small but crucial variation. The training phase of the second experiment was altered in such a way that novel *A*-ADJECTIVES appeared in contexts where they were coordinated with a complex adjectival phrase. Hence, participants watched a screen with two hamsters and heard the experimenter say *The hamster that is ablim and proud of itself moved to the star.* The subsequent experimental task remained the same as in the two previous experiments. What results do you expect? Do you think that the participants took the relative clause as a cue that *ablim* is an *A*-ADJECTIVE? In all likelihood, you do not, and you are right. The participants discounted that cue because any two coordinated adjectives would require a relative clause. The length of the coordinated adjective phrase is the simplest explanation for the speaker's choice. Accordingly, the results resembled those of experiment one rather than those of experiment two: whereas the participants were hesitant to use adjectives such as *ablim* or *adax* attributively in experiment two, they were much more ready to do so in experiments one and three.

To draw a conclusion from these observations: the constructional view of linguistic knowledge holds an explanation for the fact that speakers intuitively know when an utterance is grammatically unacceptable. All utterances that hearers process are categorised in terms of the constructions that they instantiate, and relations between constructions allow hearers to notice when one alternative is chosen despite the availability of another, more basic alternative. When such pre-emptive contexts are noticed, it leads hearers to infer constraints. Hearers interpret speakers' choices as meaningful, as reflecting grammatical conventions. A grammatically deviant sentence thus evokes the gut feeling that given the circumstances, the speaker ought to have chosen a different construction.

6.2.4 Constructions explain incidental verbatim memory

Most current models of language comprehension make the assumption that once a hearer has heard and understood a sentence, it is the general meaning of the sentence that is retained in memory while the specifics of its structure are quickly forgotten (e.g. Loebell and Bock 2003). Only in exceptional circumstances – say, in situations where it is clear that specific wordings have to be memorised or where an utterance is particularly funny or shocking – will hearers retain verbatim memories. This consensus, which is backed up by a substantial literature of empirical findings, is something of an embarrassment to Construction Grammar. If constructions are meaningful, and if meanings are memorised, why do hearers not keep a memory record of the constructional forms? What the constructional view of linguistic knowledge would predict is that forms are remembered along with meanings. In order to test whether or not this is the case, Gurevich et al. (2010) reopened the case for verbatim memory in language.

In a first experiment, they presented participants with thirty-two illustrated pages of the children's book *I Am Spider-Man*. Each picture was accompanied by three to four sentences that were presented auditorily, as recorded by a male narrator. The presentation of the entire story took around four minutes. Crucially, Gurevich et al. prepared two versions of the story that were identical in content but that differed with regard to the constructions that were used. The examples below illustrate parts of the different stories.

(9) Story version 1:   My fingers can stick to anything.
    Story version 2:   I can stick my fingers to anything.

    Story version 1:   I am strong enough to fight four bad guys at once!
    Story version 2:   Fighting four guys at once is easy for someone as strong as me.

Immediately after hearing the story, the participants were asked to perform a recognition task in which written sentences were presented on a computer screen and the participants had to decide whether or not the sentences had been part of the story. Before each sentence, a picture from the story was shown for one second. The pictures were either related to the sentence in question or unrelated. Upon reading the sentences, subjects pressed one of two keys to indicate whether they recognised a previously heard sentence. Gurevich et al. (2010: 52) found that their participants performed this task with great accuracy. Furthermore, the researchers replicated this result with a second experiment in which the story versions differed only in terms of function words. Notice that the sentences in the second pair given above contain different elements, such as *bad* in the first one and *easy* in the second one. In order to exclude possible effects due to lexical elements, all sentence pairs were constructed like the first one given above, where the only difference lies in word order and the grammatical element *I*. In a third experiment, different participants heard the *Spider-Man* story and were subsequently asked to retell the story while being prompted with the pictures. Retold sentences were counted as a match if they differed by no more than one word from the original. Again, Gurevich et al. obtained substantial evidence for verbatim memory.

It could be pointed out that in all of these experiments, the time between exposure and recall was relatively short and that this may have inflated the effect. In a final experiment, Gurevich et al. tested whether verbatim memory would still show an effect after a delay or several days. Participants were exposed to a narration of a video clip showing an episode of *Felix the Cat*. The narrator was an experimenter in the disguise of a fellow participant. Listeners were encouraged to return for another experiment after six days. On that occasion, the listeners were shown the same video clip and were asked to narrate the clip to another participant, again an experimenter in disguise. Transcriptions of the spontaneous narrations reveal a substantial ratio of sentences that fully match the utterances that the participants had heard during the first experimental session. Gurevich et al. thus maintain that verbatim memory is retained even for prolonged periods of time. This of course does not go against the finding that the extraction of general meanings also takes place, but it reconciles the constructional view of linguistic knowledge with the empirical findings of whether and how linguistic structures are memorised. On a dictionary-and-grammar view of linguistic knowledge, it would seem natural that memory of syntactic structures is quickly discarded. A constructional view predicts that verbatim memory should be retained to a substantial degree, and it explains speakers' ability to retain these memories with reference to constructions as pairings of meaning with morphosyntactic form.

6.3 Evidence from language production

6.3.1 Constructions explain reduction effects in speech

How carefully speakers enunciate their words is a matter of considerable variation. You are more likely to articulate your words carefully in situations that are formal, when your addressees are unknown to you or socially superior, or when there is ambient noise that impairs auditory comprehension. Besides these language-external variables, crucial linguistic variables concern the frequency and the predictability of the words that you are using. A word such as *and* is very frequent, which means that you have a lot of practice pronouncing it and with routine typically comes reduction. Moreover, in some contexts the word *and* is highly predictable. If a sequence of three words begins with *gin* and ends with *tonic*, the chances are that you can work out which word occurs in between. Phonetic reduction as a consequence of frequency and predictability is very well documented (e.g. Jurafsky et al. 2001). This section will make the case that this effect is observed not only on the level of words, but also on the level of constructions. That is, words are pronounced in a more reduced fashion if they occur in a construction of which they are highly typical.

Empirical evidence for this claim is presented by Gahl and Garnsey (2004), who asked their participants to read out sentences such as the following.

(10) The director suggested the scene should be filmed at night.
      The director suggested the scene between Kim and Mike.

      The confident engineer maintained the machinery of the whole upper deck.
      The confident engineer maintained the machinery would be hard to destroy.

All sentences included a complement-taking predicate such as *suggest* or *believe*; what was varied was the construction that represented the verb's complementation pattern. In the examples above, one pattern following the verbs is the THAT-LESS COMPLEMENT CLAUSE construction, while the other one is a complex noun phrase, so that the overall sentence instantiates the TRANSITIVE construction. Crucially, the verbs that were used as stimuli co-occur with these constructions to different extents. For instance, the verb *suggest* co-occurs with complement clauses more often than with direct objects, so that the first sentence given above is more likely than the second one. Conversely, the verb *maintain* is more strongly associated with the TRANSITIVE construction, so that the sentence with the complement clause would be less likely. Gahl and Garnsey told the participants that they were recording stimuli for a different experiment and asked them to read the sentences. The researchers then measured the length with which the verbs in question were pronounced. The main result is that the constructional bias of the verbs significantly correlates with reduced production (2004: 763). Verbs such as *argue, believe, claim, conclude, confess*, or *decide* are pronounced shorter when they occur in the THAT-LESS COMPLEMENT CLAUSE construction, and they are longer if they occur with a direct object. Conversely, verbs such as *accept, advocate, confirm*, or *emphasise* are reduced when occurring with a direct object, but not when they take a complement clause. Gahl and Garnsey draw the conclusion that speakers' knowledge of language includes the probabilities of co-occurrence between verbs and constructions, and that this knowledge affects reduction in speech (2004: 768). The effects that Gahl and Garnsey observe would be difficult to explain as purely collocational relations between individual words. Note that the lexical items surrounding the verbs in the stimuli sentences are exactly the same. The results only make sense in the light of constructions and their association with lexical elements.

6.3.2 Constructions explain syntactic priming, and exceptions to syntactic priming

Priming is a psychological concept that describes how the mental activation of one idea facilitates the subsequent activation of another idea. Hearing a word such as *chicken* will prime a semantically related word such as *egg*, as can be shown empirically by comparing how fast hearers react to this word, for instance in a lexical decision task that asks them to verify whether *egg* is a proper word of English. Primed with *chicken*, a word such as *egg* is verified faster than a semantically unrelated word such as *bag* (Neely 1976). The term **syntactic priming** refers to something similar, namely the phenomenon that speakers tend to repeat syntactic structures that they have recently heard or produced. Other commonly used labels for this phenomenon are structural priming or syntactic persistence. Experimental evidence for syntactic priming includes the finding that speakers who are primed with either the ACTIVE construction or the PASSIVE construction are likely to reuse the respective construction in a subsequent picture description task.

Bock (1986) devised an experiment that was presented to the participants as a memory task, in which they were asked to repeat sentences such as the following.

(11)   One of the fans punched the referee.
        The referee was punched by one of the fans.

In critical trials, these sentences were followed by a picture that the participants were asked to describe. The pictures would show scenes that lent themselves to verbalisation through either an ACTIVE construction or the PASSIVE construction. For instance, one of the pictures showed a church with lightning hitting the church steeple. Hence, the participants were able to produce an active description such as *Lightning is striking the church* or a passive description such as *The church is being hit by lightning*. Bock (1986: 364) observed an asymmetry in the responses that corresponded to the syntactic prime. If the participants had been primed with a passive sentence, the likelihood of a passive picture description increased significantly. An exactly parallel effect was obtained through priming with the DITRANSITIVE construction and the PREPOSITIONAL DATIVE construction. Repeating a sentence such as *The undercover agent sold some cocaine to the rock star* increased the likelihood that the participants used the PREPOSITIONAL DATIVE construction for the description of a scene in which a grandfather is reading a book to his grandchild. Bock's results are consistent with the idea that speakers' knowledge of language consists of a network of constructions which can be activated to greater or lesser extents at a given point in time. If a construction has been activated through recent usage, and speakers encounter a situation that is compatible with the meaning of that construction, they are thus likely to use the construction in verbalising their experience.

Syntactic priming does not only occur in the psychological laboratory, but can be observed in naturally occurring language use as well. Gries (2005) presents an analysis of corpus data in which he analyses whether the use of a DITRANSITIVE construction or a PREPOSITIONAL DATIVE construction has a measurable effect on the subsequent verbalisation of 'dative' events, that is, events in which either of the two constructions could be used. Gries retrieved several thousand pairs of dative sentences from the British component of the International Corpus of English (ICE-GB) and annotated each pair for a number of variables. The central variable, of course, was whether or not the members of the pair were structurally identical. Beyond that, it was noted whether the respective sentences were produced by the same speaker or writer, whether the main verb was the same or not, and how many sentences intervened between the sentences. These annotations allow a more detailed view on the factors that operate in syntactic priming.

Gries finds, first of all, a strong effect of syntactic priming (2005: 372). After the occurrence of a DITRANSITIVE construction, speakers reuse that construction more often than would be expected if it were by chance. With regard to the remaining variables, Gries reports that syntactic priming is especially strong if the two members of the pair contain the same main verb. This phenomenon is referred to as the **lexical boost** in the literature on syntactic priming (Pickering and Ferreira 2008). Furthermore, the priming effect is stronger when a single speaker produces both members of a pair. Priming is thus more intensive from production to subsequent production than from hearing to subsequent production. Gries also notes that the strength of priming wears off with increasing distance between the prime and the target, which is to be explained as the fading of the constructions' cognitive activation. Lastly, an important finding that emerges from the analysis is that some verbs are much more sensitive to syntactic priming than others. Gries compares the verbs *give, hand, lend, sell, send, show,* and *offer* and finds that there are substantial differences with regard to the effect strength of syntactic priming:

- *show, offer,* and *give* typically occur in DITRANSITIVE sentences, regardless of the construction that is used in the prime;
- *sell* and *hand* typically occur in PREPOSITIONAL DATIVE sentences, regardless of the construction that is used in the prime; and
- *send* and *lend* typically occur in sentences that instantiate the construction that is used in the prime.

This result is an important qualification of the overall idea of syntactic priming. Some verbs have construction-specific preferences and therefore resist priming. The effect of syntactic priming is thus carried by those verbs that alternate relatively freely between the two constructions. This result naturally integrates into a constructional view of linguistic knowledge in which constructions have collocational preferences (cf. Chapter 1, Section 1.3.4). A verb such as *show* is strongly associated with the DITRANSITIVE construction. If a speaker wants to verbalise a scene of showing – say, a boy showing his mother a scratch on his knee – speakers are inherently biased towards using the DITRANSITIVE construction. Having heard a PREPOSITIONAL DATIVE construction in the preceding context may act as a competing force, but this force would have to overcome the strong association between *show* and the DITRANSITIVE construction. More often than not, the priming effect will be neutralised.

6.3.3 Constructions explain how speakers complete sentences

Chapter 5 briefly discussed the notion of projection (Auer 2005). The fact that speakers are able to finish each other's sentences shows indirectly that their processing of language involves constant anticipation of the material that will come up next. Constructions have a rather central role to play in this process. A phrase such as *The more I read about Construction Grammar* leads hearers to anticipate the second half of the THE *X*-ER THE *Y*-ER construction, as, for instance, *the less I understand about it.* By the same token, the study by Gahl and Garnsey (2004) that was discussed above showed that in a string such as *The director suggested* the verb is produced in a more reduced fashion if the string is followed by a *THAT*-LESS COMPLEMENT CLAUSE construction, which is the option that hearers can project with greater confidence. A question of interest with regard to projection is what exactly counts as a cue for projection and how reliable those cues are. Whereas the first half of a THE *X*-ER THE *Y*-ER construction predicts the future occurrence of a second half with almost complete certainty, most cues are not as reliable. Verbs such as *suggest* or *maintain* only allow tentative predictions with regard to their complementation patterns. How can we measure and compare the strength of different cues?

A straightforward answer to that question would be that we should look at usage frequencies in order to determine what lexical and grammatical constructions are likely to co-occur. In the case of *suggest*, it is easy to measure on the basis of corpus data in how many of all instances the verb is followed by a *THAT*-LESS COMPLEMENT CLAUSE construction. If that were the case in 60 per cent of all cases, that would translate into a rather strong expectation. Measurements of simple relative frequencies would thus represent estimates of **cue validity**, a term that designates how safely you can make an assumption, given the presence of a cue. To illustrate: if I am asking you to guess what animal I am currently thinking of, the feature 'it has a trunk' has a rather high cue validity, as compared to 'it has eyes'. However, with linguistic constructions, the issue is often a little more complicated than that. Consider an auxiliary verb construction such as English *shall* followed by an infinitive. Take any corpus of English, and the most frequent verb to follow *shall* will be the verb *to be* (cf. Hilpert 2008: 43). Does that mean that hearing *shall* leads hearers to expect that *be* will be next? It has to be pointed out that *be* is a very frequent form to begin with, and it is found frequently not only after *shall*, but also after other auxiliary verbs.

Stefanowitsch and Gries (2003) make the case that the cognitive associations between constructions and the lexical elements occurring in those constructions should be measured not in simple relative frequencies, but rather in terms that show whether an element occurs with surprisingly high frequency in a construction. Consider the following contrast between the collocations *shall be* and *shall consider*. The former occurs some 2,000 times in the BNC, the latter only roughly 200 times. That is a difference of ten to one. Yet it could be argued that the collocational bond of *shall consider* is relatively stronger, because *consider* is a much less frequent verb than *be*: the BNC contains some 7,600 infinitive forms of *consider*, but more than half a million infinitives of *be*. The bottom line is that the collocation *shall consider* is surprisingly frequent, given the frequencies of its parts, whereas *shall be* is not. In fact, if the high text frequency of *be* is taken into account, then it turns out that 2,000 instances of *shall be* are significantly fewer than would be expected if it were by chance. Taking these probabilities into account would translate into the hypothesis that hearers who are exposed to the string *The international committee shall . . .* would project verbs such as *consider*, *examine*, *discuss*, or *continue*, which are not the most frequent verbs to follow *shall*, but which are verbs that follow *shall* with surprisingly high frequency (Hilpert 2008: 37).

Not everyone takes this view. Goldberg et al. (2004: 308) and more recently Bybee (2010: 97) argue that simple relative frequencies most accurately reflect cognitive associations between constructions and lexical elements. In order to investigate the issue, Gries et al. (2005) carried out a study of the *As*-PREDICATIVE construction, which is illustrated in the examples given below.

(12) The proposal was considered as rather provocative.
I had never seen myself as being too thin.
California is perceived as a place where everything is possible.

We are dealing with a PREDICATIVE construction because an entity *X* is being given the characteristic or quality *Y*, as in the PREDICATE NOMINAL construction (*Jane is a doctor*) or the PREDICATIVE ADJECTIVE construction (*The coffee is too hot*). Whereas these more basic predicative constructions include a simple copula as their main verb, the *As*-PREDICATIVE construction features a verb of perception (*see, perceive, view*) or cognition (*consider, regard, know*). These verbs occur in the construction with different frequencies. The most frequent verb is *see*, but crucially, the cue validity of that verb for the *As*-PREDICATIVE construction is relatively low. A string such as *I had never seen*... could be continued in many ways that do not involve that construction. By contrast, a string such as *The idea was hailed*... strongly cues the *As*-PREDICATIVE construction, despite the fact that the verb *hail* occurs much less frequently in the construction than *see*. Gries et al. extracted all examples of the *As*-PREDICATIVE construction from the ICE-GB, identified the verb types that occurred in the construction, and analysed their frequencies statistically in order to group the verb types into the four categories that are shown in Table 6.2 (Gries et al. 2005: 657).

Table 6.2 Verbs in the *As*-PREDICATIVE and their frequencies

	Relative frequency	
	High	Low
Surprisingly high frequency in the *As*-PREDICATIVE	define, describe, know, recognise, regard, see, use, view	acknowledge, class, conceive, denounce, depict, diagnose, hail, rate
Surprisingly low frequency in the *As*-PREDICATIVE	keep, leave, refer to, show	build, choose, claim, intend, offer, present, represent, suggest

Gries et al. (2005) then generated stimulus sentence fragments with each of the verbs in Table 6.2. Since the *As*-PREDICATIVE construction commonly involves the PASSIVE construction, both active and passive stimuli were created for each verb, such as the following.

(13)   The biographer depicted the young philosopher...
        The young philosopher was depicted...

On the basis of these stimuli, Gries et al. conducted an experiment in which participants were asked to complete the sentence fragments in the way that seemed most natural to them. The participants were told that the experiment investigated 'the kinds of English sentences that people produce'. What Gries et al. wanted to find out, of course, was which factor would lead the participants to produce an *As*-PREDICATIVE. The results indicate that surprisingly high frequency is a much better predictor for this than high relative frequency (Gries et al. 2005: 659). This is evidence that speakers of English do some rather sophisticated statistical book-keeping of the frequencies of lexical items across different constructions. A view of linguistic knowledge without reference to constructions would be at a loss when trying to explain these patterns. On a view of the construct-i-con as a repository of interconnected constructions, these results are expected as a matter of course.

6.4 Summing up

The discussion in this chapter started with the distinction of two types of evidence that could be used to support theoretical claims. First, there is evidence that we gather through the careful observation of individual linguistic forms. For instance, we might observe that the statement *That's too good a deal to pass up* contains a noun phrase that deviates from canonical noun phrase patterns, which would lead us to posit a construction (more specifically, the BIG MESS construction; cf. Van Eynde 2007). It is this kind of evidence that has primarily been at issue in the first five chapters of this book. The second type of evidence is called behavioural evidence. As the name suggests, it reflects speaker behaviour, more specifically speaker behaviour under controlled experimental conditions. In order to gather evidence of this kind, researchers typically design experiments in which one or more factors are actively manipulated. The introduction to this chapter offered an analogy in which the participants of an experiment are divided into two groups, each of which receives food of a different kind. Differences that are measured in a subsequent test could be related to the foods in question. Many linguistic experiments aim to find differences between groups of participants in this way, but it is also possible to work with a single group of participants. There, the manipulation concerns the experimental task itself, so that each participant carries out two slightly different versions of the same task. For instance, an experiment might investigate whether participants recognise English words faster if they have been primed with semantically related words. All participants in such a study would perform under two different conditions: there are trials in which prime and target are related (*chicken – egg*), and trials in which prime and target are unrelated (*chicken – bag*). Both evidence from observation and behavioural evidence are necessary for the development of linguistic theories, and even though neither can be viewed as inherently superior, behavioural evidence has one decisive advantage: if statements are to be made about cause and effect, mere observation does not yield conclusive evidence. Conversely, if the researcher manages to switch the effect on and off through active manipulation in an experiment, then she has actually identified the cause. The main point of this chapter was to review the pieces of behavioural evidence that are consonant with the constructional view of linguistic knowledge. Two major types of evidence were discussed, namely evidence from language comprehension and evidence from language production.

Experiments that investigate language comprehension present the participants with some linguistic stimulus and measure a reaction to that stimulus. Sometimes that reaction is non-linguistic, such as the press of a button; sometimes it is linguistic, as for instance the formulation of a response sentence. A first piece of evidence for Construction Grammar from language comprehension is that hearers routinely use constructions to understand the meanings of novel denominal verbs such as *to crutch, to saxophone,* or *to envelope.* Kaschak and Glenberg (2000) investigated how participants understood these verbs and found that the respective interpretations were strongly influenced by the constructional context. A second piece of evidence is provided by Bencini and Goldberg (2000), who demonstrated an influence of constructions on sentence comprehension. Participants were given the task of sorting a set of sentences according to their overall meanings, and the results showed that syntactic form had a measurable influence on the sortings. Third, knowledge of constructions relates to meta-linguistic tasks such as rating the acceptability of phrases and sentences. Using the example of *A*-ADJECTIVES as a test case, Boyd and Goldberg (2011) show that knowledge of grammatical unacceptability is the result of hearers' categorising utterances as constructions, which allows them to notice when one alternative is chosen despite the availability of another, more basic alternative. When hearers notice speakers making such choices, it triggers what Boyd and Goldberg call statistical pre-emption, that is, the inference of grammatical conventions from hearing a construction other than the one that would be expected if it were by default. A fourth piece of evidence for the constructional view of linguistic knowledge is the observation that verbatim memory is more persistent than has been generally thought. Whereas most current models of language comprehension assume an abstraction process which transfers the gist of sentences into memory but discards specifics of the morphosyntactic structure, Gurevich et al. (2010) show that hearers retain a substantial amount of verbatim memory, even when they are not explicitly asked to do so. On the view that constructions are pairings of meaning and form, that result is to be expected.

Experiments that investigate language production prompt the participants to offer a linguistic response that is audio-recorded and typically further analysed. Sometimes the task of the experiment may be just that participants are asked to read out written words or sentences; in other cases the task might be to describe a picture or a video. The chapter reviewed three pieces of evidence for Construction Grammar from language production. First, Gahl and Garnsey (2004) got participants to read sentences with complement-taking predicates such as *The director suggested the scene should be filmed at night.* One central finding of the study was that verbs were produced in a more reduced fashion if they were followed by a construction that typically co-occurs with them. Verbs such as *argue* or *suggest* are pronounced shorter when they are followed by a complement clause, and they are longer if they occur with a direct object. This result makes sense if linguistic knowledge is viewed as a repository of constructions that have associative links to lexical elements, whereas in the absence of that assumption it is hard to explain. Second, the assumption of constructions and their associations with lexical elements is consonant with findings on syntactic priming. Gries (2005) finds that use of the DITRANSITIVE construction in corpus data increases the likelihood of that construction in the expression of a following dative event. However, this effect is neutralised when the following dative event involves verbs such as *sell* or *hand*, which are strongly associated with the PREPOSITIONAL DATIVE construction. The lexical specificity of syntactic priming is problematic for accounts that aim to explain syntactic priming as a matter of form only, but the finding is fully expected on the constructional view. Third, knowledge of constructions explains how speakers complete sentence fragments. Gries et al. (2005) asked experiment participants to complete fragments such as *The young philosopher was depicted,* and noted which of their stimuli were completed with the *As*-PREDICATIVE construction. The results indicate that such continuations were especially likely if the main verb given in the stimulus was strongly associated with the construction.

In summary, there is a growing body of research that addresses language comprehension and language production from a constructional point of view. That said, since this line of work is a relatively recent enterprise, many of the findings presented in this chapter still await further substantiation through studies that replicate and extend them. Also, the thematic focus of the constructional psycholinguistic work that has been done so far is relatively narrow. Whereas quite a few studies address argument structure constructions, less work is done on morphological constructions or information structure constructions. Hence, students who are interested in the psycholinguistics of Construction Grammar will discover that this particular area offers a wealth of new and interesting dissertation topics.

Study questions

- What does it mean to 'manipulate a factor' in a psycholinguistic experiment?
- Describe the setup of the experimental tasks used by Kaschak and Glenberg (2000).
- What is the verb-centred view of sentence comprehension and what are its problems?
- Explain the concepts of statistical pre-emption and define what a pre-emptive context is. You can use the following ungrammatical example to illustrate your explanation.

  *I recommend you the white wine.

- Compare the following two sentences. Considering the findings presented by Gahl and Garnsey (2004), what would you expect with regard to the pronunciation of the adjective *easy* in these sentences?

  I found the z-score easy to interpret.
  I found the scene more easy to interpret.

- Which finding in Gries (2005) goes beyond the results of Bock (1986), and what does this finding imply with regard to the constructional view of linguistic knowledge?
- How do Gries et al. (2005) investigate whether simple relative frequencies or unexpectedly high frequencies capture more accurately speakers' cognitive associations between constructions and lexical items?

Further reading

Like the present chapter, Goldberg and Bencini (2005) offer a survey of experimental studies that yield evidence for Construction Grammar on the basis of behavioural data from language production and language comprehension. Bencini (2013) approaches the role of psycholinguistics in Construction Grammar more generally and explains a number of central issues in language processing. The concept of statistical pre-emption is further elaborated in Goldberg (2011) and Stefanowitsch (2011). On the issue of relative frequencies vs. surprisingly high frequencies, chapter 5 in Bybee (2010) presents several criticisms of Stefanowitsch and Gries (2003), to which Gries (2012) offers responses.

7 Constructions and language acquisition

7.1 Construction Grammar for kids

As the previous chapters have discussed, linguistic theories can make very different assumptions about how knowledge of language is organised in the speaker's mind. In particular, the discussion presented the constructional view of linguistic knowledge, which equates knowledge of language with a large repository of constructions, namely the contruct-i-con, and this view was contrasted with the dictionary-and-grammar view of linguistic knowledge, which separates knowledge of grammatical rules from knowledge of lexical items. These two theories not only differ with respect to the linguistic knowledge of competent adult speakers, but also make very different predictions about how children learn a first language, and how this process should be reflected in the things that young children say.

On the face of it, there appears to be quite a bit of evidence in favour of an account that equates language acquisition with the learning of words and rules. If you have taken an introductory linguistics class, you will have encountered the statement that young children do not just repeat what their caretakers say; instead, they combine words into new and original utterances that they cannot possibly have heard before. Chapter 4 has already offered the example of the wug study (Berko Gleason 1958), which demonstrated that young children routinely master the allomorphy rules of the PLURAL construction, so that they can talk about *wugs*, *heafs*, and *gutches*, choosing the right plural ending for words that they have never encountered before. Many more examples of this kind can be adduced. Consider the following authentic utterances.

(1) a. Want other one spoon, Daddy.
    b. It noises.
    c. I becamed to be Spiderman.
    d. She unlocked it open.

155

From the perspective of adult language, these utterances deviate from conventional norms, but at the same time, they reveal some rather sophisticated reasoning about linguistic generalisations. Take the first example, in which the child uses *other one* in the place of a demonstrative determiner such as *that*. The respective functions of *other one* and demonstrative *that* are clearly related, so that the child's utterance represents a reasonable guess as to what the grammar of English could be like. Likewise, the second example *It noises* betrays a generalisation across words such as *buzz*, *crash*, *roar*, or *cough*, all of which denote sounds and are used as both nouns and verbs. This kind of error is called an **overgeneralisation error**, and it is important because it signals that the child has acquired something more than just a fixed string that it can repeat. An overgeneralisation error shows that the child has learned a regularity about language. At the same time, the error shows that the child has still to acquire certain constraints on that regularity. Overgeneralisation errors are also in evidence in the third and fourth example; the form *becamed* represents a compromise between the child's having heard the irregular form *became* and knowing that regular past tense forms take a dental *-ed* suffix. The last example is a use of the verb *unlock* in the RESULTATIVE construction, which is not conventionally possible in adult usage of the construction.

Importantly, the constructional view and the dictionary-and-grammar view agree on the fact that children acquire generalisations, be they called rules or constructions. However, the two views make different predictions about the process that leads up to the adult state of linguistic knowledge. These differences are discussed in the following sections.

7.1.1 Item-based learning

On a rule-based account of language acquisition, the child has to master formal schemas that are abstract, that is, based on syntactic and part-of-speech categories. As an example, you might think of the PREDICATIVE ADJECTIVE construction, which in adult usage consists of a subject noun phrase, a copula, and an adjective. During early phases of acquisition, the child may produce utterances such as *towel wet*, which are missing certain features of the adult construction, but which are nonetheless clearly modelled on the adult construction. What the rule-based account assumes is that the child has in fact acquired the adult schema, even if the realisation of that schema is still hampered by the child's as-yet imperfect mastery of language production. This assumption is called the **continuity hypothesis**, and it states that the language of children is mentally represented by the same syntactic rules and categories as adult language (Pinker 1984). Knowing an abstract schema enables the child to formulate new and original utterances. In such utterances, a schema such as the PREDICATIVE ADJECTIVE construction is fleshed out with lexical words that are retrieved from the mental dictionary. Note that this process requires the child to have a grasp on word classes: in order to select the words for an utterance such as *towel wet* it has to be aware that *towel* is a noun and *wet* is an adjective. When learning new words, the child thus has to mark up each new word for its part-of-speech category, so that it knows how that word can be inserted into the formal schemas of its language.

The constructional account offers a very different perspective on early language learning. Most importantly, perhaps, the formal schemas that children acquire are viewed as intimately connected with the lexical material that occurs in them. It is thus assumed that children start out by learning concrete phrases that only gradually become more abstract, as the child recognises similarities across different concrete phrases. The child's mental representations of language structures are thus assumed to be different from adults' mental representations. Also on the constructional account, children are thought to acquire abstract schemas, but these are believed to be the outcome of hearing many similarly structured utterances, and they emerge only in a gradual, piecemeal fashion. This way of acquiring generalisations is referred to as **item-based learning** of linguistic schemas (Tomasello 2000a). The constructional, item-based view of language acquisition implies that children's constructions have to be studied on their own terms. The adult grammar is not to be seen as the standard that somehow underlies children's utterances; rather, the constructional view holds that children's utterances directly reflect their knowledge of language. Rather than projecting adult-like structures into the child's linguistic competence, the constructional view thus holds that what you see is what you get. This has fundamental consequences for the way in which research on language acquisition is carried out. What is studied in constructional approaches to language acquisition is how children gradually build up their construct-i-con and how that construct-i-con is restructured over the course of language acquisition.

A large part of this chapter will be devoted to the discussion of case studies that empirically test whether the item-based nature of language learning makes the right predictions about children's linguistic behaviour. We will consider how children learn abstract constructions, what factors facilitate construction learning, and how children form generalisations that eventually even go beyond single constructions. We will furthermore reassess the question how original and creative early child language really is. A robust finding across many empirical studies of language acquisition is that children are rather conservative users of language. With child language not being as creative as usually advertised, much of the initial plausibility of rule-based approaches to language acquisition is lost.

7.1.2 The sociocognitive foundation of language learning

Another fundamental difference between the constructional view and a dictionary-and-grammar view concerns the sociocognitive foundations of language learning. The formal schemas of the dictionary-and-grammar approach are in no way connected to the social environment of young children, which necessarily brings up the question how their acquisition is possible at all. How are children supposed to work out that there are grammatical categories such as subject and object, verbs, adjectives, and prepositions, and syntactic schemas such as TOUGH-RAISING or SUBJECT–AUXILIARY INVERSION? When the question is phrased in this way, the most realistic answer seems to be that they cannot possibly work out these things from the utterances they hear. The language input is too messy for that. The language that babies hear is for the most part imperfect, riddled with false starts and inaccuracies, and much too unsystematic to provide reliable and unambiguous evidence to distinguish all the grammatical structures from the possible but ungrammatical structures. This is the argument from the **poverty of the stimulus**, that is, the idea that the language input is insufficient for the acquisition of language (Chomsky 1959). If the structures of language cannot be learned from the input alone, that means that human beings must be born with an innate cognitive capacity that already specifies general grammatical principles that guide the process of language acquisition. This idea is known as the theory of **universal grammar**, which has been entertained in different versions and which is still part of current views of language acquisition (Hauser et al. 2002). Since human communication differs considerably from animal communication (Hockett 1966; Hauser 1996), universal grammar is thought to be completely disconnected from animal communication systems in evolutionary terms.

The constructional view of language acquisition does not dispute the fact that human beings are innately equipped with the ability to learn language. After all, the ability to acquire language is distinctly human. The communication systems that animals use differ in multiple respects from human language, and beyond that, humans are the only species that have developed an array of communication systems that are mutually unintelligible (Tomasello 2003: 1). Whereas animal communication systems tend to be shared across an entire species, humans can only communicate effectively with certain subgroups of their own species. Regrettably, knowing English does not automatically enable you to understand Sinhala, Finnish, or Quechua. It is thus evident that there is something special about human beings, and there is no disagreement about this point. Where the constructional approach differs from the dictionary-and-grammar view of linguistic knowledge is with regard to the question whether this special innate quality is language-specific. The assumption that is entertained by the constructional approach is that language learning depends on a set of sociocognitive abilities that are specific to humans, but not to language (Tomasello 2003: 3). As will be discussed in more detail below, these abilities make it possible for the child to acquire language in a socially grounded fashion. On the constructional view, the item-based schemas that children acquire are, via their lexical elements, tied to specific situations and situation types. This observation harks back to Goldberg's scene encoding hypothesis, but it is more encompassing than that, since Goldberg's hypothesis is about argument structure constructions only whereas the item-based schemas that characterise early child language are much more lexically specific and much less syntactically complex. On the constructional view then, children's acquisition of language is grounded in common scenes of experience that are socially shared, usually with caretakers, siblings, or peers. In order for language learning to take place, the child needs to experience these scenes and it needs to have the general sociocognitive abilities that are discussed in more detail in the following paragraphs.

The first of these abilities is the child's aptitude to engage in what is called **joint attention**. In order for language to become meaningful, the child has to be in a situation in which both the child and a caretaker focus on an object and are mutually aware of this. An everyday example of this would be a baby and her mother playing with a stuffed toy, with both alternating their eye gaze between each other and the toy. A situation of this kind is referred to as the formation of triadic joint attention, because there is a triad between the baby, the mother, and the object of joint attention. Babies start to engage in this kind of behaviour at around 9 months of age; before that they focus either on the toy or on the caretaker, but not on both at the same time (Oates and Grayson 2004). Why is this ability important? In a situation in which the baby is aware that it is experiencing the same thing as the mother, the baby associates linguistic sounds that the mother utters with the mutually shared experience. Triadic joint attention thus enables the learning of words such as *teddy*. Tomasello and Todd (1983) empirically showed that the amount of time that babies between 12 and 18 months of age spend in episodes of triadic joint attention correlates positively with the amount of vocabulary that they learn. Tomasello and Farrar (1986) further established that during episodes of triadic joint attention, both babies and caretakers talked more and for longer stretches of time than outside such episodes, and caretakers used shorter sentences and more comments. Tomasello and Farrar interpret this as a mutually reinforcing effect: joint attention provides a frame for language use, and language enables the dyad to maintain joint attention. The ability to maintain longer episodes of triadic joint attention seems uniquely human, but it has evolutionary predecessors. Dyadic joint attention, that is, affectionately looking into each other's eyes, is common, for example, in chimpanzees. Several primate species exhibit the behaviour of following gaze, which can be seen as another form of joint attention. Finally, dog owners have long known that their best friends understand pointing gestures, and this has been empirically substantiated (Kirchhofer et al. 2012). The common game of throwing a stick that a dog may then fetch even has elements of triadic joint attention.

A second sociocognitive ability that underlies language acquisition is **intention reading**, that is, babies' predisposition to interpret other people's actions as purposeful and goal-directed. Commonly used in connection with this idea is the term **theory of mind**, which denotes babies' understanding that other people have mental states such as intentions, desires, or beliefs. Toddlers around 16 months of age understand other people's intentions, which is evidenced by the observation that they selectively imitate actions that they see as purposeful, but not actions that produce accidental results (Carpenter et al. 1998). Intention reading is crucial for language learners because they have to interpret utterances as expressions of what other people think, want, like, or dislike. The association of linguistic sounds with communicative intentions motivates the early use of phrases such as *bye-bye daddy* or *more juice*, and as the child becomes familiar with phrases of this kind, it enters a position in which it can analyse these phrases into their component parts and thus acquire productive schemas, rather than just fixed strings. The question to what extent non-human species are capable of intention reading has yet to receive a final answer. However, there are experiments comparing reactions of apes and 2-year-old children to novel communicative signs that show children's unparalleled readiness to attribute communicative intentions to other people (Tomasello et al. 1997). Primates do, however, show some capacity to distinguish intentional from non-intentional actions (Call and Tomasello 1998). Suffice it to say here that mind-reading is something that human beings can hardly suppress whereas it is not done as a matter of course by non-human species.

Third, the ability of **schematisation** allows children to see the similarities between phrases such as *more juice*, *more apple*, and *more noodles* and to abstract from these phrases a pattern such as *more X*, which contains an open 'slot' into which other linguistic elements can be inserted. This element need not always be a noun, as attested utterances such as *more sing* or *more hot* illustrate. A few schemas with open slots that are typically found in the early construct-i-con of English-speaking children are listed below (cf. Braine 1976; Tomasello 2007; Diessel 2013).

(2) *Schema*   *Examples*
    all X   all done, all wet
    where's X   where's daddy?, where's cookie?
    let's X   let's go!, let's find it!
    I'm X-ing it.   I'm holding it, I'm pulling it.

Varying the items that can fill those slots is what linguistic creativity is like in children between 2 and 3 years of age (Lieven et al. 2003; Dąbrowska and Lieven 2005). The empirical observation that creative utterances of young children usually just vary a single element of a well-established pattern is evidence for the piecemeal construction of generalisations. Isolated examples of child language may give the appearance that the child has mastered an abstract pattern such as the PASSIVE construction, the DITRANSITIVE construction, or even SUBJECT–AUXILIARY INVERSION, but when these examples are seen in the context of the utterances that the child has previously heard and produced, it turns out that the child produces variations on a known theme. Schematisation of this kind is fundamental to human cognition. Human beings use their ability to form schemas not only in language but, in fact, in a wide array of activities. For instance, the act of unlocking a door with a key and opening it is a complex activity that has a number of open variables, that is, what specific key is necessary, whether the door is opened by pulling or pushing, whether I need to press a handle or turn a knob, and so on and so forth. If I have formed a concept of 'opening a door', I have in fact generalised over all of these variables and created a cognitive schema. Given the pervasiveness of schematisation in non-linguistic thought, it should not be surprising that it is found even in animal species that are not closely related to human beings. For instance, dogs that have learned to retrieve a ball or a stick have mentally abstracted over the individual balls or sticks they have been trained with. The trick will thus work just as well with a new, similar object that the dog owner throws in the right way.

Fourth, **role reversal and imitation** play a decisive role for the maintenance of triadic joint attentional frames and by extension for the early acquisition of language. Communication by means of linguistic signs is bi-directional, so that both communicating parties are simultaneously both senders and receivers of messages. This design feature of human language makes it differ from most systems of animal communication (Hockett 1966). The ability to imitate the linguistic sounds produced by others is quite trivially a fundamental prerequisite for learning language, but less trivially the child also has to have the ability to understand and reverse the respective roles of sender and recipient in order to engage in true communication. That is, at some point young children understand that they, too, can name an object and thus direct someone else's attention to it. What this boils down to is the insight that language is symbolic: it consists of form–meaning pairs that are intersubjectively shared, that is, mutually known to a speaker and a hearer. As a consequence, these symbolic units can be used to direct other people's attention towards things and issues that need not even be present in the current extralinguistic context. Non-human primates and human infants before the onset of triadic joint attention seem to lack this insight. For instance, Tennie et al. (2012) show that chimpanzees fail to imitate other's actions, such as raising their clasped hands or turning their back towards a wall, even if they have observed other chimpanzees receiving a reward for those actions. The chimps are perfectly capable of realising that they, too, would like a reward. What is missing is the ability to imagine themselves in the role of the trained chimpanzee who performs the necessary behaviour. The somewhat surprising conclusion is that apes are not 'aping' quite as naturally as humans are.

Fifth, language learning could not happen without the general cognitive skill of **pattern recognition**. This concerns in particular the ability of young infants to detect statistical regularities in the language that they hear. As it turns out, infants that do not yet themselves produce linguistic sounds are already extremely attentive listeners. By listening to the speech that is produced in their immediate environment they learn which sounds tend to occur in sequence. Hence, long before children begin to produce their native language, they already have a robust understanding of its phonotactic properties. This knowledge is then available to the child during the phase of early word learning, where it can help the child to detect word boundaries. To illustrate: Saffran et al. (1996) demonstrate that 8-month-old infants learn statistical patterns of an ambient auditory speech stream even from very short episodes of exposure. In an experiment, babies were exposed to 2-minute recordings of nonce trisyllabic words such as *bidaku, padoti, golabu, tupiro*, and so on. Importantly, the speech stream provided no acoustic cues to word boundaries, so that the only cues to 'wordhood' were the transitional probabilities from one syllable to the next: the syllable *bi* was always followed by *da*, but the syllable *ku* was only followed by *pa* one time out of three. During a subsequent test phase, Saffran et al. presented the infants with words that they had heard before and with new words that 'violated' the transitional probabilities that the infants had heard, for instance *pabiku* (*pa* should have been followed by *do*, not by *bi*). The infants showed greater interest towards these 'non-words', as measured by looking times in a conditioned head-turn experiment. Evidently, the infants were surprised to hear the word *pabiku*. What this finding suggests is that infants perform some rather sophisticated book-keeping on the transitional probabilities of neighbouring sounds. Having knowledge of this kind makes the later process of word learning much easier, and thus the need to posit innate, language-specific learning mechanisms is lessened. Unlike capabilities such as intention reading or imitative learning, pattern recognition in the auditory speech stream has also been documented for tamarin monkeys (Ramus et al. 2000), so again, this human capability has evolutionary predecessors.

Summing up this section, the constructional view of language acquisition is based on the assumption that language learning depends on and emerges out of the interaction of several domain-general cognitive abilities. Some of these abilities, for instance schematisation and auditory pattern recognition, are shared by non-human species, while other abilities, like triadic joint attention, intention reading, and imitative learning, are distinctly human. All of them are necessary for language learning to occur. The next section discusses in more detail the actual process of language learning, as illustrated by a number of case studies from children who acquire English as their first language.

7.2 Evidence for the item-based nature of language learning

The part of language acquisition that is of particular interest from a constructional perspective is the one that takes place in the period between 18 and 24 months of age, which is when children start to produce multiword utterances. As discussed above, these utterances take place in triadic joint attentional frames in which both the child and a caretaker jointly focus on an object or an activity. Children's early multi-word utterances thus have the purpose of directing the caretaker's attention to particular aspects of the joint activity. For example, in the joint activity of a meal time, the child might utter constructs such as the following.

(3) more juice
     juice in there
     my noodles
     noodles hot

These four particular examples can be analysed as **pivot schemas**, which represent the first internally complex constructions that children master when starting to use language productively. Pivot schemas consist of a fixed, unchanging part and an open slot into which different elements can be inserted. In an utterance such as *my noodles* the element *my* is the pivot, while the element *noodles* fills the slot that can, on other occasions, be filled with elements that designate items to which the child claims ownership, as in *my shoe, my doll, my key,* and so on. Pivot schemas thus represent linguistic generalisations, and there is even evidence that children between 18 and 24 months of age generalise across multiple pivot schemas. Tomasello et al. (1997) exposed children to novel nouns in contexts such as *Look! The wug!*, which were then spontaneously reproduced by the children in several other pivot schemas such as *Wug did it* or *I see wug.* The adult syntactic category of nouns can thus be seen to emerge from successive generalisations across very simple constructions that at first have strong lexical restrictions. Tomasello et al. (1997) further found that the adult syntactic category of verbs poses greater difficulties with regard to generalisations across multiple pivot schemas. When the children were prompted with novel verbs, as in *Look what Ernie's doing to Big Bird! It's called meeking!*, the children did not reproduce *meeking* in pivot schemas that were in their active construct-i-con. Conceivable responses such as *Ernie meeking* or *I'm meeking Big Bird* were simply not produced.

Why do the linguistic elements that we, in the description of adult syntax, refer to as nouns and verbs pattern so differently in child language? Tomasello (1992) proposes an explanation that he calls the **verb island hypothesis**. The verb island hypothesis states that verbs during early language acquisition form islands of organisation, so that each verb is limited to a single argument structure pattern (cf. Chapter 3 on verbal argument structure). Tomasello bases this hypothesis on data from a longitudinal case study of a single child. The data show that while the child mastered multiple pivot schemas that involved verbal elements, the child tended to create one-to-one mappings of verbs and argument structure patterns that were only gradually extended to allow multiple argument structure patterns for the same verb. The general nature of Tomasello's findings has been corroborated by other studies (e.g. Lieven et al. 1997). What the verb island hypothesis suggests is that it may be relatively easy for the child to come up with a category that generalises over the noun slot in pivot schemas such as *there's X, my X, more X, X in there*, and so on, while it is relatively difficult to generalise across pivot schemas such as *I'm X-ing, don't X me, I X-ed it*, and so on. Furthermore, the restrictions of verbs to particular argument structure patterns suggests that young children do not form abstract generalisations such as subject and direct object; rather, they operate with more concrete roles, such as 'sitter' and 'thing to sit on' for the verb *sit*.

Eventually of course, children do learn that verbs can be used across several patterns of argument structure. Brooks and Tomasello (1999) studied this process on the basis of an experiment in which they trained children between 2 and 4 years of age to use the PASSIVE construction. Under natural conditions, the PASSIVE construction is a late-comer in the construct-i-con of a learning child: full passives with a *by*-phrase are rarely produced before the age of 4 years, while shorter forms such as *The bunny got caught* do appear earlier, but are also rare. The PASSIVE construction is an interesting test case for the constructional, item-based view of language acquisition, since the constructional view and the dictionary-and-grammar view predict different patterns of learning. Specifically, if knowledge of the PASSIVE construction is conceived of as a grammatical rule, then the child should, upon hearing a verb in the PASSIVE, understand that this verb can also be used in the ACTIVE construction. To take a concrete example, an utterance such as *Look! Big Bird is getting zibbed by Ernie* should lead the child to conclude that *Ernie zibbs Big Bird* is a possible sentence of English. To test this hypothesis, Brooks and Tomasello exposed children to scenes in which the experimenter performed transitive actions that were described as *meeking* and *tamming*. In *meeking* actions, a puppet was using a rope to pull a toy up a ramp. In *tamming* actions, another puppet swung on a suspended rope, knocking a toy off a pedestal. The children were divided into two groups that were exposed to different linguistic descriptions of these actions. One group heard descriptions that were exclusively instantiating the ACTIVE construction, and the other group only heard instances of the PASSIVE construction. The examples below illustrate the descriptions produced by the experimenter.

(4) *Active training*
    Look, Big Bird is going to meek something
    Big Bird is going to meek the car!
    Who's going to meek the car?
    Did you see who meeked the car?

Passive training
Look, the car is going to get meeked!
The car is going to get meeked by Big Bird.
Yes, the car is getting meeked by Big Bird.
What's going to get meeked?

In a subsequent test phase, the experimenter tried to elicit descriptions of the same actions from the children, using three different kinds of question. In a neutral condition, the experimenter simply asked a question such as *What happened?*. In the patient-focused condition the questioned element corresponded to the undergoer of *meeking* or *tamming*, yielding questions such as *What happened to the car?* Finally, the agent-focused condition involved questions such as *What did the Big Bird do?*, which focused on the participant who was actively *meeking* or *tamming*. These questions were designed to elicit different constructions as answers. The best match for an agent-focused question in terms of information packaging (cf. Chapter 5) is the ACTIVE construction. So, given a discourse situation that calls for an ACTIVE, did the PASSIVE-trained children also offer that construction?

Brooks and Tomasello report that only some of the PASSIVE-trained children generalised the verbs *meeking* and *tamming* to the ACTIVE construction (1999: 34). In a group of children that were around 3.5 years of age, roughly half of the group offered ACTIVE responses; younger children around 2.5 years of age did so in only 15 per cent of all cases. What makes these results remarkable is that they cannot be explained in terms of knowledge of grammatical rules, or the absence thereof. The children that were tested had an active command of the ACTIVE construction, and they had received training in the PASSIVE construction. Yet many of them did not generalise from the PASSIVE to the ACTIVE. Predictably, the results for the reverse condition were even more drastic. Children who learned a new verb in the ACTIVE construction would, in the overwhelming majority of cases, reproduce the verb exclusively in that construction, no matter what type of question was asked. The study thus shows that children are using verbs conservatively, even at advanced stages of language learning, and it further shows that there are asymmetries with regard to generalisations from one construction to another. Specifically, a generalisation from the PASSIVE to the ACTIVE appears to be cognitively easier than the reverse. This, of course, reflects the greater basicness of the ACTIVE construction, and also its greater type frequency, that is, the range of different verbs that children have already encountered in that construction.

Further evidence for the item-based nature of language learning comes from a series of studies by Elena Lieven and colleagues, who investigated just how creative and original young children's utterances really are. Recall that the purported creativity of child language is a main argument for the idea that children acquire productive syntactic rules, and by extension for the claim that children must be endowed with innate language-specific knowledge so that they are able to acquire those abstract rules. In order to assess the creativity of child language, Lieven et al. analysed longitudinal corpus data consisting of recordings of a 2-year-old child that were made at closely spaced intervals, one hour per day, five days a week, for six weeks (2003: 336). All of the child's multi-word utterances during the last recorded hour – 295 in total – were identified and taken as a representation of the child's linguistic competence. For each of those utterances, Lieven et al. investigated whether it was newly and originally constructed from a syntactic rule, or whether the previous recordings contained 'predecessors', that is, utterances that were either completely identical or that differed in only minor ways. An exhaustive analysis of the child's utterances allowed Lieven et al. to quantify how much of a child's linguistic output is actually creative.

Given a research setup of this kind, what would you expect? Take a guess at the percentage of the child's utterances that are creative, and write that number on a piece of paper, or in the margin of this page, for future reference. Lieven et al. identified predecessors of the child's utterances by looking for previous utterances in the corpus that were produced by either the child or a caretaker. A predecessor was counted as such if it shared a consecutive sequence of morphemes with the target utterance; for each predecessor it was determined whether it differed from the target utterance in terms of morpheme substitution, morpheme add-on, morpheme drop, morpheme insertion, or morpheme rearrangement, as shown in the examples below.

(5)	Change	Target	Predecessor
	substitution	I got the butter	I got the door
	add-on	Let's move it around	Let's move it
	drop	And horse	And a horse
	insertion	finished with your book?	finished your book?
	rearrangement	Away it goes	It goes away

For each target utterance, it was determined how many steps, in terms of the changes shown in (5), were necessary to relate it to a predecessor. For 63 per cent of the target utterances (n = 186), this was not even necessary, as they had been produced in completely identical fashion before. Only 109 of the child's utterances were novel. Of these, 81 differed from earlier utterances in a single morphemes, with substitutions

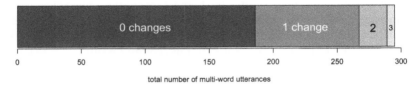

Figure 7.1 Operations required to link target utterances with predecessor utterances

being the most typical scenario. Only 6 utterances, or 2 per cent of the entire language output, required three or more steps between target and predecessor. Figure 7.1 (adapted from Lieven et al. 2003: 344, table 2) visualises these findings.

Note that utterances that require two or more changes do include examples in which target and predecessor differ in the word length of a single constituent. For instance, to get from *Girl's playing falling down* to *Girl's not playing tennis here*, three steps are needed: one for the insertion of *not*, one for the add-on of *here*, and one for the substitution of *tennis* for *falling down*. The basic conclusion from the quantitative results is that there was fairly little novelty in the language output of the child. The largest chunk of utterances with a single change between target and predecessor involved the process of substitution, which is compatible with the idea of pivot schemas that contain a fixed element and an open slot. While the results of Lieven et al.'s study represent only a single child, further studies have yielded highly compatible findings. For instance, Dąbrowska and Lieven (2005) studied the acquisition of English *Wh*-QUESTIONS in two children at age 2 and 3, respectively. Again, the data on which the investigation is based are a dense sequence of recordings, the last of which is searched for target utterances that are then linked to predecessor utterances from earlier recordings. In line with what has been discussed so far, many of the target questions were mere repetitions of questions that the child had heard or uttered before. Most novel questions could be derived from predecessors with just a single operation of change (2005: 451), yielding distributions that are similar to the one shown in Figure 7.1. Again, the most frequent process of change is substitution, typically the replacement of a nominal constituent with another (2005: 452). As perhaps expected, there is an effect of age. For both children, the ratio of creative questions is lower at age 2 than at age 3. Is this perhaps the onset of syntactic, rule-based creativity?

Analysing those questions that resist an explanation in terms of predecessor utterances, Dąbrowska and Lieven come to a very different conclusion. Consider some of the questions for which no reasonable predecessors could be found (2005: 454).

(6) Do you want to football?
Which ones go by here?
What's called the newsagent man?
Where is Deepa come with you?

Dąbrowska and Lieven note that a majority of non-derivable target questions do not conform to adult-like conventions. Evidently enough, the children extrapolate from their knowledge of English when they produce these questions, trying out something new. However, what the questions show is that they have not, in fact, acquired a rule that can be used to generate possible grammatical WH-QUESTIONS of English. Rather, the examples reflect a process of 'tinkering' with bits and pieces that the child has heard before, and which are put together in ways that are almost right, but not quite. The bottom line is that when children use language creatively, they do so in ways that are not at all predicted by the dictionary-and-grammar view of linguistic knowledge.

7.3 From item-based schemas to constructions

How do children get from pivot schemas and verb islands to the abstract argument structure constructions that were discussed in Chapter 3 of this book? A necessary prerequisite for this is children's ability to generalise across verbs, which in most English-speaking children gradually develops over the third year of life. Such generalisations are in evidence when children who are presented with a verb in just one constructional context later use that verb in other constructional contexts, as in Brooks and Tomasello's (1999) study of the PASSIVE construction. A useful research strategy to investigate children's beginning ability to use constructions productively involves the use of novel verbs (*meeking*, *tamming*, etc.) and novel constructions, that is, word order patterns that do not exist in ordinary English and that the child thus does not know. Applying this strategy, Akhtar (1999) exposed children aged between 2;8 and 4;4 to sentences with novel verbs in three different word orders, as shown in the examples below.

(7) Elmo dacking the car.   subject – verb – object
Elmo the car gopping.   subject – object – verb
Tamming Elmo the car.   verb – subject – object

These sentences were presented as descriptions of transitive actions: the verb *dacking* described knocking a toy down a ramp, *gopping* was used for situations in which a toy was catapulted off a platform, and *tamming* referred to placing a toy on a surface. All children were exposed to all of the three word orders. After exposure, the children were prompted to re-enact the actions and verbalise what they had done. Sentences with the novel verbs were recorded and analysed with regard to the word order that the children used.

What Akhtar found was that verbs that were presented in SVO word order (*Elmo dacking the car*) were accurately reproduced in that order by all children, regardless of age. With regard to verbs in the other two word orders, there was an effect of age: the 4-year-old children most of the time 'corrected' the word orders to SVO, whereas children aged 2 and 3 were more conservative. In roughly half of all trials, they used the novel verbs in the SOV and VSO orders in which they had heard them; in the other half of the trials, they produced an SVO order (Akhtar 1999: 346). What this observation suggests is that even 2-year-olds have formed a rudimentary concept of the TRANSITIVE construction that is available as an alternative to pivot schemas and verb islands. Their wavering between the syntactic pattern that was heard and the canonical SVO order indicates a tension between an attested item-based structure and a budding generalisation. In the 4-year-olds in Akhtar's study, that constructional generalisation has become entrenched enough so that the children use it with transitive verbs that they have heard only in other syntactic contexts. The TRANSITIVE construction thus appears to develop a stronger mental representation over time. Another observation is important. Across the three age groups, a substantial number of children showed intra-speaker variation, so that they reproduced unusual word orders on some occasions and switched to SVO on other occasions (1999: 349). This result is at odds with the predictions of the dictionary-and-grammar view of linguistic knowledge. On that approach, word order should be acquired as a grammatical rule that is subsequently applied across the board. Akhtar's findings portray the learning of constructional generalisations thus as a continuation of the gradual, item-based process that characterises early language acquisition.

The idea that even argument structure constructions emerge as generalisations over item-based structures that become increasingly more abstract is fleshed out in a study by Casenhiser and Goldberg (2005), who note that many constructions that young children regularly hear show a skewed distribution with regard to the verbs that occur with them. Constructions such as the DITRANSITIVE construction, the GOAL-DIRECTED MOTION construction, and the CAUSED MOTION construction all occur with a verb that is highly frequent and that represents the core of the constructional meaning, as shown below.

(8) *Construction*   *Most Frequent   Example*
                                        Verb

   DITRANSITIVE   give   I give you the ball.
   GOAL-DIRECTED MOTION   go   That goes in the box.
   CAUSED MOTION   put   I put it here.

The main idea that Casenhiser and Goldberg investigate in their study can be called the **skewed frequency hypothesis.** What this hypothesis boils down to is the claim that a skewed distribution of verbs, with a centre of gravity represented by one highly frequent verb, is a design feature of constructions that facilitates the acquisition of their form and meaning. Adopting the research strategy used by Akhtar (1999), Casenhiser and Goldberg designed novel verbs and a novel construction for their study, which were put together in sentences such as *The rabbit the hat moopoed.* Stimuli sentences such as these were presented to children between 5 and 7 years of age, delivered as auditory descriptions of short video clips in which toys appeared in a location. As you might expect, the video for *The rabbit the hat moopoed* showed a rabbit coming out of a hat. *The monster the cloth keeboed* showed a puppet monster appearing from underneath a blanket. The task that the children had to accomplish after being exposed to these stimuli was to match a previously unheard sentence such as *The sailor the pond neeboes* with one of two simultaneously playing videos showing a sailor and a pond. Whereas one showed the sailor appearing, the other showed the sailor moving continuously across the pond. Trials were counted as successes if the children selected the scene of appearance. Now, instead of comparing children of different ages, Casenhiser and Goldberg randomly assigned the participating children to one of two groups. One group was exposed to a set of stimuli with a skewed verbal distribution, while the other group heard a set of stimuli in which the frequency of verb types was more balanced. The verbs the two groups heard were the following.

(9) Skewed: 4 × moopo, 1 × vako, 1 × suto, 1 × keebo, 1 × fego
    Balanced: 2 × moopo, 2 × vako, 2 × suto, 1 × keebo, 1 × fego

A third group of children acted as a control group and watched the videos without any accompanying sound.

Casenhiser and Goldberg observe that the three groups obtained different results in the experimental task. Predictably, the control group performed at the level of chance. The balanced frequency group performed better, but the best results were obtained by the skewed frequency group, yielding positive evidence for the skewed frequency hypothesis. This result is compatible with the view that language learning involves cognitive mechanisms that are not inherently specific to language. Casenhiser and Goldberg (2005: 506) review several psychological studies that indicate that category learning in general is facilitated by frequent exposure to central, prototypical members of the respective categories.

7.4 The acquisition of complex sentences

Adult syntax, in written as well as in spoken language, is characterised by complex constructions that involve the combination of several clausal structures. Diessel (2013: 361) distinguishes three main types that are illustrated below.

(10) *Construction Type*   *Example*
     COMPLEMENT CLAUSE   I think <u>it's in here</u>.
     RELATIVE CLAUSE   This is the pig <u>that ran away</u>.
     ADVERBIAL CLAUSE   We can play <u>if you want</u>.

These three construction types emerge in different ways. Diessel and Tomasello (2001) study how the first type, COMPLEMENT CLAUSE, develops in the speech of English-speaking children between 1 and 5 years of age.

While adult COMPLEMENT CLAUSE constructions such as *I believe John to be innocent* exhibit a hierarchical structure of a superordinate matrix clause *I believe* and a subordinate complement clause *John to be innocent*, it is questionable that children's early complement clauses, such as *I think Daddy's sleeping* or *See if Mommy's there*, are structured in the same way. Instead, Diessel and Tomasello argue that strings such as *I think* and *See if* should be seen as the fixed part of pivot schemas that accommodate a clausal structure in their open slot (*I think ___, See if ___*). Evidence for this claim comes from longitudinal corpus data that represent the language output of seven children. The data show that children's earliest complement clauses occur with a limited set of verbs (*see, think, want,* etc.) and usually the first person singular pronoun *I*. Complement-taking pivot schemas function as epistemic markers (*I think, I guess*), modal markers (*I wish, I hope*), and directives (*want, see, look, remember*), so that COMPLEMENT CLAUSE constructions are grounded in communicative situations that the child frequently experiences. Over time, children's complement-taking structures evolve from formulaic parts of a pivot schema to the fully fledged matrix clauses that characterise adult syntax. So examples such as *I know this piece go* gradually give way to examples such as *This airplane doesn't know where it's going*. In contrast to the former, the latter has a full noun phrase as a subject, it includes a marker of negation, and the subject is anaphorically referenced in the complement clause, which is thus clearly hierarchically subordinate to the matrix clause. On the whole, the acquisition of COMPLEMENT CLAUSE constructions thus strongly resembles the item-based learning process that is at work in the acquisition of argument-structure constructions.

RELATIVE CLAUSES, as discussed in Chapter 3, are FILLER-GAP constructions which contain a verbal argument that appears in a non-canonical position. For instance, the direct object in the sentence *Bob didn't eat the sandwich* appears directly following the verb, whereas in the RELATIVE CLAUSE construction *That's the sandwich that Bob didn't eat* the direct object actually precedes the verb. The noun phrase *the sandwich*, that is, the 'filler', thus appears in a non-argument position. Since the verb *eat* is not followed by any linguistic material, we speak of that position as a 'gap'. Understanding the relationship between filler and gap has been seen as the prime obstacle that children face in the acquisition of RELATIVE CLAUSE constructions. A basic psycholinguistic finding that relates to this issue is the observation that some relative clauses are more difficult to process than others. Consider the examples below, which indicate the canonical argument positions of the fillers with co-indexed blanks.

(11)   The detective$_i$ who ___$_i$ observed John was clever.
       The detective$_i$ who John observed ___$_i$ was clever.
       Give me the ball$_i$ that ___$_i$ hit the girl.
       Give me the ball$_i$ that the girl threw ___$_i$.

When listeners are confronted with constructed examples such as these, which express all major constituents with full lexical phrases, a robust finding emerges. Out of the four sentences, listeners find the first one easiest to process (Wanner and Maratsos 1978, amongst many others). The first example is called a SUBJECT RELATIVE CLAUSE because the gap represents the subject constituent of the relative clause: the detective does the observing. Compare this to the second example, in which the gap represents the object constituent. Here, the detective is being observed and the construction is therefore called an OBJECT RELATIVE CLAUSE. The roles of subject and object in the relative clause are independent of the role of the same referent in the matrix clause, as is shown by the third and fourth examples. Now, why should object relative clauses be more difficult to process? An explanation that has been invoked is the relative distance between filler and gap. In the first and third examples, that distance is considerably shorter than in the second and fourth. The longer the distance between filler and gap, the longer the listener has to keep the filler in working memory, until its syntactic role has become clear. This represents a cognitive effort that might be too hard for young children, which would explain why children's first relative clauses are subject relative clauses.

However, the distance between filler and gap might not be the whole story. Also among children's early relative clause constructions are object relative clauses such as the following.

(12) That's the yoghurt$_i$ that I want ___$_i$!
       What's that$_i$ you have ___$_i$?

Diessel and Tomasello (2005) point out that the constructed examples on which most psycholinguistic studies of relative clause comprehension have been based are very different from the authentic relative clauses that children hear and produce. Sentences such as *The senator that the reporter attacked responded immediately* are grammatically correct examples of written English, but you are in fact unlikely to read anything like that outside linguistic research laboratories. What Diessel and Tomasello question is thus whether research based on constructed examples accurately reflects what ordinary speakers, including young children, do when they are processing relative clauses. The technical term for idea that experimental tasks should closely reflect naturally occurring behaviour is **ecological validity**. The constructional view of language acquisition makes a very different prediction about children's early relative clauses. Children would simply be expected to have the least difficulties with RELATIVE CLAUSE constructions that they hear and use frequently. Children's input contains a large number of subject relative clauses, but also a large number of PRESENTATIONAL OBJECT RELATIVE CLAUSE constructions, that is, utterances such as *That's the one I want* or *Here's the block I was looking for*. With regard to the latter, a frequency-based account predicts little difficulty whereas an account based on the distance between filler and gap would predict substantial difficulties. In order to test which of these predictions is borne out, Diessel and Tomasello (2005) presented 4-year-old children with different relative clause constructions, as illustrated below.

(13) *Construction*   *Example*
       SUBJECT RELATIVE CLAUSE   There's the boy who played in the garden.

       AGENT RELATIVE CLAUSE   There's the farmer who saw Peter.
       PATIENT RELATIVE CLAUSE   That's the girl who the boy teased.
       INDIRECT OBJECT RELATIVE   There's the girl that he borrowed
          CLAUSE   a ball from.

OBLIQUE RELATIVE CLAUSE That's the car that Peter ran away from.
GENITIVE RELATIVE CLAUSE That's the boy whose cat ran away.

The task that the children had to do was simple: they were asked to repeat back to the experimenter what they had just heard. A trial was counted as a success if the child repeated exactly what it had heard. In the case of lexical mistakes, such as saying *man* instead of *farmer*, the trial was counted as a partial success.

What Diessel and Tomasello found was that children performed better with subject relative clauses than with agent relative clauses (2005: 888). This is inconsistent with the distance-based hypothesis, since the distance in both construction types is the same. The researchers further found that there were no differences across patient relative clauses and indirect object relative clauses. Again, this is inconsistent with the distance-based hypothesis, since the distance is greater in the latter type. Lastly, the researchers observed that children almost invariably failed to reproduce genitive relative clauses, despite a very short distance between filler and gap. An analysis of the children's errors showed that the typical pattern was a shift towards subject relative clauses. Upon hearing a sentence such as *There is the horse that the little cat jumped on yesterday*, some children produced *There is the horse that jumped on the cat yesterday*, accepting semantic implausibility in exchange for the benefit of a well-known structure. In summary, while some of Diessel and Tomasello's results are consistent with the distance-based hypothesis, there is evidence to suggest that the frequency of constructions has a decisive role to play in the learning process. Structures that the child frequently hears are thus more successfully reproduced.

The last category of complex sentences to be discussed in this section is the one of ADVERBIAL CLAUSE constructions. Adverbial clauses represent perhaps the prototypical idea of subordinate clauses in adult syntax, which are linked to a full main clause through a subordinating conjunction such as *because, if,* or *while*. In order to understand children's acquisition of these structures, it is necessary to come to terms with the idea that children learn them on the basis of spoken examples, not the carefully edited examples that occur in writing, and that mostly shape our idea of what subordinate clauses are like. Diessel (2004: 160) points out that children start using conjunctions such as *because* not for the purpose of linking a main clause with a subordinate clause. Rather, children's early utterances with *because* function as autonomous, stand-alone answers to questions, as in the following examples.

(14) Adult: Why should they come from Africa?
     Child: Because they live in Africa.

(15) Child: You can't have this.
     Adult: Why?
     Child: Cause I'm using it.

Diessel studied how five children between 2 and 5 years of age used conjunctions such as *and, because, but,* and *so,* finding that consistently, the unbound use of conjunctions precededs and outnumbered the bound use of those elements (2004: 160ff).

Combinations of main and adverbial clauses continue to pose a major challenge for young language learners well into childhood. Their production only gets under way with children's growing ability to plan complex bi-clausal utterances, and even children between 6 and 7 years of age still show processing difficulties when they are confronted with sentences such as *The boy jumped over the fence before he patted the dog* (Bowerman 1979). Findings about the acquisition of adverbial clauses thus echo many of the points that have been made earlier in this chapter. In particular, the result that children's first uses of adverbial clauses are not, syntactically speaking, subordinate clauses calls into question the idea that children might be acquiring a new syntactic rule that would allow them to construct complex sentences.

7.5 Summing up

Any theory of linguistic knowledge makes predictions about how children acquire that knowledge. This chapter made the point that Construction Grammar makes predictions that differ in many ways from earlier theories that stand more in the tradition of partitioning linguistic knowledge into a system of grammatical rules and a mental lexicon that contains words and idioms. On such a view, the task of language learning seems almost impossibly hard if the child does not have recourse to some innate knowledge to fall back on. How is the child to work out abstract and complex syntactic relations purely on the basis of patchy and noisy input? The constructional view of language acquisition holds that this is simply the wrong question to ask. Specifically, it is the wrong question because a central underlying assumption, namely the continuity hypothesis, does not hold. The continuity hypothesis states that the language of children is mentally represented by the same syntactic rules and categories as adult language. However, children do not in fact need to work out abstract and complex syntactic relations; what they do need to work out is what their caretakers and peers have in mind when they utter linguistic sounds. Empirical data show that children do so in an item-based fashion, learning bit by bit and generalising gradually from the bits that are in place. Language acquisition, on this view, rests on a number of sociocognitive skills, including the ability to form triadic joint attention, intention reading, the ability to form schemas, imitation, and pattern recognition. Some of these abilities are shared by humans and several non-human species; others, notably the ability to sustain longer periods of triadic joint attention, seem to be distinctive of human beings.

The item-based nature of early language learning is characterised by the formation of pivot schemas, which can be thought of as mini-constructions with a fixed pivot and an open slot into which the child may insert different linguistic elements. At first, the mutual connections between these pivot schemas are weak or even non-existent, as posited in the verb island hypothesis. It is only with the child's growing experience with language that generalisations across pivot schemas are formed, which eventually result in an adult-like syntactic competence.

The chapter reviewed evidence that called into question the idea that children's language production is too creative to be learned from the input alone. Studies that track children's language production over time robustly find that children experiment very cautiously with language, and that if they do, the results tend to deviate from conventional adult usage. This result casts doubt on the assumption that children acquire syntactic rules that allow them to use language productively. Rather, the item-based strategies that very young children apply in the acquisition of pivot schemas seem to be continued into the processes of learning more abstract constructions, such as argument structure constructions and even complex clausal constructions. The chapter reviewed evidence for the gradual strengthening of abstract constructions such as the TRANSITIVE construction, and it explained the skewed frequency hypothesis, which views the distributions of verbs in constructions as a design feature that boosts learnability. A final section on complex sentences discussed how children acquire complement clauses, relative clauses, and adverbial clauses. Studies investigating these processes have found that the frequency of structures in the input is an important predictor of children's early proficiency with these structures, and it was also shown that children use adverbial clauses as independent utterances before they integrate them into complex sentential constructions.

Study questions

- What is an overgeneralisation error and why are these errors interesting?
- What is the continuity hypothesis?
- Explain the argument from the poverty of the stimulus.
- Why is the ability to engage in joint attention important for word learning?
- Michael Tomasello is equally well known for his work on language acquisition and his research on primate cognition. Read one of his studies of non-human behaviour (cooperation, gesture, deception, etc.) and determine what the results say about differences from the cognitive skills of human beings (for instance, Hare and Tomasello 2005 is an interesting paper on dogs' cognitive skills).
- What is a pivot schema? Give examples.
- The CHILDES database is a large collection of corpus data, including many transcriptions of child language that were used in the studies described in this chapter. Find the CHILDES database online, download a batch of files, and familiarise yourself with the format of the data.
- What is the verb island hypothesis?
- What is the skewed frequency hypothesis?
- Explain how the distance-based account makes different predictions about the acquisition of relative clauses from those of a frequency-based account.

Further reading

An authoritative and highly readable introduction to the field of language acquisition from a constructional perspective is Tomasello (2003), while two shorter articles (Tomasello 2000a, 2000b) are useful primers. Diessel's (2013) chapter in *The Oxford Handbook of Construction Grammar* offers another concise overview that summarises the most important ideas. A book that is highly to be recommended is Ambridge and Lieven (2011), which presents a comprehensive overview that contrasts the constructional approach with other approaches, notably generative grammar. In order to gain a more thorough insight into the practices of first language acquisition research, it is useful to read a few experimental and corpus-based studies such as the ones reviewed in this chapter. Examples of papers that make important points in clear, student-friendly writing include Brandt et al. (2009), Dąbrowska et al. (2009), Lieven et al. (2009), and Wonnacott et al. (2012).

8 Language variation and change

8.1 Language myths

Grammar is a subject that in all likelihood has formed part of your school curriculum. It is also a subject that is almost universally hated by students. Ask a few friends of yours who are not studying linguistics what they remember about their grammar lessons, and they will claim two things. First, they have forgotten every single thing they were supposed to learn. Second, they have made their way through life quite successfully without knowing any of those things. It is probably true that your friends do not remember particulars, such as the distinction between restrictive and non-restrictive relative clauses and how to mark that distinction through the use of a comma. However, while school lessons usually fail to instil a lasting intellectual appreciation of grammar, they tend to be successful in the propagation of several fundamental misconceptions about language. Most students will readily adopt these ideas as their own and remember them throughout their entire lives. One such idea is that grammar is a set of rules specifying what is right and wrong in language use. Ignore the rules, and marks in red ink will follow. The proposal that linguistic **variation** is a perfectly normal thing is met with suspicion. If the question comes up whether it is right to say *the man whom I thanked* or *the man that I thanked*, and you point out that either one is fine, your non-linguist friends will interpret this as a feeble attempt to cover up the fact that you have forgotten the proper rule.

Another powerful, almost universally shared belief is that young people do not know how to speak, let alone write, proper English any more. People are aware that linguistic **change** is under way, and usually this is seen as cause for alarm. The perception of language decay is voiced over and over again. Whereas once we had Shakespearean sonnets, we now have text messages whose impoverished linguistic quality is plainly visible in words such as *gr8* or *ROFL* and of course the complete absence of punctuation and proper orthography. If you mention to non-linguists that perpetual change is very much the natural state of a living language, and that all fears of decay, which are documented across every recorded period of history, have ultimately proved to be unfounded (cf. Deutscher 2005: ch. 3), they will tell you that this time around, things are different. The technological advances of the last decades, so the argument goes, have changed the way we communicate more fundamentally than anything else that happened in the past. It is certainly true that only a generation ago, the prospect of everybody having small handheld devices that allow the instant exchange of spoken and written messages with people all across the globe would have seemed a little futuristic. Nonetheless, there are reasons to believe that technology of this kind only has a very minor influence on the way in which language changes (Baron 2008). The idea that grammar unambiguously specifies what is right and wrong and the idea that language is currently undergoing a decay are **language myths**, that is, ideas that are fundamentally at odds with reality, but that nonetheless remain unchallenged in popular discussions (Bauer and Trudgill 1998). Linguists of different theoretical persuasions agree on relatively few issues, but the fact that variation and change are fundamental aspects of language that are furthermore deeply interconnected is a point on which everybody in the field agrees. This chapter discusses the role of variation and change in a constructional model of linguistic knowledge. It will become apparent that variation and change have a very natural place in that model and that the very architecture of the construct-i-con actually predicts that language use should be characterised by variation and change.

In order to make that argument, this chapter will go over the following ideas. Section 8.2 introduces the concept of variation, that is, the idea that a speaker can say the same thing in different ways. The section discusses examples of variation within single constructions and examples of variation across pairs of constructions. Section 8.3 turns to the issue of variation between different groups of speakers. It is clear that there is not just 'the English language', but rather a multitude of Englishes. Speakers use English in different ways depending on where they live, who their peers are, and how they fit into the social order of their community. The section will explore the implications of inter-speaker variability for the constructional view of linguistic knowledge. Section 8.4 discusses the role of language change in Construction Grammar. The section will spell out how historical language change relates to the main topics of the previous sections, namely intra-speaker and inter-speaker variability. Section 8.5 concludes the chapter.

8.2 Constructional variation

8.2.1 There's more than one way to do it

What does it mean to say that there is variation in a construction? In the simplest of terms, it means that there is always more than one way to use a construction. For instance, speakers of English have different ways of pronouncing a lexical construction such as *secretary*. Depending on their speech rate at the time of pronouncing the word, the result might consist of four syllables, as in /ˈsɛ.krɪ.tə.ɹɪ/, or it might have only three syllables, as in /ˈsɛ.krɪ.tɹɪ/. Besides variation in the quantity or length of how a word is realised, there is of course also qualitative variation, so that the same phonological segments are produced, albeit in qualitatively different ways. To illustrate, the same speaker might say /ˈsɛ.krɪ.tə.ɹɪ/ on some occasions but /ˈsɛ.krɪ.tə.ri/, with a higher final /i/, on other occasions. Different ways of pronouncing the same word reflect variation at the formal pole of a lexical construction. Recall that a construction is defined as a generalisation that speakers make: a certain form corresponds to a certain meaning. Taken together, these two poles form a symbolic unit. What constructional variation shows is that generalisations of this kind are not quite as simplistic as a one-to-one mapping of a single, invariant form to a single, invariant meaning. Rather, both the formal pole and the meaning pole of a construction should be seen as containing information on several variants – formal variants of the construction as well as meaning variants. If I know the word *secretary*, that knowledge includes the fact that the word can be pronounced in different ways, and also, reflecting variation on the meaning pole, that the word can be used with several different meanings. Besides the meaning of 'an assistant for office work', the word has several other meanings, depending on its context. The term *secretary of state* refers to a high political office and *a wooden secretary* refers to a piece of furniture. Variation at the meaning pole of a construction is thus very much at issue in cases of polysemy. The basic take-home message is that constructions are **many-to-many mappings**, connecting a set of related forms to a set of related meanings. This idea might strike you as a very basic, almost trivial observation: lexical words are associated with a range of different pronunciations and a range of different meanings. That sounds plausible, but is that really all there is to variation in constructions?

As the previous chapters of this book have discussed, constructions range from the very simple and specific to the very complex and abstract, and it is variation in more complex constructions that will occupy us most in the rest of this chapter. For instance, Chapter 3 has already pointed to the meaning variation that can be observed in the S-GENITIVE construction. The examples in (1) illustrate once more that this morphosyntactic construction encodes several different types of semantic relation that are grouped around the prototype of possession (Taylor 1989).

(1) John's book
John's office
John's train
the country's president
yesterday's sad events
inflation's consequences

The S-GENITIVE construction can be used to convey that someone owns a certain object, but the examples reveal a network of extended meanings beyond that central sense. Parallel observations were made concerning meaning variation in the DITRANSITIVE construction (Goldberg 1995) and in MODAL AUXILIARY constructions (Sweetser 1990). Different senses of these constructions are connected via metaphorical and metonymic links (cf. Chapter 3, Section 3.2.2), just as in the example of the different senses of *secretary*. Lexical and grammatical constructions thus behave very similarly with regard to variation at their meaning poles. But what about formal variation in grammatical constructions? It appears that the forms of grammatical constructions can vary in different ways from the forms of lexical constructions. To begin with, complex constructions like the S-GENITIVE construction occur with a wide range of lexical words, and therefore their actual pronunciations exhibit massive variation. The only commonality at the phonological pole of the examples in (1) is that all of them contain an alveolar fricative in the role of the genitive *s*. Beyond the lexical variation, it could be argued that there is actually not much variation going on in the S-GENITIVE construction: the genitive *s* simply connects two nominals, which, we might admit, can be realised in different ways, perhaps being preceded by a determiner (*the country's president*) or an adjective (*yesterday's sad events*). It is, however, interesting to consider the limits of that variation. For instance, formations such as **John's it*, with a pronominal second nominal, are ungrammatical, as is **that's window* (in the sense of 'the window of that one'), in which the first nominal is a demonstrative. So, even in the S-GENITIVE, not just any nominal will do; some nominals are used while others are not. This variation reflects knowledge of language that speakers have and that Construction Grammarians should try to work out. In order to illustrate formal variation in abstract syntactic constructions in some more detail, the following section discusses the example of relative clauses.

8.2.2 *Variation in syntactic constructions: the example of relative clauses*

The RELATIVE CLAUSE construction has already been introduced briefly in Chapters 3 and 6. Relative clauses instantiate the NOUN PHRASE construction, and they belong to the family of FILLER-GAP constructions (Sag 2010). As the examples in (2) show, relative clauses come in a wide range of structural variants.

(2) That's the cat that ran away.
     That's the cat that I saw yesterday.
     That's the cat that I told you about.
     That's the cat I saw yesterday.
     That's the solution suggested by our team of experts.
     That's the proper thing to do.

All of the above examples are what are called presentational relative clauses that occur within a PREDICATE NOMINAL construction of the form *That's NP*. The construction types that will be compared in the following represent the NP of that PREDICATE NOMINAL construction. The above examples can be contrasted in terms of several **variables**, that is, features that can be realised in two or more different ways. The following paragraphs discuss three of those variables.

A particularly important variable with regard to relative clauses concerns the grammatical role of the nominal constituent that is relativised and hence appears as a 'gap' in the relative clause (cf. the discussion of fillers and gaps in Chapter 3). Consider the first three examples: *the cat that ran away, the cat that I saw yesterday,* and *the cat that I told you about.* Note that the grammatical role of the relativised nominal *the cat* is different across the three relative clauses. In the first example, *the cat* is understood as the subject of the verb phrase *ran away;* in the second example, *the cat* is understood as the object of the verb *saw.* This motivates a terminological distinction of SUBJECT RELATIVE CLAUSES and OBJECT RELATIVE CLAUSES (Huddleston and Pullum 2002: 1044). In the third example, *the cat* is neither the subject nor the object of the relative clause. Rather, as the topic about which something has been said, it functions as an **oblique**, defined here as an object that is marked by a preposition. Examples with this kind of relativised nominal are called OBLIQUE RELATIVE CLAUSES. Besides SUBJECT, OBJECT, and OBLIQUE RELATIVE CLAUSES there are further types of grammatical roles that can appear as gaps, but the distinction between those three already serves to illustrate the variability of the grammatical role.

A second variable is the presence or absence of a **relativiser**, that is, an element that introduces a relative clause and explicitly marks it as such. A comparison between the first three examples and the fourth example shows that some relative clauses are introduced by a relativiser, here the relative pronoun *that*, whereas some other relative clauses are uttered without a relativiser. Notably, OBJECT RELATIVE CLAUSES display variation in this regard: *the cat that I saw* and *the cat I saw* are both well-formed relative clauses. By contrast, the SUBJECT RELATIVE CLAUSE **That's the cat ran away* is not an acceptable sentence in standard British or American English. That said, SUBJECT RELATIVE CLAUSES without relativisers are fully acceptable in certain varieties of English such as Hong Kong English and Newfoundland English (Kortmann and Lunkenheimer 2013). Differences between varieties of English will be discussed in more depth in Section 8.3. For now, the focus lies on variability that pertains to the linguistic knowledge of a single speaker, called intra-speaker variability. A speaker of standard American English may form OBJECT RELATIVE CLAUSES with or without a relativiser, and in the former case, there is furthermore a choice between the generic relativisers *that* and *which*, and the relative pronouns *who*, *whom*, and *whose*, which go along with specific types of relativised constituents.

A third variable becomes apparent when the first four examples are compared with the fifth and sixth example. Whereas the earlier examples showed relative clauses with finite, fully inflected verb forms (e.g. *the cat that ran away*), the last two examples contain verbs that are non-finite, that is, a participle in the fifth example (*the solution suggested by our team*) and an infinitive in the sixth one (*the thing to do*). Note that the variable of finiteness covaries with the presence or absence of a relativiser: non-finite relative clauses disallow the use of a relativiser (**the solution which suggested by our team*, **the thing that to do*). Speakers intuitively know how to form relative clauses with these different verb forms, and so the variable of finite and non-finite relative clauses must be part of the formal pole of the RELATIVE CLAUSE construction.

The three variables described in the above paragraphs by no means exhaust the entire variability that is found in English relative clauses (see Wiechmann to appear for a comprehensive overview), but they should suffice to illustrate the complexity of linguistic generalisations at the level of syntactic constructions. To posit that there is a RELATIVE CLAUSE construction in English is to commit to the claim that speakers generalise across the entire space of variability, viewing all different examples of relative clauses as instances of the same, highly abstract grammatical category. Whether speakers actually arrive at such high-level generalisations or whether they use more local generalisations at a lower level of abstraction is being investigated in current work (Perek 2012). Looking at the variability that is inherent in the syntactic constructions that make up the grammar of English thus teaches us an important lesson: constructions, that is, linguistic generalisations, are not fixed schematic templates, like assembly instructions that allow only a single correct way of constructing a complex whole. By way of an analogy, it might not be too far-fetched to compare constructions to the theme of a jazz standard like *Smoke Gets in Your Eyes*. When musicians play the song, the melody is reproduced in recognisable ways, but there is room for modification and improvisation. And like musicians who have a 'feel' for the modifications that do and do not work, speakers intuitively know when it 'sounds right' to leave out the relativiser of a relative clause or to choose a non-finite verb rather than a fully inflected one. Variation in the usage of constructions is thus an important topic for Construction Grammar, but taking variation seriously also means that the job of describing linguistic knowledge gets a lot harder. Recall that the traditional goal of grammatical description is to distinguish grammatical utterances from ungrammatical utterances. Doing this is already quite a difficult task. Now, with variation entering the picture, we do not merely want to distinguish between black and white, that is, ungrammatical and grammatical, but rather, we acknowledge that there is a continuum with shades of grey between the end points of black and white, and we want to explain why there is this continuum. Why does a certain form 'sound better' than another form in one context but not in another? What are the variables that are at play? How do those variables relate to one another? It may seem to you at this point that asking these questions is more likely to result in utter confusion rather than in an improved understanding of speakers' linguistic knowledge. The following paragraphs will try to clear matters up a little bit by discussing how corpus data can be used to investigate constructional variation.

8.2.3 Analysing variation between constructions

The analysis of linguistic variation has only recently been put on the research agenda of Construction Grammarians, who are thus relative late-comers to a phenomenon that has already been studied intensively for several decades within the tradition of **quantitative sociolinguistics** (Tagliamonte 2006; Trousdale 2010). Sociolinguists following the approach developed by William Labov (Labov 1994, 2001) have known for a long time that speakers realise constructions in different ways, and that these different realisations are not random, but highly predictable on the basis of social factors such as age or ethnicity, or linguistic factors such as the morpho-phonological context of a given utterance. To illustrate, more than forty years ago Labov (1969) had already showed that variable usage of the copula *be* in African American Vernacular English (AAVE), more specifically Philadelphia AAVE, followed a system of rules that could be described in terms of both linguistic and social factors. In the parlance of sociolinguistics, these are known as **language-internal factors** and **language-external factors** respectively. The variation that Labov analysed concerned the presence or absence of the copula in examples such as the following.

(3) She ['s/ø] the first one.
We ['re/ø] on tape.
He ['s/ø] gon' try to get up.
His wife [is/ø] suppos' a be getting money.

Non-use of the copula was shown to be more likely in sentences with pronominal subjects, as opposed to subjects expressed by full lexical forms. The zero variant was also more likely if the following syntactic constituent was a form of *gonna* rather than a predicate nominal or a predicative adjective. A social factor that Labov took into account was the speech situation: when interviewed in a group, the participants used the zero variant more often than when they were interviewed individually. There were furthermore differences between different groups of AAVE speakers, so the language-external variable of the peer network had an effect.

Labov proposed that cases of variability should be thought of as grammatical rules that are contingent on a number of factors, with each of those factors influencing the likelihood of the rule being either applied or not applied. The technical term that is associated with this proposal is the **variable rule**. So a rule such as 'the copula *be* is expressed as zero in AAVE' is inherently variable: speakers apply it on some occasions but not on others. This means that the application of the rule is **probabilistic**, and the presence or absence of certain contextual features makes it more or less likely that the rule will in fact apply. As was explained, the rule is especially likely to apply if the subject of the utterance is pronominal, if the utterance contains *gonna*, and if the utterance is made in a group interview. But even when all of these factors come together, there remains a small chance that the rule does not apply, so that the speaker ends up pronouncing a form of the copula.

Studies of variable rules have mostly been carried out with the aim of showing how variation in language use correlates with non-linguistic, social distinctions. Their main purpose is thus not to provide a model of what speakers know when they know a language, which you recognise as the fundamental goal of Construction Grammar. Nonetheless, the tools of quantitative sociolinguistics have proven to be immensely useful, and indeed indispensible, for constructional research. In particular, the concept of a variable rule has informed research on related argument structure constructions (cf. Chapter 2) such as the member constructions of the DATIVE ALTERNATION or the LOCATIVE ALTERNATION. Consider, once again, two examples of the DITRANSITIVE construction and the PREPOSITIONAL DATIVE construction.

(4) John gave his favourite aunt Mary   DITRANSITIVE
    the book.
    John gave the book to his favourite   PREPOSITIONAL DATIVE
    aunt Mary.

How does the idea of a variable rule carry over to the use of these constructions? Like the contrast between /ˈsɛ.krɪ.tə.rɪ/ and /ˈsɛ.krɪ.trɪ/ or the contrast between a copula form and a zero variant, the DATIVE ALTERNATION represents a possibility for speakers to say something in two different ways. Both member constructions of the DATIVE ALTERNATION can be used to express the idea of a transfer. This does not mean that the two constructions are seen as semantically equivalent. There is merely an area of semantic overlap, that is, a certain range of ideas that can be expressed through both the DITRANSITIVE construction and the PREPOSITIONAL DATIVE construction. Given that alternative ways of saying things are usually not random but governed by linguistic and social determinants, it makes sense to investigate the conditions under which speakers choose either one or the other of the two constructions. The literature that addresses this question is so large that any attempt to review it in this book is bound to be less than satisfying. The DATIVE ALTERNATION has been such a popular topic that one could actually compare that linguistic body of research to the biological study of the fruit fly, which has been analysed as a model organism in genetics, physiology, and pathogenesis, amongst other fields. So, at the obvious risk of giving short shrift to a lot of important findings, what have linguists learned about the DATIVE ALTERNATION? Bresnan et al. (2007) offer a summary of linguistic factors that govern speakers' choices between the two constructions. As the following paragraphs will outline, these factors concern distinctions that pertain to practically all levels of linguistic structure: morpho-phonology, syntax, semantics, and information packaging (cf. Chapter 5).

While information packaging was named last in that list, the distinction between given and new information is actually one of the most fundamental determinants of speakers' choices in the DATIVE ALTERNATION. The distinction between given and new matters chiefly for two of the three arguments of the respective constructions: the theme, that is, the element that is transferred, and the recipient, that is, the participant that represents the end point of the transfer (cf. Chapter 2 for a discussion of these thematic roles). Let us focus on the role of the theme first. Consider the following constructed dialogue that is concluded by two possible utterances by speaker B.

(5) A: Do we have any more wine?
    B: No, I'm afraid there's nothing left.
    A: But we had that last bottle of Merlot!
    B: Yes, but...
         ... I gave John that last one.   DITRANSITIVE
         ... I gave that last one to John.   PREPOSITIONAL DATIVE

Being forced to choose between those two conclusions of the dialogue, which one would you prefer? In experimental studies that use stimuli of this kind (Bresnan 2007), speakers of American English show a strong preference for the PREPOSITIONAL DATIVE, and you probably do, too. In the example, the theme, that is, *that last bottle of Merlot*, represents shared knowledge of the two speakers. With themes that are given, speakers prefer to use the PREPOSITIONAL DATIVE because that allows them to reserve the utterance-final position for the actual focus of the utterance (cf. Chapter 5). In the example above, the element in focus is *John*, whose role as the recipient of the last bottle of Merlot represents new information. With the role of the recipient, speakers' respective preferences are precisely reversed. Consider the following, modified version of the dialogue you just read.

(6) A: Do we have any more wine?
    B: No, I'm afraid there's nothing left.
    A: But it's John's birthday and I need to bring something!
    B: Yes, well...
         ... you could give John some
         chocolates.   DITRANSITIVE
         ... you could give some
         chocolates to John.   PREPOSITIONAL DATIVE

In this context, many speakers find that the DITRANSITIVE sounds considerably better. Corpus data show that this is not only an intuition that speakers have when they judge experimental stimuli, but that this distribution of given and new information also characterises the naturally occurring usage of the two constructions (Bresnan et al. 2007). Hence, when speakers verbalise the idea of a transfer, they choose a construction with information packaging properties that match the current set of ideas that are shared between the speaker and the hearer.

The variable of givenness is closely correlated with three syntactic variables. First, there is the distinction of whether theme and recipient are expressed by pronouns or full lexical noun phrases. The former strongly tend to represent given information, which is not necessarily so with the latter. The DITRANSITIVE construction is thus used disproportionally often with pronominal recipients (*You could give him some chocolates*) whereas it actually disallows pronominal themes (**You could give John it*). The second syntactic variable that ties in with the issue of givenness is the status of theme and recipient as either definite noun phrases or indefinite noun phrases. Given information tends to be expressed with definite noun phrases, whereas a primary function of indefinite articles is the introduction of new referents into the conversation. Third, themes and recipients can be expressed through syntactic units that differ in length. Naturally, pronouns are shorter than full lexical phrases, and new pieces of information tend to require relatively lengthier descriptions, so this variable also aligns with the remaining ones. In accordance with the principle of end weight (cf. Chapter 5), long themes nudge speakers towards using the DITRANSITIVE construction whereas long recipients are used more often with the PREPOSITIONAL DATIVE construction.

A semantic variable concerns the distinction of different kinds of transfer that can be expressed through the constructions of the DATIVE ALTERNATION. Concrete transfers (*give John some chocolates*) contrast with intended transfers (*promise John some chocolates*), metaphorical transfers (*give the idea some thought*), and transfers of information (*tell John a story*). These different types of transfer do not lend themselves equally well to the use with both constructions. For instance, certain metaphorical transfers are not felicitously expressed with the PREPOSITIONAL DATIVE construction.

(7) This light gives me a headache.
     ?This light gives a headache to me.

With regard to semantic properties of theme and recipient also, it is possible to identify variables that affect speakers' choices. The contrast between animate and inanimate recipients is responsible for the different acceptability judgements in the following examples.

(8) John threw his keys to the floor.
     *John threw the floor his keys.

Another important variable that pertains not just to the utterance itself but to the prior speech situation is the question whether or not a member construction of the DATIVE ALTERNATION has been uttered in the preceding context. Corpus studies show that speakers are more likely to use a given syntactic construction if they have recently either heard that construction or even produced it themselves (Szmrecsanyi 2006). This phenomenon, which is called **structural priming** or **morphosyntactic persistence**, not only accounts for variation in the DATIVE ALTERNATION but has been shown to be at work in a wide range of other morphosyntactic alternations.

Among the variables that only have a minor impact on the alternation, one might name the variable of whether the theme is either concrete (*give John some chocolates*) or abstract (*give John a hint*) and the variable of whether the theme is in the singular (*a box of chocolates*) or in the plural (*some chocolates*). Abstract themes induce a slight bias towards the DITRANSITIVE, while plural themes pull speakers towards the PREPOSITIONAL DATIVE.

All of the variables that have been discussed up to now, with the exception of the length of theme and recipient, reflect distinctions between two or at most a handful of possible values. Givenness was discussed as a binary variable that takes either given or new as its value; the variable of transfer sense distinguished between a small number of different types of transfer. It was mentioned earlier in this chapter that one source of variability in syntactic constructions is their ability to co-occur with many different lexical elements. As a case in point, both the DITRANSITIVE construction and the PREPOSITIONAL DATIVE construction occur with a large set of ditransitive verbs, notably *give, send, offer, sell,* and so on. The variable of the verb that occurs in a member construction of the DATIVE ALTERNATION is one that has hundreds of different levels. Depending on how large a corpus one has at hand, the number of different verbs that appear may get fairly large. Nonetheless, it is useful to consider this variable, because as was pointed out in Chapter 1, speakers' knowledge of collocational relations between verbs and constructions forms an integral part of the linguistic knowledge that Construction Grammarians aim to model. Native speakers know intuitively that **John explained me the problem* is not an acceptable sentence of English, but second language learners of English have to learn the idiosyncrasy of *explain* as an exception. Gries and Stefanowitsch (2004a) compare the observed and expected frequencies of verbs in the DATIVE ALTERNATION, which allows them to identify verbs that are particularly typical of either the DITRANSITIVE construction or the PREPOSITIONAL DATIVE construction. As it turns out, verbs such as *give, tell,* and *show* are strongly associated with the former, while speakers prefer to use verbs such as *bring, play,* and *take* with the latter. These preferences can partly be explained as reflexes of semantic variables such as a dispreference for inanimate recipients in the DITRANSITIVE: you can *bring your dog to the office,* but you cannot **bring the office your dog.*

Given all of this information on variation between the DITRANSITIVE construction and the PREPOSITIONAL DATIVE construction, you can imagine that a variable rule governing the use of the two construction will be highly complex. What a rule of this kind would state is that the idea of a transfer is likely to be expressed as a DITRANSITIVE if the recipient is given, pronominal, and animate, the theme is new and a long lexical phrase, the kind of transfer is a transfer of information, and the verb that is used is *give,* as in an example such as *John gave me the idea of painting the house purple* (compare *John gave the idea of painting the house purple to me*). Quantitative techniques that work on the basis of corpus data (cf. Baayen 2008 and Gries 2013 for overviews) allow rather precise assessments of the relative impacts of each variable, and experimental studies show that the behaviour of speakers in forced choice tasks and grammaticality judgement tasks is highly compatible with those corpus-based results (Bresnan 2007; Bresnan and Hay 2008; Bresnan and Ford 2010). This means that the close analysis of variation between constructions allows us to build detailed and realistic models of selected parts of the construct-i-con. It goes without saying that the DATIVE ALTERNATION is merely a very small part of the construct-i-con, but as the example of the fruit fly in biology shows, it is sometimes very useful to have precise knowledge of a small slither of reality because that knowledge may in the end generalise to other phenomena. More specifically, we know that all kinds of constructions exhibit variation, and we further know that some variables – among them syntactic length, animacy, and givenness – matter across a wide range of different constructions (Szmrecsanyi 2006). If the goal of Construction Grammar is to create a realistic image of what it is that speakers know, working out how speakers choose between alternative constructions is an important part of the enterprise.

8.3 Constructional variation across groups of speakers

When we are talking about the grammar of English and mean speakers' linguistic knowledge by that, we are obviously making an abstraction: different speakers of English have very different ways of talking, which reflect individual differences in linguistic knowledge. 'The grammar of English' would thus be something of a compromise between these bodies of knowledge, perhaps some general traits that all speakers more or less agree on. Yet it is questionable whether such a compromise would be an appropriate object of scientific inquiry because inter-speaker variation is found even in what we think of as very general constructions. Consider the following examples, none of which are compatible with the linguistic knowledge of a speaker of standard American English, but all of which form part of speakers' knowledge in at least one of the world's **varieties of English**.

(9) *Example*

Example	*Description*
There's no one does that any more.	subject relative without relativiser
This our problem is very serious.	determiner doubling
I eaten my lunch.	perfect without auxiliary *have*
This is better as the other one.	comparative *as*
The boys was there, Mary weren't.	was/weren't polarity split
They ride bikes is what they do.	full clauses as cleft focus phrase
As I said it before, this is a problem.	resumptive *it*

These examples, which are based on data from the electronic World Atlas of Varieties of English (eWAVE) database (Kortmann and Lunkenheimer 2013), show that variability between different groups of speakers runs much deeper than, say, the British–American contrast between /təˈmɒːtəʊ/ and /təˈmeɪtəʊ/. Relative clauses, noun phrases, the perfect, comparison, negation, clefting, and pronoun usage are fundamental and basic domains of grammar, and in all of these there is variation. What this means is that the quest for a compromise between all varieties of English is likely to be a problematic enterprise. Rather, the goal of constructional research should be to account for speakers' knowledge in a certain variety of English. This goal of course includes the objective of accounting for differences in the use of a construction across two or more varieties, or the question of how a construction is used by different social groups within a single variety. Let us consider two studies that pursue questions of this kind.

Bresnan and Hay (2008) compare the member constructions of the DATIVE ALTERNATION across American English and New Zealand English. As was discussed in the previous section, the DITRANSITIVE construction and the PREPOSITIONAL DATIVE construction are both used for the verbalisation of transfers, and speakers probabilistically choose between the two constructions on the basis of several factors, including the givenness of theme and recipient and the type of transfer that is at issue. These factors impact speakers' choices with different strengths (Bresnan et al. 2007). A reasonable question to ask is whether the relative force of these factors is the same across different varieties of English. Bresnan and Hay (2008) gathered examples of the DITRANSITIVE construction and the PREPOSITIONAL DATIVE construction with the verb *give* from corpora of American English and New Zealand English to compare the effects of givenness, animacy, length, and so on across the two varieties. A first result of Bresnan and Hay's analysis is that these factors do have effects in the same direction across both varieties. A theme that represents given information thus biases both American and New Zealand speakers towards the PREPOSITIONAL DATIVE construction. A second result is that the effect strengths of givenness, length, and transfer type are statistically indistinguishable across the two varieties. As far as these factors are concerned, speakers' knowledge of the two constructions is thus remarkably similar. A third result, however, is that American and New Zealand speakers differ with regard to the factor of animate and inanimate recipients. Speakers of New Zealand English make greater use of the DITRANSITIVE construction with inanimate recipients in examples such as *give the door a push* or *give the economy a boost*. Despite this difference, the overall picture that emerges is that even complex variable rules can exist in very similar forms across different varieties of English.

By the same token, there are also cases of constructions differing across two varieties where such differences would not necessarily be expected. One such example is the *INTO*-CAUSATIVE construction, which is illustrated below.

(10) He tricked me into believing the story.
      They forced him into signing his resignation.

The *INTO*-CAUSATIVE construction has been studied by Gries and Stefanowitsch (2004b), who observe that the construction varies at its meaning pole between a sense that involves causation by trickery and another one that encodes causation by force. The above examples respectively instantiate these meanings. Wulff et al. (2007) compare the construction across corpora of British and American English, finding that there are differences with regard to the lexical verbs that are typically used. With regard to the finite main verb of the construction, an asymmetry between British and American usage concerns verbs of physical violence (*bounce, push, throw, force*, etc.) and verbs of persuasion (*talk, coax, entice, threaten*, etc.). The former class of verbs is disproportionally often found in the British data, while the latter is characteristic of American examples, allowing Wulff et al. to summarise their findings in the title 'Brutal brits and persuasive Americans'. To be sure, both classes of verbs are routinely used by both American and British speakers, and given a single example, one would be hard pressed to match the utterance with one of the varieties. Nonetheless, what these results show is that speakers' knowledge of the construction is subtly different across the two varieties. While the syntactic form of the construction is identical across both varieties, the variation at the semantic pole of the construction, its 'meaning potential' (Wulff et al. 2007: 278), is not.

To sum up this section, the study of constructional variation across different groups of speakers represents one of the current frontiers of Construction Grammar; there simply is not a lot of research. One reason for this is that variation has traditionally not been a central concern for constructional research, and another is that differences of the kind discussed in this section are not easily revealed through native-speaker intuitions, which have remained the evidence of choice for Construction Grammarians for a very long time (cf. the discussion in Chapter 1). However, as experimental and corpus-based methods are increasingly becoming the norm in constructional research, it is now fully feasible to analyse phenomena of inter-speaker variation, and research of this kind is likely to play a significant role in the further refinement of Construction Grammar as a theory of linguistic knowledge.

8.4 Constructional change: variation across time

The introduction to this chapter discussed several language myths – deep-seated, flawed beliefs about language. One myth that was not mentioned is the belief that there is a single correct way to use a linguistic form that needs to be preserved. For instance, best-selling style guides will tell you that the adverb *hopefully* should not be used in a sentence such as *Hopefully I'll be leaving tomorrow*, that is, unless you are actually planning to leave in a hopeful frame of mind. The word *hopefully* is to be used only as a manner adverb, as derived from the adjective *hopeful*. The underlying logic of this proposal is that there is a 'right' way to use a word, and by that logic, any process of change that leads speakers to use a linguistic form in a way that deviates from earlier usage is to be condemned. What is slightly self-defeating about that argument is that these days, very few speakers actually use *hopefully* in the sense of 'full of hope'. Or when was the last time you hopefully checked your inbox? Change is the natural state of a living language, and this is the case because variation characterises language at all levels of its organisation. Speakers use linguistic forms in different ways, and over time, variants that appeal to other speakers tend to proliferate. The appeal of a variant may be due to intrinsic qualities, such as its usefulness or ease of production or processing, or it may be due to extrinsic reasons, such as the social prestige of the speakers that started using it, or the nature of the idea it describes. For instance, there is a reason that the euphemistic labels for disadvantaged minorities, public toilets, and bodily disabilities are regularly updated: As speakers strive to express themselves in socially acceptable ways, they prefer to use variants that are just a bit more indirect than what is commonly used, and as a consequence, older euphemisms end up being perceived as too direct (cf. Keller 1994).

Coming back to constructions, how does the enterprise of Construction Grammar relate to language change? The discussion earlier in this chapter developed the idea that speakers' knowledge of constructions represents many-to-many mappings that involve a set of related forms and a set of related meanings. Speakers know that a construction can be realised formally in a number of different ways, and they know that the construction has the potential to convey a range of different meanings. Knowledge structures of this kind are susceptible to change. The case of *hopefully* illustrates this. A speaker of American English who grew up after the 1950s will recognise the sense 'full of hope' as a possible meaning of the word, but at the same time that speaker will know that *hopefully* is first and foremost used as a pre-posed sentence adverb in the sense of 'I hope'. By the same token, you will probably share the intuition that *the man whom I thanked* sounds somewhat old-fashioned when compared to *the man that I thanked*. In that sense, your cognitive representation of the RELATIVE CLAUSE construction differs from the representation that earlier generations of speakers would have had.

Differences between different historical stages of a single variety of English can be analysed with the same tools that are applied for the comparison of contemporary varieties of English. Typically, research of this kind resorts to corpora, since the historical varieties of English are fairly well- documented. To give an example, Wolk et al. (2013) carry out a study that follows the model of Bresnan and Hay's (2008) investigation of the DATIVE ALTERNATION, but instead of contrasting American and New Zealand English, Wolk et al. compare the use of the DITRANSITIVE and the PREPOSITIONAL DATIVE construction across different periods of Late Modern English. Speakers during those periods had slightly different ways of using those constructions, for instance with regard to the factor of animate and inanimate recipients. These corpus-based results allow researchers to make very precise 'educated guesses' as to the constructional knowledge that speakers used to have. Regrettably, of course, it is impossible to test those claims experimentally: there simply are no speakers of Late Modern English left who could be asked into the laboratory. Yet it is possible to study more recent processes of change with currently living speakers of different ages, say, around 20, 45, and 70 years of age. If it emerges that old speakers use a constructional variant that is used less by middle-aged speakers and even more rarely by young speakers, it can be concluded that this is a variant on its way out of the language system. Studies taking this analytical approach are called **apparent-time** studies (Bailey 2008), as opposed to **real-time** studies that compare data from different historical periods.

To sum up the preceding paragraphs, the diachronic approach to Construction Grammar studies variation in language use over time. Via studying historical variation in language use, it aims to work out differences between the linguistic knowledge of speakers at different points in time. The historical record of language use shows that constructions change. What makes the study of historical change so challenging is that constructions can in fact change with regard to several different aspects, including not only their form and meaning, but also their frequency of use and their association with social traits of the speakers who are using them. To capture all of these aspects, Hilpert (2013: 16) proposes the following definition of constructional change:

(11) Constructional change selectively seizes a conventionalized form–meaning pair of a language, altering it in terms of its form, its function, any aspect of its frequency, its distribution in the linguistic community, or any combination of these.

This definition starts with the idea of a construction as a conventionalised pair of form and meaning (cf. the definition of constructions in Chapter 1). The most basic changes that can happen to a construction concern meaning and form. Over time, speakers may use a construction with a new meaning that is extended from an older one, as in the case of sentence-adverbial *hopefully*. They may also use the construction in a new form that is an altered variant of an older form. A typical process in this regard is the phonological reduction of frequent constructions, as for instance *gonna* from *be going to*. Another common process of formal change in constructions is known as **host-class expansion** (Himmelmann 2004), which captures the idea that a slot in a construction may over time come to accommodate different types of structural units. Patten (2010) reports on the historical development of the *IT*-CLEFT construction (cf. Chapter 5). *IT*-CLEFTs show a diachronic development towards a diversified repertoire of syntactic phrase types that can appear in the focus phrase of the construction. Consider the following examples:

(12) It was the butler that killed her.
      It is in December that she's coming.
      It is here that we met.
      It is vacuuming the floor that I hate most.

In the first example, the focus phrase contains a nominal, while the second example has a prepositional phrase, and the third one an adverbial. The fourth example has a gerund -*ing* clause as the focus phrase. Patten (2010: 229) shows that the noun phrase pattern is the earliest one that is attested, the remaining ones successively coming in at later stages. What this means is that the class of syntactic units that can be used as focus phrases increasingly expands; hence the term host-class expansion.

The above definition of constructional change further states that a construction can change with regard to any aspect of its frequency. This statement first and foremost covers the event of a construction becoming used more or less often over time. Relative clauses with the relativiser *whom* are a good example of a construction gradually fading out of usage. As was discussed in Chapter 6, speakers keep track of the frequencies with which they hear a construction used, so they know whether a construction is common or rather uncommon in day-to-day language use. Yet there is much more to the statement that constructions change with regard to frequency. The most important aspect of this statement concerns the fact that constructions have variants, and that these variants may change in terms of their relative frequencies. At the risk of boring you, let us return to the DITRANSITIVE construction just one more time. As a speaker of English, whether native or second language learner, you have knowledge of that construction, and your knowledge includes the fact that there is a variant of the construction in which the recipient is not a single animate human being, as in the following examples.

(13) Let's give the potatoes five more minutes.
      John gave the swing a push.
      Mary earned her country a gold medal in the Winter Olympic Games.

Not only do you know that such examples are possible, your mental representation of the DITRANSITIVE construction also includes a record of how often you can expect to hear such examples, as opposed to DITRANSITIVE clauses with animate recipients. In the many-to-many mapping of forms and meanings that make up your knowledge of the DITRANSITIVE construction, some variants are represented more strongly than others, so that they are activated more easily, processed faster, and produced more often. Over time, the relative frequencies of constructional variants may change, and the cognitive representation of those variants will change accordingly.

Constructional change also has a social dimension, such that a construction may change from being used by a specific subgroup of the speech community to being used by a larger part of the community. Your knowledge of a construction includes knowledge of the social contexts in which it is appropriate to use that construction. In some constructions, these contexts may be quite restrictive. Take for instance the word *dude*, which is a lexical noun that has acquired grammatical function as a term of address in American English (Kiesling 2004). The following examples offer two tokens of usage.

(14)   It was great, dude. I really liked it.
       Dude, you need to borrow that DVD. It's freakin' rad.

Clearly, *dude* indexes an informal, conversational register, and it tends to be used by younger speakers, but there is more to it than that. Kiesling (2004: 285) analyses authentic uses of the term and finds that *dude* is unevenly distributed across female and male speakers: mostly, *dude* is used by males to address other males. Female speakers use *dude* to a much lesser extent, and if they do, they prefer to use it in same-sex conversations. What speakers do when they use *dude* is thus to signal male-stereotyped camaraderie. This only works between certain speakers. Imagine your linguistics professor handing you back a term paper and saying *Dude, that's a straight A!* The chances are that despite the good news, a few seconds of awkward silence would follow. Now, whether or not *dude* will spread out to other demographics, including linguistics professors, is a matter of speculation. However, there are documented cases of constructions that speakers perceived as restricted at first and which subsequently spread to ever larger groups of language users and to a greater range of registers, spoken as well as written ones. Mair and Leech (2006) note that phenomena such as negative contraction (*don't, isn't*), the Get-PASSIVE (*something gets eaten*), and singular *they* (*If anyone still needs a handout they should see me after class*) are increasingly establishing themselves in written genres, and these authors propose the term **colloquialisation** for this. What this boils down to is that knowledge of constructions includes knowledge of who is likely to say what in what kinds of situation, and over time that knowledge may change.

8.5 Summing up

This chapter began by pointing out that variation and change, contrary to what many laypeople believe, are fundamental and natural characteristics of language. Variation in language means that speakers have a certain amount of freedom to say the same thing in different ways. Change in language is a direct outcome of variation: given a construction that has multiple variants, speakers may reduce their usage of some of those variants while creating other variants that are then used to an increasingly greater extent. It was argued that variation and change naturally fit into the constructional view of linguistic knowledge. Constructions, as symbolic units, have a formal pole and a functional pole. The main point of this chapter was to illustrate that at both of these poles, there is variation, so that knowledge of a construction is in fact knowledge of a many-to-many mapping of several related forms to several related meanings. Variation at the meaning pole of a construction includes patterns of polysemy in lexical words such as *strong* (*strong fighter, strong coffee, strong feelings*) and in constructions such as the S-GENITIVE construction (*John's book, yesterday's events*) or the DITRANSITIVE construction (*John gave Mary the book, I gave the idea some thought*). Variation at the formal pole includes different pronunciations of the same word, but also different syntactic realisations of the same complex construction. Recall the example of the IT-CLEFT construction, which accommodates different types of structure in its focus phrase (*It was the butler that killed her, It was here that we met*, etc.). Another example of formal variation that was offered discussed different realisations of the RELATIVE CLAUSE construction. The discussion introduced the concept of a variable as a constructional feature that speakers can realise in two or more ways. With regard to relative clauses, important variables include the grammatical role of the relativised constituent, the presence or absence of a relativiser, and the verb form of the relative clause, which may be finite or non-finite. It was argued that constructional variation is an integral part of speakers' knowledge of language: speakers know how a construction can vary, that is, what variants are possible and what variants are not.

The chapter further pointed out that the study of variation in constructions and between constructions has its roots in the research tradition of quantitative sociolinguistics. The discussion introduced the concept of a variable rule, that is, a rule that is applied probabilistically: several language-internal and language-external factors influence the likelihood of such a rule being applied. Most studies that operate with this concept cast variable rules as binary choices, so that speakers may choose to use one construction from an alternating pair of constructions. An example that was presented in some detail was the DATIVE ALTERNATION, in which speakers' choices between the DITRANSITIVE construction and the PREPOSITIONAL DATIVE construction hinge on variables such as the givenness of theme and recipient, the length of theme and recipient, the animacy status of the recipient, and several others. Current research combines both experimental and corpus-based methods to investigate constructional variation, and approaches of this kind can identify with great precision the relative impacts that different variables have on speakers' linguistic behaviour.

The final parts of the chapter were concerned with constructional variation across different varieties of English, including not only varieties that are spoken in different areas of the world, but also varieties that were spoken during different historical periods. It was argued that Construction Grammar should not strive to model a compromise between the different bodies of knowledge that different speakers of English have. Rather, the goal should be to account for the knowledge that reasonably well-defined groups of speakers have. Individual differences of course also remain when such an approach is taken. The example of the DATIVE ALTERNATION was used to illustrate how constructional knowledge may differ rather subtly from one variety of English to another one. The example of the *INTO*-CAUSATIVE construction illustrated cross-varietal differences in the collocational preferences of a construction. The methodologies that are applied in studies of constructions across different Englishes are put to use in similar ways in diachronic research on constructional change. The discussion offered a definition of constructional change and illustrated the ways in which constructions can change with several examples. Importantly, constructions may change not only with regard to form and meaning, but crucially also with regard to aspects of their frequency and their distribution in the community of speakers.

Study questions

- Give an example of linguistic variation from your own language use. What are the factors that make you say the same thing differently in different situations?
- Why do language variation and change have such a bad reputation among non-linguists?
- Look up the web page of the eWAVE (www.ewave-atlas.org) and find out in what varieties, besides Hong Kong English and

Newfoundland English, subject relative clauses without relativisers are acceptable.

- What is a variable rule? Give an example.
- What does it mean to say that a language-external factor has a probabilistic effect on a variable rule? Give an example.
- Do some bibliographical research and find another morphosyntactic alternation that has been studied with the approach used by Bresnan et al. (2007).
- What is morphosyntactic persistence?
- What is the difference between apparent-time studies and real-time studies?
- The term of address *dude* is restricted with respect to the speakers that use it. Can you come up with other examples of constructions that are used only by specific groups in the speech community?
- The Corpus of Historical American English (COHA) is a great resource in which to learn about constructions that have changed in frequency over the past two hundred years. Look up the web page (http://corpus.byu.edu/coha) and search for the words *whom*, *chap*, and *dude*. Feel free to continue searching!

Further reading

Hoffmann and Trousdale (2011) have edited a special issue of the journal *Cognitive Linguistics* on the topic of 'Variation, change and constructions in English'. Their introduction to the special issue, as well as the contributions themselves, illuminate the topic from different angles. Hoffmann and Trousdale's (2013) *Oxford Handbook of Construction Grammar* contains several chapters on variation and change; in particular, the contributions by Östman and Trousdale, Fried, and Hollmann continue lines of thought that were developed in this chapter. A resource that is extremely useful for the exploration of constructional variability between different varieties of English is the *Mouton World Atlas of Variation in English* (Kortmann and Lunkenheimer 2013), especially since it is accompanied by a web-based database that is free to use (www.ewave-atlas.org). Finally, Hilpert (2013) presents several case studies of constructional change that illustrate how variation in constructional usage develops over time.

9 Concluding remarks

The introduction of this book asked the question what speakers know when they know a language. The very short answer to that question was given right then and there: speakers know constructions. The simplicity of that answer is deceptive, of course. The subsequent chapters of this book have tried to articulate the many different ideas that this simple sentence entails: constructions comprise everything from monomorphemic words to complex syntactic constructions; they connect a formal pole with a meaning pole, each of which is characterised by variation; they are hierarchically organised and interconnected through links such as instantiation links or subpart links; they are learned through exposure to language use; they serve to evoke parts of semantic frames and to present those ideas in ways that facilitate successful communication. They are automatically accessed by hearers when they process language; they change over time; they exhibit subtle or not so subtle differences from one variety of English to another. The list could go on, but you get the general idea: behind the simple statement that speakers know constructions lies a view of linguistic knowledge that comprises a network of ideas – a linguistic theory – and the purpose of this book was to introduce you to that theory.

Now that you have a rough idea of Construction Grammar as a linguistic theory, there are two next logical steps. A first step would be to increase your expertise and explore the Construction Grammar literature, following your own interests. It was mentioned in the preface to this book that what is presented here is just one particular flavour of Construction Grammar; you are now sufficiently versed in the basics to learn about and appreciate the differences between approaches such as Cognitive Construction Grammar (Goldberg 1995, 2006), Cognitive Grammar (Langacker 1987), Radical Construction Grammar (Croft 2001), and Sign-Based Construction Grammar (Boas and Sag 2012). In order to get a first overview, start with the respective articles in Hoffmann and Trousdale's *Oxford Handbook of Construction Grammar*

(2013). In deepening your knowledge of Construction Grammar, you might also proceed by following up on a specific area of Construction Grammar that particularly suits your interest. For instance, if first language acquisition is what you are interested in, there is a world of constructional research for you to explore. Tomasello (2003) continues to be a great reference to start with, even though a lot of fascinating new results have emerged since it was published. If you would like to find out more about the psycholinguistic side of constructional research, start with Goldberg (2006) and Bencini (2013). It is always a good idea to look up people's professional web pages to find out about their most recent work. Many researchers keep copies of their articles online, so that looking up someone's web page might even save you a trip to the library.

A second important step would be to engage with Construction Grammar in your own work. Throughout this book, it was emphasised that Construction Grammar is a theory that makes testable predictions and that these predictions need to be evaluated on the basis of empirical data. If you are a student planning to write a first long essay, the idea of having to deal with data might make you a little uneasy. However, engaging with empirical linguistic data, be it collected from a corpus, during an experiment, or from the responses of a questionnaire, is not witchcraft, and dealing with such data will tell you more about language than any amount of reading that you could do in the same time. Be sure to ask for help; discuss your plans with your lecturers and your fellow students. When you are starting out, it is not a bad strategy to model your own work on a study that someone else has already done. You can use other sources of data or tweak the research question a little bit. In such cases, do not be afraid to send the original author an email, asking for advice. Yes, researchers are usually busy, but getting an email from someone who is reading and appreciating their work will generally make them happy.

Now, what could be a manageable research project for a long essay on Construction Grammar? One type of study could be called the 'oddball construction' essay. Several classic studies in Construction Grammar deal with patterns such as *What's that scratch doing on my desk?* or *I wouldn't read, let alone review, a book by that guy.* An essay of this kind identifies an idiosyncratic construction and offers an analytical sketch, typically describing the constraints and unexpected properties of that construction. Showing that a construction deviates from more canonical patterns of English adds to the body of evidence that speakers must have a tremendous amount of construction-specific knowledge. In Chapter 1, this was metaphorically described as the 'growth of the appendix'. A second type of essay that merits discussion involves the replication of a published experimental study. Experimental research in Construction Grammar is still in its infancy, but there are quite a few studies out there that do not require the use of specialised software or expensive machinery. Studies such as Bencini and Goldberg (2000), Gurevich et al. (2010), or Dąbrowska (2010) can be replicated, that is, repeated with similar or identical stimuli but with different participants, using your own computers and props that you can make from office materials. Do not worry that simply repeating an existing study might not yield anything of worth: the replication of studies is a very important part of science, and besides that, retracing the steps of experienced researchers makes you learn a lot. A third type of essay uses corpus data to study variation in the use of a construction. Studies of this kind take a construction and explore how it varies with regard to structure and to meaning, across varieties, and perhaps across different groups of speakers, or across different periods of time. Doing this does not necessarily require that you are already familiar with corpus-linguistic methods, but it certainly requires you to take the plunge and get the skills that enable you to answer your research question. For starters, you might use online resources such as Mark Davies' suite of corpora (http://corpus.byu.edu), which allow you to collect data via a web page, without any need for specialised software. Wiechmann and Fuhs (2006) point towards useful pieces of software for the analysis of conventional corpora. If you decide that you want to pursue corpus linguistics in more depth, Gries (2009) is a highly recommended resource. As it is needless to say, these suggestions do not begin to cover the spectrum of studies that could be done. Follow your interests, ask for advice, and be ready to learn.

To conclude, this book hopefully leaves you wanting to find out more about Construction Grammar. As was pointed out earlier, the theory is under development, which means that many issues still need to be worked out. Also, connections between Construction Grammar and related fields of inquiry are currently being developed. It therefore remains to be seen what the future holds for Construction Grammar. At the same time, if you would like to play a part in shaping that future, there is ample opportunity.

References

Aarts, Bas (2000), 'Corpus linguistics, Chomsky and fuzzy tree fragments', in Christian Mair and Marianne Hundt (eds), *Corpus Linguistics and Linguistic Theory*, Amsterdam: Rodopi, pp. 5–13.

Akhtar, Nameera (1999), 'Acquiring basic word order: Evidence for data-driven learning of syntactic structure', *Journal of Child Language* 26: 339–56.

Ambridge, Ben and Adele E. Goldberg (2008), 'The island status of clausal complements: Evidence in favor of an information structure explanation', *Cognitive Linguistics* 19/3: 349–81.

Ambridge, Ben and Elena Lieven (2011), *Child Language Acquisition: Contrasting Theoretical Approaches*, Cambridge: Cambridge University Press.

Arnon, Inbal and Neal Snider (2010), 'More than words: Frequency effects for multi-word phrases', *Journal of Memory and Language* 62/1: 67–82.

Aronoff, Mark (1976), *Word Formation in Generative Grammar*, Cambridge, MA: MIT Press.

Auer, Peter (2005), 'Projection in interaction and projection in grammar', *Text & Talk* 25/1: 7–36.

Baayen, R. Harald (2008), *Analyzing Linguistic Data*, Cambridge: Cambridge University Press.

Bailey, Guy (2008), 'Real and apparent time', in Jack K. Chambers, Peter Trudgill, and Natalie Schilling-Estes (eds), *The Handbook of Language Variation and Change*, 2nd edn, Oxford: Blackwell, pp. 312–31.

Baron, Naomi S. (2008), *Always On: Language in an Online and Mobile World*, Oxford: Oxford University Press.

Bauer, Laurie (2006), 'Compounds and minor word-formation types', in Bas Aarts and April McMahon (eds), *The Handbook of English Linguistics*, Malden: Blackwell, pp. 483–506.

Bauer, Laurie and Antoinette Renouf (2001), 'A corpus-based study of compounding in English', *Journal of English Linguistics* 29: 101–23.

Bauer, Laurie and Peter Trudgill (eds) (1998), *Language Myths*, London: Penguin.

Behaghel, Otto (1932), *Deutsche Syntax. Bd. IV: Wortstellung, Periodenbau*, Heidelberg: Winter.

Bencini, Giulia M. L. (2013), 'Psycholinguistics', in Thomas Hoffmann and

Graeme Trousdale (eds), *The Oxford Handbook of Construction Grammar*, New York: Oxford University Press, pp. 379–96.

Bencini, Giulia M. L. and Adele E. Goldberg (2000), 'The contribution of argument structure constructions to sentence meaning', *Journal of Memory and Language* 43/4: 640–51.

Berko Gleason, Jean (1958), 'The child's learning of English morphology', *Word* 14: 150–77.

Boas, Hans C. (2003), *A Constructional Approach to Resultatives*, Stanford: CSLI.

Boas, Hans C. (2005), 'Determining the productivity of resultative constructions: A reply to Goldberg & Jackendoff', *Language* 81/2: 448–64.

Boas, Hans C. and Ivan A. Sag (eds) (2012), *Sign-Based Construction Grammar*, Stanford: CSLI.

Bock, J. Kathryn (1986), 'Syntactic persistence in language production', *Cognitive Psychology* 18: 355–87.

Booij, Geert (2009), 'Construction morphology and compounding', in Rochelle Lieber and Pavel Stekauer (eds), *The Oxford Handbook of Compounding*, Oxford: Oxford University Press, pp. 201–16.

Booij, Geert (2010), *Construction Morphology*, Oxford: Oxford University Press.

Booij, Geert (2012), *The Grammar of Words: An Introduction to Linguistic Morphology*, Oxford: Oxford University Press.

Booij, Geert (2013), 'Morphology in Construction Grammar', in Thomas Hoffmann and Graeme Trousdale (eds), *The Oxford Handbook of Construction Grammar*, New York: Oxford University Press, pp. 255–73.

Bowerman, Melissa (1979), 'The acquisition of complex sentences', in Michael Garman and Paul Fletcher (eds), *Studies in Language Acquisition*, Cambridge: Cambridge University Press, pp. 285–305.

Boyd, Jeremy K. and Adele E. Goldberg (2011), 'Learning what not to say: The role of statistical preemption and categorization in "a"-adjective production', *Language* 81/1: 1–29.

Braine, Martin D. S. (1976), *Children's First Word Combinations*, Chicago: University of Chicago Press.

Brandt, Silke, Evan Kidd, Elena Lieven, and Michael Tomasello (2009), 'The discourse bases of relativization: An investigation of young German and English-speaking children's comprehension of relative clauses', *Cognitive Linguistics* 20/3: 539–70.

Bresnan, Joan (2007), 'Is syntactic knowledge probabilistic? Experiments with the English dative alternation', in Sam Featherston and Wolfgang Sternefeld (eds), *Roots: Linguistics in Search of Its Evidential Base*, Berlin: Mouton de Gruyter, pp. 77–96.

Bresnan, Joan and Marilyn Ford (2010), 'Predicting syntax: Processing dative constructions in American and Australian varieties of English', *Language* 86/1: 186–213.

Bresnan, Joan and Jennifer Hay (2008), 'Gradient grammar: An effect of animacy on the syntax of *give* in New Zealand and American English', *Lingua* 118/2: 245–59.

Bresnan, Joan, Anna Cueni, Tatiana Nikitina, and R. Harald Baayen (2007), 'Predicting the dative alternation', in Gerlof Boume, Irene Kraemer, and Joost Zwarts (eds), *Cognitive Foundations of Interpretation*, Amsterdam: Royal Netherlands Academy of Science, pp. 69–94.

Brooks, Patricia and Michael Tomasello (1999), 'Young children learn to produce passives with nonce verbs', *Developmental Psychology* 35: 29–44.

Bybee, Joan L. (2010), *Language, Usage, and Cognition*, Cambridge: Cambridge University Press.

Call, Jody and Michael Tomasello (1998), 'Distinguishing intentional from accidental actions in orangutans (*Pongo pygmaeus*), chimpanzees (*Pan troglodytes*), and human children (*Homo sapiens*)', *Journal of Comparative Psychology* 112/2: 192–206.

Carpenter, Malinda, Nameera Akhtar, and Michael Tomasello (1998), 'Fourteen- through 18–month-old infants differentially imitate intentional and accidental actions', *Infant Behavior and Development* 21: 315–30.

Casenhiser, Devin and Adele E. Goldberg (2005), 'Fast mapping of a phrasal form and meaning', *Developmental Science* 8: 500–8.

Chafe, Wallace (1976), 'Givenness, contrastiveness, definiteness, subjects, topics, and point of view', in Charles N. Li (ed.), *Subject and Topic*, New York: Academic Press, pp. 25–55.

Chafe, Wallace (1987), 'Cognitive constraints and information flow', in Ross Tomlin (ed.), *Coherence and Grounding in Discourse: Outcome of a Symposium*, Amsterdam: John Benjamins, pp. 21–51

Chomsky, Noam A. (1959), 'Review of *Verbal Behavior*. By B. F. Skinner', *Language* 35/1: 26–58.

Croft, William A. (2001), *Radical Construction Grammar: Syntactic Theory in Typological Perspective*, Oxford: Oxford University Press.

Croft, William A. and D. Alan Cruse (2004), *Cognitive Linguistics*, Cambridge: Cambridge University Press.

Culicover, Peter W. and Ray S. Jackendoff (1999), 'The view from the periphery: The English comparative correlative', *Linguistic Inquiry* 30: 543–71.

Dąbrowska, Ewa (2008), 'Questions with long-distance dependencies: A usage-based perspective', *Cognitive Linguistics* 19/3: 391–425.

Dąbrowska, Ewa (2010), 'Naive v. expert intuitions: An empirical study of acceptability judgments', *Linguistic Review* 27: 1–23.

Dąbrowska, Ewa and Elena Lieven (2005), 'Towards a lexically specific grammar of children's question constructions', *Cognitive Linguistics* 16/3: 437–74.

Dąbrowska, Ewa, Caroline Rowland, and Anna Theakston (2009), 'The acquisition of questions with long-distance dependencies', *Cognitive Linguistics* 20/3: 571–97.

Davies, Mark (2010), *The Corpus of Historical American English (COHA): 400+ Million Words, 1810–2009*, available online at http://corpus.byu.edu/coha.

Deutscher, Guy (2005), *The Unfolding of Language*, New York: Holt.

Diessel, Holger (2004), *The Acquisition of Complex Sentences*, Cambridge: Cambridge University Press.

Diessel, Holger (2013), 'Construction Grammar and first language acquisition', in Thomas Hoffmann and Graeme Trousdale (eds), *The Oxford Handbook of Construction Grammar*, Oxford: Oxford University Press, pp. 347–64.

Diessel, Holger and Michael Tomasello (2001), 'The acquisition of finite complement clauses in English: A corpus-based analysis', *Cognitive Linguistics* 12: 1–45.

Diessel, Holger and Michael Tomasello (2005), 'A new look at the acquisition of relative clauses', *Language* 81/1: 1–25.

Du Bois, John (1985), 'Competing motivations', in John Haiman (ed.), *Iconicity in Syntax*, Amsterdam: John Benjamins, pp. 343–65.

Evans, Vyvyan and Melanie Green (2006), *Cognitive Linguistics: An Introduction*, Edinburgh: Edinburgh University Press.

Fillmore, Charles J., Paul Kay, and Mary Catherine O'Connor (1988), 'Regularity and idiomaticity in grammatical constructions: The case of *let alone*', *Language* 64/3: 501–38.

Fillmore, Charles J., Russell R. Lee-Goldman, and Russell Rhodes (2012), 'The FrameNet Constructicon', in Hans C. Boas and Ivan A. Sag (eds), *Sign-Based Construction Grammar*, Stanford: CSLI, pp. 283–99.

Fried, Mirjam and Jan-Ola Östman (eds) (2004), *Construction Grammar in a Cross-Language Perspective*, Amsterdam: John Benjamins.

Gahl, Susanne and Susan M. Garnsey (2004), 'Knowledge of grammar, knowledge of usage: Syntactic probabilities affect pronunciation variation', *Language* 80/4: 748–75.

Ghomeshi, Jila, Ray Jackendoff, Nicole Rosen, and Kevin Russell (2004), 'Contrastive focus reduplication in English (The *salad-salad* paper)', *Natural Language and Linguistic Theory* 22: 307–57.

Gibson, Edward and Eva Fedorenko (2010), 'Weak quantitative standards in linguistic research', *Trends in Cognitive Sciences* 14/6: 233–4.

Giegerich, Heinz (2004), 'Compound or phrase? English noun-plus-noun constructions and the stress criterion', *English Language and Linguistics* 8/1: 1–24.

Goldberg, Adele E. (1995), *Constructions: A Construction Grammar Approach to Argument Structure*, Chicago: University of Chicago Press.

Goldberg, Adele E. (2001), 'Patient arguments of causative verbs can be omitted: The role of information structure in argument distribution', *Language Sciences* 23: 503–24.

Goldberg, Adele E. (2003), 'Constructions: A new theoretical approach to language', *Trends in Cognitive Sciences* 7/5: 219–24.

Goldberg, Adele E. (2006), *Constructions at Work: The Nature of Generalization in Language*, Oxford: Oxford University Press.

Goldberg, Adele E. (2011), 'Corpus evidence of the viability of statistical preemption', *Cognitive Linguistics* 22/1: 131–54.

Goldberg, Adele E. (2013), 'Constructionist approaches', in Thomas Hoffmann and Graeme Trousdale (eds), *The Oxford Handbook of Construction Grammar*, Oxford: Oxford University Press, pp. 19–31.

Goldberg, Adele E. and Farrell Ackerman (2001), 'The pragmatics of obligatory adjuncts', *Language* 77/4: 798–814.

Goldberg, Adele E. and Giulia M. L. Bencini (2005), 'Support from language processing for a constructional approach to grammar', in Andrea Tyler (ed.), *Language In Use: Cognitive and Discourse Perspectives on Language and Language Learning*, Washington, DC: Georgetown University Round Table on Languages and Linguistics, pp. 3–18.

Goldberg, Adele E. and Ray S. Jackendoff (2004), 'The English resultative as a family of constructions', *Language* 80/4: 532–67.

Goldberg, Adele E., Devin M. Casenhiser, and Nitya Sethuraman (2004), 'Learning argument structure generalizations', *Cognitive Linguistics* 15/3: 286–316.

Green, Georgia M. (1985), 'The description of inversions in Generalized Phrase Structure Grammar', *Berkeley Linguistics Society* 11: 117–46.

Gregory, Michelle and Laura A. Michaelis (2001), 'Topicalization and left-dislocation: A functional opposition revisited', *Journal of Pragmatics* 33/11: 1665–706.

Grice, Herbert Paul (1975), 'Logic and conversation', in Peter Cole and Jerry Morgan (eds), *Syntax and Semantics. Vol. 3*, New York: Academic Press, pp. 41–58.

Gries, Stefan T. (2004), 'Shouldn't it be breakfunch? A quantitative analysis of the structure of blends', *Linguistics* 42/3: 639–67.

Gries, Stefan T. (2005), 'Syntactic priming: A corpus-based approach', *Journal of Psycholinguistic Research* 34/4: 365–99.

Gries, Stefan T. (2009), *Quantitative Corpus Linguistics with R: A Practical Introduction*, London: Routledge.

Gries, Stefan T. (2011), 'Corpus data in usage-based linguistics: What's the right degree of granularity for the analysis of argument structure constructions?', in Mario Brdar, Stefan T. Gries, and Milena Žic Fuchs (eds), *Cognitive Linguistics: Convergence and Expansion*, Amsterdam and Philadelphia: John Benjamins, pp. 237–56.

Gries, Stefan T. (2012), 'Frequencies, probabilities, association measures in usage-/exemplar-based linguistics: Some necessary clarifications', *Studies in Language* 36/3: 477–510.

Gries, Stefan T. (2013), *Statistics for Linguistics with R*, 2nd edn, Berlin: Mouton de Gruyter.

Gries, Stefan T. and Anatol Stefanowitsch (2004a), 'Extending collostructional analysis: A corpus-based perspective on "alternations"', *International Journal of Corpus Linguistics* 9/1: 97–129.

Gries, Stefan T. and Anatol Stefanowitsch (2004b), 'Co-varying collexemes in the *into*-causative', in Michel Achard and Suzanne Kemmer (eds), *Language, Culture, and Mind*, Stanford: CSLI, pp. 225–36.

Gries, Stefan T. and Stefanie Wulff (2005), 'Do foreign language learners also have constructions? Evidence from priming, sorting, and corpora', *Annual Review of Cognitive Linguistics* 3: 182–200.

Gries, Stefan T., Beate Hampe, and Doris Schönefeld (2005), 'Converging evidence: Bringing together experimental and corpus data on the association of verbs and constructions', *Cognitive Linguistics* 16/4: 635–76.

Griffiths, Patrick (2006), *An Introduction to English Semantics and Pragmatics*, Edinburgh: Edinburgh University Press.

Gropen, Jess, Steven Pinker, Michelle Hollander, Richard Goldberg, and Ronald Wilson (1989), 'The learnability and acquistion of dative alternation in English', *Language* 65/2: 203–57.

Gurevich, Olya, Matt Johnson, and Adele E. Goldberg (2010), 'Incidental verbatim memory for language', *Language and Cognition* 2/1: 45–78.

Halliday, M. A. K. (1967), 'Notes on transitivity and theme in English. Part 2', *Journal of Linguistics* 3: 199–244.

Hankamer, Jorge and Ivan A. Sag (1976), 'Deep and surface anaphora', *Linguistic Inquiry* 7/3: 391–428.

Hare, Brian and Michael Tomasello (2005), 'Human-like social skills in dogs?', *Trends in Cognitive Science* 9: 439–44.

Haspelmath, Martin and Thomas Müller-Bardey (2004), 'Valency change', in Geert Booij, Christian Lehmann, and Joachim Mugdan (eds), *Morphology: A Handbook on Inflection and Word Formation. Vol. 2*, Berlin: de Gruyter, pp. 1130–45.

Hauser, Marc D. (1996), *The Evolution of Communication*, Cambridge, MA: MIT Press.

Hauser, Marc D., Noam A. Chomsky, and Tecumseh W. Fitch (2002), 'The faculty of language: What is it, who has it, and how did it evolve?', *Science* 298: 1569–79.

Hay, Jennifer (2002), 'From speech perception to morphology: Affix-ordering revisited', *Language* 78/3: 527–55.

Hay, Jennifer and Ingo Plag (2004), 'What constrains possible suffix combinations? On the interaction of grammatical and processing restrictions in derivational morphology', *Natural Language and Linguistic Theory* 22: 565–96.

Healy, Alice F. and George A. Miller (1970), 'The verb as the main determinant of sentence meaning', *Psychonomic Science* 20: 372.

Herbst, Thomas and Katrin Götz-Votteler (eds) (2007), *Valency: Theoretical, Descriptive and Cognitive Issues*, Berlin: de Gruyter.

Herbst, Thomas, David Heath, Ian Roe, and Dieter Götz (2004), *A Valency Dictionary of English*, Berlin: de Gruyter.

Hilferty, Joseph (2003), 'In defense of grammatical constructions', PhD dissertation, University of Barcelona.

Hilpert, Martin (2006), 'Distinctive collexemes and diachrony', *Corpus Linguistics and Linguistic Theory* 2/2: 243–57.

Hilpert, Martin (2008), *Germanic Future Constructions: A Usage-Based Approach to Language Change*, Amsterdam: John Benjamins.

Hilpert, Martin (2013), *Constructional Change in English: Developments in Allomorphy, Word Formation, and Syntax*, Cambridge: Cambridge University Press.

Himmelmann, Nikolaus P. (2004), 'Lexicalization and grammaticization:

Opposite or orthogonal?', in Walter Bisang, Nikolaus P. Himmelmann, and Björn Wiemer (eds), *What Makes Grammaticalization: A Look from its Components and its Fringes*, Berlin: Mouton de Gruyter, pp. 21–42.

Hockett, Charles F. (1966), 'The problem of universals in language', in Joseph H. Greenberg (ed.), *Universals of Language*, Cambridge, MA: MIT Press, pp. 1–29.

Hoffmann, Thomas (2013), 'Abstract phrasal and clausal constructions', in Thomas Hoffmann and Graeme Trousdale (eds), *The Oxford Handbook of Construction Grammar*, Oxford: Oxford University Press, pp. 307–28.

Hoffmann, Thomas and Graeme Trousdale (2011), 'Variation, change and constructions in English', *Cognitive Linguistics* 22/1: 1–23.

Hoffmann, Thomas and Graeme Trousdale (eds) (2013), *The Oxford Handbook of Construction Grammar*, Oxford: Oxford University Press.

Hopper, Paul J. and Sandra A. Thompson (1980). 'Transitivity in grammar and discourse', *Language* 56/2: 251-99.

Huddleston, Rodney and Geoffrey K. Pullum (2002), *The Cambridge Grammar of the English Language*, Cambridge: Cambridge University Press.

Imo, Wolfgang (2007), *Construction Grammar und Gesprochene-Sprache-Forschung: Konstruktionen mit zehn matrixsatzfähigen Verben im gesprochenen Deutsch*. Tübingen: Niemeyer.

Israel, Michael (1996), 'The *way* constructions grow', in Adele Goldberg (ed.), *Conceptual Structure, Discourse and Language*, Stanford: CSLI, pp. 217–30.

Jurafsky, Daniel, Alan Bell, Michelle Gregory, and William D. Raymond (2001), 'Probabilistic relations between words: Evidence from reduction in lexical production', in Joan L. Bybee and Paul J. Hopper (eds), *Frequency and the Emergence of Linguistic Structure*, Amsterdam: John Benjamins, pp. 229–54.

Kaschak, Michael and Arthur Glenberg (2000), 'The role of affordances and grammatical constructions in language comprehension', *Journal of Memory and Language* 43: 508–29.

Kay, Paul and Charles J. Fillmore (1999), 'Grammatical constructions and linguistic generalizations: The *What's X Doing Y?* construction', *Language* 75/1: 1–33.

Keller, Rudi (1994), *On Language Change: The Invisible Hand in Language*, London: Routledge.

Kiesling, Scott (2004), 'Dude', *American Speech* 79/3: 281–305.

Kintsch, Walter (1998), *Comprehension: A Paradigm for Cognition*, Cambridge: Cambridge University Press.

Kirchhofer, Katharina C., Felizitas Zimmermann, Juliane Kaminski, and Michael Tomasello (2012), 'Dogs (*Canis familiaris*), but not chimpanzees (*Pan troglodytes*), understand imperative pointing', *PLoS ONE* 7/2: e30913.

Kortmann, Bernd and Kerstin Lunkenheimer (eds) (2013), *The Mouton World Atlas of Variation in English*, Berlin: de Gruyter.

Labov, William (1969), 'Contraction, deletion, and inherent variability of the English copula', *Language* 45/4: 715–62.

Labov, William (1994), *Principles of Linguistic Change. Vol. I: Internal Factors*, Oxford: Blackwell.

Labov, William (2001), *Principles of Linguistic Change. Vol. II: Social Factors*, Oxford: Blackwell.

Lakoff, George (1974), 'Syntactic amalgams', *Chicago Linguistics Society* 10: 321–44.

Lakoff, George (1987), *Women, Fire, and Dangerous Things: What Categories Reveal about the Mind*, Chicago: University of Chicago Press.

Lakoff, George and Mark Johnson (1980), *Metaphors We Live By*, Chicago: University of Chicago Press.

Lambrecht, Knud (1994), *Information Structure and Sentence Form: Topic, Focus and the Mental Representations of Discourse Referents*, Cambridge: Cambridge University Press.

Lambrecht, Knud (2001a), 'A framework for the analysis of cleft constructions', *Linguistics* 39/3: 463–516.

Lambrecht, Knud (2001b), 'Dislocation', in Martin Haspelmath, Ekkehard König, Wulf Oesterreicher, and Wolfgang Raible (eds), *Language Typology and Language Universals: An International Handbook. Vol. 2*, Berlin: Walter de Gruyter, pp. 1050–78.

Langacker, Ronald W. (1987), *Foundations of Cognitive Grammar. Vol. 1: Theoretical Prerequisites*, Stanford: Stanford University Press.

Langacker, Ronald W. (1995), 'Raising and transparency', *Language* 71/1: 1–62.

Leino, Jaakko (2013), 'Abstract phrasal and clausal constructions', in Thomas Hoffmann and Graeme Trousdale (eds), *The Oxford Handbook of Construction Grammar*, Oxford: Oxford University Press, pp. 329–44.

Levin, Beth (1993), *English Verb Classes and Alternations: A Preliminary Investigation*, Chicago: University of Chicago Press.

Levin, Beth and M. Rappaport Hovav (2005), *Argument Realization*, Cambridge: Cambridge University Press.

Lieven, Elena, Julian Pine, and Gillian Baldwin (1997), 'Lexically-based learning and the development of grammar in early multi-word speech', *Journal of Child Language* 24/1: 187–219.

Lieven, Elena, Heike Behrens, Jenny Speares, and Michael Tomasello (2003), 'Early syntactic creativity: A usage-based approach', *Journal of Child Language* 30: 333–70.

Lieven, Elena, Dorothé Salomo, and Michael Tomasello (2009), 'Two-year-old children's production of multiword utterances: A usage-based analysis', *Cognitive Linguistics*, 20/3: 481–508.

Lindquist, Hans (2009), *Corpus Linguistics and the Description of English*, Edinburgh: Edinburgh University Press

Loebell, Helga and J. Kathryn Bock (2003), 'Structural priming across languages', *Linguistics* 41/5: 791–824.

Mair, Christian (1987), '*Tough*-movement in present-day British English: A corpus-based study', *Studia Linguistica* 41/1: 59–71.

Mair, Christian and Geoffrey Leech (2006), 'Current changes in English syntax', in Bas Aarts and April McMahon (eds), *The Handbook of English Linguistics*, Oxford: Blackwell, pp. 318–42.

Mayerthaler, Willi (1981), *Morphologische Natürlichkeit*, Wiesbaden: Athenaion.

Michaelis, Laura A. (2004), 'Type shifting in Construction Grammar: An integrated approach to aspectual coercion', *Cognitive Linguistics* 15/1: 1–67.

Michaelis, Laura A. and Knud Lambrecht (1996), 'Toward a construction-based theory of language function: The case of nominal extraposition', *Language* 72/2: 215–47.

Neely , James H. (1976), 'Semantic priming and retrieval from lexical memory: Evidence for facilitatory and inhibitory processes', *Memory & Cognition* 4: 648–54.

Newman, John and Sally Rice (2006), 'Transitivity schemas of English EAT and DRINK in the BNC', in Stefan T. Gries and Anatol Stefanowitsch (eds), *Corpora in Cognitive Linguistics: Corpus-Based Approaches to Syntax and Lexis*, Berlin: Mouton de Gruyter, pp. 225–60.

Oates, John and Andrew Grayson (2004), *Cognitive and Language Development in Children*, Oxford: Blackwell.

Patten, Amanda L. (2010), 'Grammaticalization and the *it*-cleft construction', in Elizabeth C. Traugott and Graeme Trousdale (eds), *Gradience, Gradualness and Grammaticalization*, Amsterdam: John Benjamins, pp. 221–43.

Payne, Thomas (1997), *Describing Morphosyntax: A Guide for Field Linguists*, Cambridge: Cambridge University Press.

Perek, Florent (2012), 'Alternation-based generalizations are stored in the mental grammar: Evidence from a sorting task experiment', *Cognitive Linguistics* 23/3: 601–35.

Pickering, Martin and Victor S. Ferreira (2008), 'Structural priming: A critical review', *Psychological Bulletin* 134/3: 427–59.

Pinker, Steven (1984), *Language Learnability and Language Development*, Cambridge, MA: Harvard University Press.

Pinker, Steven (1989), *Learnability and Cognition: The Acquisition of Argument Structure*, Cambridge, MA: MIT Press.

Plag, Ingo (1999), *Morphological Productivity: Structural Constraints in English Derivation*, Berlin: Mouton de Gruyter.

Plag, Ingo (2003), *Word-Formation in English*, Cambridge: Cambridge University Press.

Prince, Ellen (1978), 'A comparison of *wh*-clefts and *it*-clefts in discourse', *Language* 54/4: 883–906.

Prince, Ellen (1981), 'Toward a taxonomy of given–new information', in Peter Cole (ed.), *Radical Pragmatics*, New York: Academic Press, pp. 223–56.

Quirk, Randolph, Sidney Greenbaum, Geoffrey Leech, and Jan Svartvik (1985), *A Comprehensive Grammar of the English Language*, New York: Longman.

Ramus, Franck, Marc D. Hauser, Cory Miller, Dylan Morris, and Jacques Mehler (2000), 'Language discrimination by human newborns and by cotton-top tamarin monkeys', *Science* 288: 349–51.

Ross, John Robert (1967), 'Constraints on variables in syntax', PhD dissertation, MIT.

Ruppenhofer, Josef (2005), Regularities in null instantiation, Ms.

Ruppenhofer, Josef and Laura A. Michaelis (2010), 'A constructional account of genre-based argument omissions', *Constructions and Frames* 2: 158–84.

Saeed, John (2003), *Semantics*, 2nd edn, Oxford: Blackwell.

Saffran, Jenny R., Richard N. Aslin, and Elissa L. Newport (1996), 'Statistical learning by 8–month-olds', *Science* 274: 1926–8.

Sag, Ivan A. (2010), 'English filler-gap constructions', *Language* 86/3: 486–545.

Sag, Ivan A., Thomas Wasow, and Emily Bender (2003), *Syntactic Theory: A Formal Introduction*, 2nd edn, Stanford: CSLI.

Sato, Yoruke (2010), 'Complex phrase structures within morphological words: Evidence from English and Indonesian', *Lingua* 120/2: 379–407.

Schütze, Carson T. (1996), *The Empirical Base of Linguistics: Grammaticality Judgments and Linguistic Methodology*, Chicago: University of Chicago Press.

Siegel, Dorothy (1974), 'Topics in English morphology', PhD dissertation, MIT.

Spencer, Andrew (1988), 'Bracketing paradoxes and the English lexicon', *Language* 64/3: 663–82.

Stefanowitsch, Anatol (2003), 'Constructional semantics as a limit to grammatical alternation: The two genitives of English', in Günter Rohdenburg and Britta Mondorf (eds), *Determinants of Grammatical Variation in English*, Berlin and New York: Mouton de Gruyter, pp. 413–41.

Stefanowitsch, Anatol (2006), 'Negative evidence and the raw frequency fallacy', *Corpus Linguistics and Linguistic Theory* 2/1: 61–77.

Stefanowitsch, Anatol (2008), 'Negative entrenchment: A usage-based approach to negative evidence', *Cognitive Linguistics* 19/3: 513–31.

Stefanowitsch, Anatol (2011), 'Constructional preemption by contextual mismatch: A corpus-linguistic investigation', *Cognitive Linguistics* 22/1: 107–29.

Stefanowitsch, Anatol and Stefan T. Gries (2003), 'Collostructions: Investigating the interaction of words and constructions', *International Journal of Corpus Linguistics* 8/2: 209–43.

Stemberger, Joseph P. and Brian MacWhinney (1988), 'Are inflected forms stored in the lexicon?', in Michael Hammond and Michael Noonan (eds), *Theoretical Morphology*, New York: Academic Press, pp. 101–16.

Sweetser, Eve (1990), *From Etymology to Pragmatics: Metaphorical and Cultural Aspects of Semantic Structure*, Cambridge: Cambridge University Press.

Szmrecsanyi, Benedikt (2006), *Morphosyntactic Persistence in Spoken English: A Corpus Study at the Intersection of Variationist Sociolinguistics, Psycholinguistics, and Discourse Analysis*, Berlin: Mouton de Gruyter.

Tagliamonte, Sali A. (2006), *Analysing Sociolinguistic Variation*, Cambridge: Cambridge University Press.

Takahashi, Hidemitsu (2012), *A Cognitive Linguistic Analysis of the English Imperative: With Special Reference to Japanese Imperatives*, Amsterdam: John Benjamins.

Taylor, John R. (1989), 'Possessive genitives in English', *Linguistics* 27: 663–86.

Taylor, John R. (1996), *Possessives in English: An Exploration in Cognitive Grammar*, Oxford: Oxford University Press.

Taylor, John R. (2012), *The Mental Corpus: How Language is Represented in the Mind*, Oxford: Oxford University Press.

Tennie, Claudio, Josep Call, and Michael Tomasello (2012), 'Untrained chimpanzees (*Pan troglodytes schweinfurthii*) fail to imitate novel actions', *PLoS ONE* 7: e41548.

Thompson, Sandra A., and Paul J. Hopper (2001), 'Transitivity, clause structure, and argument structure: Evidence from conversation', in Joan L. Bybee and Paul J. Hopper (eds), *Frequency and the Emergence of Linguistic Structure*, Amsterdam: John Benjamins, pp. 27–60.

Tomasello, Michael (1992), *First Verbs: A Case Study of Early Grammatical Development*, Cambridge: Cambridge University Press.

Tomasello, Michael (2000a), 'The item based nature of children's early syntactic development', *Trends in Cognitive Sciences* 4: 156–63.

Tomasello, Michael (2000b), 'Do young children have adult syntactic competence?', *Cognition* 74: 209–53.

Tomasello, Michael (2003), *Constructing a Language: A Usage-Based Theory of Language Acquisition*, Cambridge, MA: Harvard University Press.

Tomasello, Michael (2007), 'Construction Grammar for kids', *Constructions*, Special Vol. 1, available online at http://elanguage.net/journals/constructions.

Tomasello, Michael and Michael Jeffrey Farrar (1986), 'Joint attention and early language', *Child Development* 57: 1454–63.

Tomasello, Michael and Jody Todd (1983), 'Joint attention and lexical acquisition style', *First Language* 4: 197–212.

Tomasello, Michael, Nameera Akhtar, Kelly Dodson, and Laura Rekau (1997), 'Differential productivity in young children's use of nouns and verbs', *Journal of Child Language* 24: 373–87.

Trousdale, Graeme (2010), *An Introduction to English Sociolinguistics*, Edinburgh: Edinburgh University Press.

Van Eynde, Frank (2007), 'The Big Mess construction', in Stefan Müller (ed.), *Proceedings of the HPSG-07 Conference*, pp. 415–33.

van Marle, Jaap (1985), *On the Paradigmatic Dimension of Morphological Creativity*, Dordrecht: Foris.

Wanner, Eric and Michael Maratsos (1978), 'An ATN approach to comprehension', in Morris Halle, Joan Bresnan, and George Miller (eds), *Linguistic Theory and Psychological Reality*, Cambridge: Cambridge University Press, pp. 119–61.

Wasow, Tom and Jennifer E. Arnold (2003), 'Postverbal constituent ordering in English', in Günther Rohdenburg and Britta Mondorf (eds), *Determinants of Grammatical Variation in English*, The Hague: Mouton, pp. 120–54.

Wiechmann, Daniel (to appear), *Understanding Relative Clauses: A Usage-Based View on the Processing of Complex Constructions*, Berlin: de Gruyter.

Wiechmann, Daniel and Stefan Fuhs (2006), 'Concordancing software', *Corpus Linguistics and Linguistic Theory* 2/1: 109–30.

Wolk, Christoph, Joan Bresnan, Anette Rosenbach, and Benedikt Szmrecsanyi

(2013), 'Dative and genitive variability in Late Modern English: Exploring cross-constructional variation and change', *Diachronica* 30/3.

Wonnacott, Elizabeth, Jeremy Boyd, Jennifer Thomson, and Adele E. Goldberg (2012), 'Input effects on the acquisition of a novel phrasal construction in five year olds', *Journal of Memory and Language* 66: 458–78.

Wulff, Stefanie, Anatol Stefanowitsch, and Stefan T. Gries (2007), 'Brutal Brits and persuasive Americans: Variety-specific meaning construction in the *into*-causative', in Günter Radden, Klaus-Michael Köpcke, Thomas Berg, and Peter Siemund (eds), *Aspects of Meaning Construction*, Amsterdam: John Benjamins, pp. 265–81.

Zeschel, Arne (2009), 'What's (in) a construction?', in Vyvyan Evans and Stéphanie Pourcel (eds), *New Directions in Cognitive Linguistics*, Amsterdam: John Benjamins, pp. 185–200.

Index